Books by Roger P. Bolton

Just A Little Talk With God
The Debacle In Washington
& What We Must Do About It
Justified Anger
E. J., Mountain Doctor
And The Challenge in Ellijay

Available on Kindle only:
To The Parents of My Grandchildren
Granddads Political Comments

WHY DONALD TRUMP WON

Why would the best want to become like the rest?

Roger P. Bolton

ISBN: 1541038886
ISBN 13: 9781541038882
Library of Congress Control Number: 2016920706
CreateSpace Independent Publishing Platform
North Charleston, South Carolina

To my family

Spouse: Jane

Children: Julie, David, Karen

Fantastic Grandchildren:

Cameron
Jackson
Connor
Olivia
Hannah
Ashlee
Blake

PREFACE

What you are about to read are the actual things written over the last several years regarding what has been happening to our country as politicians in Washington have taken it upon themselves to change what has made this nation the greatest nation in the history of the world.

Most of what has been written pertains to why there has been such effort to change this country totally different from what it has been. Even though we have been the greatest nation, many liberal politicians really believe they have a better idea, one that will make us an even better nation. The basic problem with this is that they are trying to do things other nations have already tried to do but have failed.

Successful athletic teams learned a lesson a long time ago, and it is often heard this way: "Go with what brung us here." This is poor English, but it states a truth, and that is: Don't change what has made you successful. Work on what has worked, but make it better. For things that have not worked, either discard them or find a way to make them work for you.

There is no nation or individual, for that matter, who does not need to learn to do things better. That is the task that will always be before us as individuals or a nation. That is the task of each athlete, no matter how good he/she is: to learn to do things better.

The presidential election of 2016 has surprised many people, and many are perplexed regarding how a newcomer to politics could win over a person with decades of experience.

(The things written in this book will point to what has been happening in the past few decades, particularly the last one, to get us to the point where the American people have said, "Whoa," to the powers that be. The basic message to those who wish to change us is, "We will not let you completely destroy our Constitution and replace it with something that is far inferior.")

INTRODUCTION

WHY DID TRUMP WIN?

Put simply, Trump won because enough Americans realized that Obama and the democrats were rapidly dismantling what has made the United States the greatest nation in the history of the world, and that, if changes were not made, we would continue to lose the freedoms we have all enjoyed.

The vote to elect Trump was not only a repudiation of Obama and what he has done to this country, but, it was, also, a repudiation of the work of liberals over the past several decades as they have sought to make governmental dependents of millions of Americans. As a result, we now find almost fifty percent of Americans groveling at the government trough looking for more and more free stuff.

What voters finally realized is that the liberals/progressives, primarily democrats, joined by a few republicans and independents, were committed to replacing constitutional government with socialism, a form of government that has never achieved what we have achieved under our form of government.

One of the things that was entailed in this was the change of who served whom. The Constitution calls for elected officials to serve the citizens of this country. Socialism requires citizens to serve government, and, unfortunately, this is the direction we have been headed for several decades.

The work to undo the damage caused by Congress and the presidents will be difficult, and the American people will deal with some hard times as corrections and restorations are made. The future course of this country has been damaged by those who think they have found a better way than constitutional government, and we will all feel effects as we move back toward again being the Greatest Nation.

Restoring this country will not be easy for most of us, but return to constitutional government is far better than moving on into liberalism/socialism.

(Note to the reader: Because this material was written over a period of several years, there is some redundancy as a subject again claimed my attention and was considered worth additional comments. Most of what is written is not dated, but you will be able to get an idea about dates from the content.)

TABLE OF CONTENTS

Preface   vii
Introduction   ix

Section One Surprise And Some Reasons Why   1
Chapter 1   The Presidential Election: What Happened?   3
Chapter 2   The Trump Phenomenon   5
Chapter 3   Stunned   7
Chapter 4   It Is More Than Sour Grapes Or Sore Losers   10
Chapter 5   Plugging The Holes In The Boat   12
Chapter 6   The Day America Could Have Died   14
Chapter 7   It Just May Not Be Anger   17
Chapter 8   No Savior For The American People   21
Chapter 9   Sinking Into Mediocrity   23
Chapter 10   Things That Have Diminished This Country   25
Chapter 11   A Different Quality Of People   29
Chapter 12   The Greatest Damage   31
Chapter 13   Thumbing Their Noses At The American People   35
Chapter 14   Why Would The Best Want To Become Like
             The Rest Anyway?   37
Chapter 15   They Stopped Dreaming And Marching   40

Chapter 16   The Work Of The Great Divider   44
Chapter 17   The Inability To Understand   47
Chapter 18   Where We Have Come From   50
Chapter 19   What Has Happened To Us?   53
Chapter 20   Failure In What We Have Done   56
Chapter 21   Needed: More Rich People   59
Chapter 22   The Will Of The People   61
Chapter 23   So Many Things To Do   63
Chapter 24   Abandoning The Constitution   65

Section Two Changing The Greatest Nation   67
Chapter 25   Thinking About Things   69
Chapter 26   The Destruction Of America   71
Chapter 27   Distraught Over Trump's Election   73
Chapter 28   Crying College Students   75
Chapter 29   Not Understanding What Happened   77
Chapter 30   Bankrupt, But Won't Face The Fact   79
Chapter 31   Awakening The Sleeping Giant   81
Chapter 32   The Results Of Brainwashing   83
Chapter 33   Majoring On The Bad Stuff   86
Chapter 34   Big Difference Between Socialism &
             Constitutional Government   89
Chapter 35   Failure To Ask Questions   91
Chapter 36   Mostly Self-Inflicted   93
Chapter 37   A Clear Difference Between Republicans &
             Democrats   95
Chapter 38   Because Of Who I Am   97
Chapter 39   If Black People Ever Figure It Out   99
Chapter 40   The Harm Of Doing For Others   102
Chapter 41   Looking At The Dark Side   104
Chapter 42   Black Lives Matter....Really???   107
Chapter 43   Needed In Washington: A New Kind Of
             Politician   109

Chapter 44   A Nation Of Wimps   111
Chapter 45   Failure To Understand   112
Chapter 46   The Last Time I Checked   113
Chapter 47   Dramatic Change Needed In Washington   116
Chapter 48   What About Fair Share?   119
Chapter 49   The Greatest Damage To Poor People   122
Chapter 50   The Power Of Indoctrination   125
Chapter 51   Good People: Where Are They?   127
Chapter 52   Used & Abused   129
Chapter 53   The Value Of One Human Being   131
Chapter 54   Disregarding The Constitution   134
Chapter 55   The Devastating Work Of Liberals   136
Chapter 56   The Need To Replace The Politicians In
              Washington   138
Chapter 57   Identification Of The Non-Productive   141
Chapter 58   Inferiority Guaranteed   142
Chapter 59   Make Them Think What We Want Them
              To Think   145

Section Three More Things To Consider   147
Chapter 60   A Great Opportunity Missed   149
Chapter 61   Being Used And Unaware Of It   152
Chapter 62   The Failure Of Money   154
Chapter 63   It's Time To Think About Things   156
Chapter 64   Time To Hit The "Restore" Button   159
Chapter 64   The Art Of Producing Worthless People   163
Chapter 65   Becoming Like The World   166
Chapter 66   Politicians Then, Politicians Now   168
Chapter 66   Learning *From* Britain's Eu Exit   171
Chapter 67   When You Don't Know What To Do, Do
              Something Anyway   173
Chapter 68   Primitive Mind In Control   175
Chapter 69   To Be Or Not To Be? Still The Question   177

Chapter 70   Products Of Where We Come From   179
Chapter 71   Lack Of Identity   182
Chapter 72   Used And Abused, But Don't Know It   185
Chapter 73   Time For Black Leaders To Do Their Job 188

Section Four Over And Beyond   191
Chapter 74   Another Look At This Political Mess   193
Chapter 75   Escaping The Primitive Mind   196
Chapter 76   Just Don't Think About It   198
Chapter 77   Comfortable In One's Own Skin   200
Chapter 78   When Brains Don't Work Right   202
Chapter 79   Hornswoggled Americans   204
Chapter 80   Dysfunction In Our Face   206
Chapter 81   Trouble In America   208
Chapter 82   Letter To A Politician   210
Chapter 83   Insulted And Unaware Of It   212
Chapter 84   Liberalism's Worst Damage   214
Chapter 85   Victims Of Socialism   216
Chapter 86   Replace The Judge: Now Or Later?   219
Chapter 87   When Voting: Use Emotion Or Reason?   221
Chapter 88   Never Should A Man Abandon Himself   224
Chapter 89   Martin Luther King, Jr's. "Dream": Abandoned 226
Chapter 90   The Costs Of Indoctrination/Brain-Washing 229
Chapter 91   When You Don't Know What To Do, Do
             Something Anyway (One More Look)   231
Chapter 92   Hypocrisy On Full Display   234
Chapter 93   Choosing To Be Ignorant   236
Chapter 94   Building My Own Future   238
Chapter 95   Dictators-In-Waiting   241
Chapter 96   Indoctrination: More Powerful Than Education 243
Chapter 97   When Others Offend You   246
Chapter 98   Being Comfortable With One's Beliefs   248
Chapter 99   What Politicians Have Done To Me...
             And Others   250

Chapter 100 Failing To Deal With The Real Problem   253
Chapter 101 Time To Change Mental Health Programs   255
Chapter 102 Freedom Or License   257
Chapter 103 Americans: A Choice Has To Be Made   259
Chapter 104 Americans: Stupid, Insane Or Both?   261
Chapter 105 If You Are Going To Understand Obama   264
Chapter 106 Looking Only At The Dark Side   265
Chapter 107 Christianity Under Attack   267
Chapter 108 How Democrats Treat Poor People   270
Chapter 109 What About The Value Of Political
             Experience?   273
Chapter 110 The Steady Rise Of A New Holocaust   275
Chapter 111 When You Arrive In Washington, Check Your
             Brain At The Potomac   277
Chapter 112 Liberals: Expert Hornswogglers   279
Chapter 113 We Should Pay Attention   281
Chapter 114 Is It Time To Clean House?   283
Chapter 115 Treaties And Agreements Between Nations   286
Chapter 116 Preparing To Repeat History   288
Chapter 117 We Don't Want To Deal With That   290
Chapter 118 Abandoning The Constitution   292
Chapter 119 The Price Of Liberalism   294
Chapter 120 Retreat Into Barbarism   296
Chapter 121 The New World Order   297

Section Four Finding Our Way   299
Chapter 122 My Ego: In The Hands Of Others?   301
Chapter 123 The Need For Renouncers   303
Chapter 124 Escaping The Need To Think   305
Chapter 125 Wanting Things That Cannot Be   307
Chapter 126 There Are Reasons We Are The Greatest
             Nation   309
Chapter 127 Liberalism: Keeping People Inferior And Poor   312
Chapter 128 Free Money Or Shall I Earn It?   314

Chapter 129 The Value Of Treaties And Agreements 316
Chapter 130 No Ground To Stand On 318
Chapter 131 Learning To Live With Each Other 320
Chapter 132 Resignation To The Will Of Others 323
Chapter 133 The Road From Freedom To Chaos Is Short 325
Chapter 134 Science And Technology Have Not Delivered What Man Needs 328
Chapter 135 Evil In Its Purest Form 330
Chapter 136 True Colors Always Show 332
Chapter 137 Savages Among Us 334
Chapter 138 Choosing Other Than The Certain Minimum 336
Chapter 139 Whence All This Crime? 338
Chapter 140 The Inquisition: With Us Again? 340

Section Five Maintaining Awareness 343
Chapter 141 Brains Are For Thinking 345
Chapter 142 Some Things Need To Be Said 348
Chapter 143 It Is Time 353
Chapter 144 Keeping America Safe 355
Chapter 145 The Law And Me 357
Chapter 146 A Lesson To Learn 358
Chapter 147 Looking Success Straight In The Eye 360
Chapter 148 Leaving The Past Behind 362
Chapter 149 On The Same Road…Again 365
Chapter 150 Political Correctness Or Political Control 367
Chapter 151 Learning About The Work Of A Chief Executive Officer 369
Chapter 152 Enjoying "Woe Is Me" 371
Chapter 153 My Thin Skin 373
Chapter 154 Success: Available To Everyone 375
Chapter 155 American Citizens: "Reduce The Size Of Government" 377
Chapter 156 Why We Do The Things We Do 379

Chapter 157   When My Neighbor Throws Rocks   381
Chapter 158   Hate: On The Rise, Again   383
Chapter 159   Control, Mastery And Maturity   386
Chapter 160   Treating Failure As Success   389
Chapter 161   Something To Remember Now & When
              We Vote   391
Chapter 162   What Happened To All The Gumption?   392
Chapter 163   The High Costs Of Brainwashing   393
Chapter 164   A Flourishing Life   397
Chapter 165   Freedom To Fly High   399
Chapter 166   A Word To Politicians   401
Chapter 167   Looking For The Promised Land   403
Chapter 168   Capturing People: As Easy As Capturing
              Wild Pigs   407
Chapter 169   Let's Quit Being Offended   409
Chapter 170   Obama Got Part Of What He Wanted   411
Chapter 171   Finances Should Be Better   413
Chapter 172   The News Media And Mind Control   414
Chapter 173   Now, What Do We Americans Do?   416

Conclusion: 419

SECTION ONE

Surprise and Some Reasons Why

CHAPTER 1

THE PRESIDENTIAL ELECTION: WHAT HAPPENED?

B ottom line: The American people would not allow the Democratic Party to completely eliminate constitutional government. Had Mrs. Clinton won, it would have been only a matter of time until the Constitution of the United States was completely eliminated, to be found only in history books.

For decades, liberal democrats have been on a course to replace our constitutional government with socialism, a form of government that majors on taking from productive people and giving to people who choose not to take care of themselves. This greatest nation in history has been built on opportunities for success being given to everyone: each person is encouraged to be productive and take care of himself/herself.

Many people choose to do nothing and live off the labor of others. This is the reason socialism has become so popular, and democrats have taken advantage of this, in effect saying to them, "Vote for us and we will tax the successful and give to you." Many have responded to this, and have gathered at the trough provided by democrats. This has resulted in a waste of the potential of millions of Americans as they have done nothing to develop their talents and abilities.

Then along comes a man who hates the United States, becomes president and works to diminish this nation any way he can, including ignoring the Constitution as he wishes, diminishing the military, diminishing the space program, taking freedoms from people, including freedom of speech, attacking our major religion by promoting another, by the misuse of executive orders to change what he does not like, and many other things. The Democratic Party has fully supported him in their drive to force socialism on this country, making it quite clear that they have no use for constitutional government.

It has taken the American people quite a while to realize and understand what the Democratic Party has been trying to do for the past several decades, which is nothing short of destroying the Constitution by replacing it with socialism, and, understanding this, have now said, "We will not permit this."

CHAPTER 2

THE TRUMP PHENOMENON

A lot of people are scratching their heads trying to figure out why Donald Trump has become so popular. He is saying a lot of things that have attracted a large following, something that is difficult to figure out.

But, is this so difficult to figure out? The Trump phenomenon is happening because of the utter disgust and anger productive Americans have toward what the politicians in Washington have done to this great country over the past few decades. At one time, not too long ago, we were the greatest nation the world has ever known, but professional politicians have been whittling away at this greatness, and have reduced us to a nation where we are much less than we once were.

There was a time when people came to America for a chance to work hard and enjoy the results of their labor. They are the ones who produced the greatest country. Now people are flocking here because they can become members of the great horde of people receiving government money extracted from the earnings of hard-working families. Some foreigners, who have contributed zero work in our country, are living on more money per month than citizens who have worked all their lives and paid taxes.

We how have over 40 million people receiving money from our government. In a nation that has been built on grit and determination, this should never be. We have been a nation of productive people working and taking care of ourselves. We now are fast becoming a nation of people being taken care by other people, which is abandonment of what has made us the greatest nation in the history of the world. We are fast becoming a shadow of what we once were.

Some current politicians running for office are shouting, "Vote for us, and we will give you even more things." This is attracting the ear of those who fail to understand that this is an unhealthy dependence because it eliminates self-care, which is a hallmark of good mental health. Mentally healthy people always care for themselves, producing what is needed to make life good.

Many of our citizens have awakened to the reality of what our politicians in Washington have done to us, and their evaluation of something gone wrong is spilling over as trump is giving voice to their feelings. What we need to realize is that anger that is based on evaluation is a healthy anger, not a destructive one. Good anger is something that can lead us to make decisions that are best for our country. Good decisions are not made when bad anger is in control. Good decisions come out of healthy anger because it leads us to deal with the issues that have led us to be what we now are. What is involved following healthy anger is concentration on how to deal with the issues that have led us to be what we now are. This will involve a lot of thought, which will enable us to properly evaluate why we are now where we are, and what we must do to again become a beacon of freedom and hope for the world.

Dealing with the kind of damage done by politicians over the past few decades will not be easy, and good minds, free of the wrong kind of anger, will be needed for this.

CHAPTER 3

STUNNED

The word "stunned" may be the best word to use to describe the reaction of many Americans to the election of Donald Trump as our next president. There have been all kinds of reaction to his election, from the crowds who march, proclaiming, "Not our president," to those who see this as nothing more than a "Brexit" vote, suggesting that voters simply didn't know what they were doing.

On the contrary, this vote for president was a reaction of people who believe government under our Constitution is the way things should be in this country, not what has been coming from our current politicians in Washington or from those who have been victims of some effective brainwashing, i.e. students in and from our colleges, and people who have been receiving free money printed by our government.

The United States became the greatest nation in the world because the Constitution offered people the opportunity to build lives as they desired, not as the political powers desired. In other words, citizens have been free to build their own lives as they desired, not as circumscribed by the politicians in Washington.

The politicians in Washington, according to our Constitution, are supposed to serve us citizens. We are not supposed to serve politicians, but the politicians have effectively reversed this, and this is the great problem voters have with the power structure now in Congress and the White House. It is not the job of citizens to do what politicians want us to do; their job is to move in the direction the citizens want.

In the current system in Washington, money has bought the allegiance of poor people. It has bought the allegiance of employees in government, as Obama gave them undeserved raises, making them earn much more than they could in comparable jobs in the private sector. It has bought the allegiance of people on Wall Street by rigging the system so they could dramatically increase their "earnings," and this has led to the virtual elimination of the middle class in this country. It has bought the allegiance of non-productive people as they have received free money from Washington.

In addition to these things, what is supposed to be an educational system in our colleges has been dumbed down in many colleges and universities to nothing more than a program of indoctrinating people to think what they are told to think. This was a preliminary to getting people to believe that socialism is superior to constitutional government. Socialism has never been equal to constitutional government, and it never will be because it takes the control of one's life out of the individuals' hands and places it in the hands of politicians, many of whom are not capable of forming their own thoughts.

Did the voters do the wrong thing in electing Donald Trump to be president? No, they did not. Had Mrs. Clinton won, the Constitution would have been confined to the history books, and the people in Washington would have been free to call the shots for the kind of life every American would have. This is not what this country has been about, and, if we ever go there, the life of each individual will become dependent on what the politicians in Washington decide it will be. We would then become an "also-ran" country of people marching to the beat of the politicians in Washington, not to our own beat as provided by our Constitution.

"Stunned?" Yes, that may be the best word to use in describing the reaction of many people to the election of Donald Trump as president.

CHAPTER 4

IT IS MORE THAN SOUR GRAPES OR SORE LOSERS

The reaction of the democrats is leading some people to say, "It's just sour grapes" or, "They are sore losers." But, their reaction goes far beyond this. For decades, long before many people alive today were born, the democrats have been trying to fundamentally change how our country is governed. They do not like constitutional government, and wish to do away with it..

They almost got what they wanted. Had Mrs. Clinton won the presidency, they would have taken the final step of discarding the Constitution of The United States. This is what they have been in the process of doing for a long time. The many welfare programs they have pushed through Congress, although sounding good because a small percentage really did need assistance, was a great leap forward in making millions of willing participants dependent on government. This was a huge step in replacing constitutional government with socialism.

The democrats had worked their program well, year after year, and there was a steady increase in the number of people who supported what they were doing. They believed they could take the final step this year of eliminating the Constitution and replacing it with socialism.

This accounts for the sour grapes and the democrats appearing to be such poor losers. They have seen the election of Mr. Trump over Mrs. Clinton as the destruction of their dreams, and they are a shattered people at this time.

The person they counted on to help them take the final step toward socialism, Obama, has failed to drive the last nail in the coffin. He created as much division in this country as he could, so much so that he can be called "The Great Divider." He took us rapidly toward becoming a third-world country, about as far as he could take us, but enough Americans caught on to what was happening to call a halt to it.

The people who are now demonstrating, rioting, and coming up with all kinds of things to discredit Trump's election are expressing disappointment and grief over their loss. They are acting like third-world people. They are not true Americans who respect the guidelines of the Constitution.

In the previous two presidential elections, millions of Americans disliked the election of Obama, but they did not demonstrate or riot. They were good Americans, and let our guiding document, the Constitution, guide them. That is what good Americans do, and that is what should be happening now.

Continuing to have fits over not getting their way is a certain sign they do not believe in our Constitution, and, because of this, it can be said that they are not good Americans. The framers of the Constitution wrote it to protect the people of this great nation from those who might think they had a better idea.

CHAPTER 5

PLUGGING THE HOLES IN THE BOAT

Everyone knows that, if the boat you're in has holes in it, it will sink if you do not plug those holes. Everyone knows that, right?

Apparently, many do not believe this. At the present time, the financial boat of the United States has many holes in it and is on the verge of sinking, but many are suggesting that, rather than plug some of the holes, more holes should be bored.

"Let's go on spending what we have been spending; everything is going to be okay. And, while we are at it, let's drill a few more holes by passing this new legislation we are putting on the books." The concept of making things worse does not seem to be on the horizon for politicians who are addicted to developing new ways to spend more money.

Both republicans and democrats have for decades been drilling more holes in our financial boat by figuring out ways to spend more and more of our tax money. It seems, however, that many republicans have now realized that endless spending has greatly crippled our financial viability, and desire to start plugging the holes in this boat, but the democrats give no sign of wanting to do so. Rather, they say, "Uncover all the holes you are trying to plug. Everything is going to be okay. All we have to do is print more money."

Democrats seem to be following the philosophy that, if you just keep on doing things that have not worked long enough, eventually they will begin to work. In better circles, this is known as stupidity.

We are in great need of new people to operate the financial boat of the United States. We need people who understand that our leaky boat must be repaired. It is sinking, and the same old inattention to the holes is drowning us all. Astute people all around the world, through the money they have loaned us to stay afloat, are poised to call in our debt and, not only put us on our financial knees, but lay us prostrate as a totally bankrupt nation.

Our administration and Congress have played the fool by trying to remedy problems that only citizens can remedy. They have positioned themselves as the great saviors of those who have shown no interest in lifting themselves to a better life, and they have plunged us further into the weakness of a people who have no clue as to what being real Americans is all about.

With all haste, we need to plug the holes in our boat. Returning to what we have been doing is a certain disaster. We need to have people in Washington who are aware this disaster is actually happening, but too many of them are trying to row the boat with their heads so high in the air they cannot see all the water accumulating at their feet.

Many citizens believe the current politicians in Washington have no ability to make things better for our country, and that whatever they do will make things worse. It is a matter of how much worse things will be. Until we replace those who now operate the boat, the plugs will not be put in place and the water around our feet will get deeper, and the time will come when the holes can no longer be plugged.

CHAPTER 6

THE DAY AMERICA COULD HAVE DIED

The United States has been a great nation, made so because it gave everyone, regardless of where they originated, the chance to make something of themselves through personal grit and determination. For the first time in the history of the world, people could become what they wanted to become because of the freedoms they were offered. No political body would keep people from living in freedom and achievement.

We struggled for a long time in our quest for freedom for everyone, and many people had to pay high prices in this quest, i.e. the Civil War and the other wars we have fought. We were approaching the time when, regardless of color, we could all stand shoulder to shoulder. MLK, Jr. moved us a long way toward this, and full equality seemed only a matter of time. But, he was assassinated, and the movement he was on was derailed.

The chance to stand tall with everyone was still available, but some people did not want everyone in this great nation to rise and learn that the best life anyone can have is the one they build for themselves. A group of politicians realized that assuming personal responsibility for oneself, which includes preparation and often struggle, would remove millions of people from their influence. People who take care of themselves don't want others to take care of them.

How to make people want to be cared for was the subject pursued, and the quest to make people want to be cared for became the goal. By whom? By people who believe in socialism, a form of government that convinces people that the government, i. e. politicians, can take better care of them than they can take care of themselves.

As a result, a group of politicians developed government giveaway programs, things we now call the "Welfare System." Many people saw this as an opportunity to stop marching toward equality, and signed up for the government programs, never realizing they were settling for a way of life far inferior to the one they could build for themselves. Now, in 2016 we are awash with multiple government programs that have destroyed personal initiative and accomplishment, and millions of people live wasted lives.

The day America would have died was the day a majority of citizens could have turned down the chance to build their dreams on personal effort, and accept additional giveaways from the giveaway crowd in Washington.

Who are these people who stepped in and offered millions a chance to avoid the responsibility of personal care? Simply put, they are liberals who do not believe people can take care of themselves, and need politicians to do it for them.

These people are not hard to identify. They go by the name of democrats, and they are convinced they know how to take better care of people than people themselves know. Democrats might protest this evaluation of them, but the writing has been clearly on the wall. This was seen a long time ago by none other than Norman Mattoon Thomas, six times Socialist Party candidate for President of the United States who, in a 1944 speech said, "The American people will never knowingly adopt socialism. But, under the name of 'liberalism,' they will adopt the socialist program, until one day America will adopt it without knowing how it happened." He further said, because of this, he no longer needed to run for President of the United States, and, "The Democratic Party has adopted our platform."

Had the democrats won the presidential election, they would have completed their "coup" of replacing our Constitutional Government, which offers freedom to be what we want to be, with socialism, where life for each of us is determined by the liberal politicians in Washington.

If enough people had scrambled to be taken care of by the politicians in Washington, then the taps could have been played for the death of America. That day could have happened in November if Mrs. Clinton had been elected President of the United States. It was quite clear she does not believe in the Constitution or Bill of Rights, she wants to continue bringing people from the Middle East to this country, and that she would take away more of the freedoms that have made America a great nation. The coup would have been complete had she received the most votes, and became our next president. But, that did not happen, thankfully.

CHAPTER 7

IT JUST MAY NOT BE ANGER

Some people who are mystified about the election of Donald Trump are taking the position that this vote for him was by angry people. They may be entirely wrong about this. Even Bill Clinton has said the voting was by angry white men.

Proper evaluation by thinking people may have been what prompted their vote. Weighing the pros and cons of constitutional government against what the move toward socialism has been doing resulted in many people deciding that constitutional government is far superior to socialism. Socialism makes dependents out of people by taking money from the rich and giving to those who, even though able-bodied, choose not to work. This is a totally unfair system, but liberals were speeding us toward it.

What thinking Americans saw developing over the past several decades were efforts by liberal politicians to completely change what has made America a great nation. This thing of people standing on their own two feet, getting a job, and becoming productive is what resulted in us standing taller than other nations, and we did not want to be drug down to become a third-world country, which seems to be where recent politicians have been taking us.

There are many things some Americans don't like. In the last eight years, our debt has almost doubled to 20 trillion dollars, and the powers of the last few years had planned to keep the deficits piling up with no end in sight. What happened to Greece could be seen rapidly approaching our country. Thinking people don't want this to happen, and realize that getting a handle on this will be awfully difficult, but it must be done.

Our military has been drastically cut, and, withdrawing from Iraq opened the door for the growth of ISIS. Radical Muslims are committed to the destruction of America, and we need leadership who understand their goal of destroying this nation. Hillary Clinton was committed to continuing Obama's policies, and this meant continuing to allow dangerous people to easily enter this country, doing little to nothing anywhere to confront the worst enemy we have in today's world.

The number of people holding jobs and contributing to the welfare of this nation is far below what it should be. The official unemployment rate is a big lie because we now have more people not working than ever before in our history. This is an effort by current politicians to make a bad situation look good, and it is entirely false.

In the past eight years, we have been reduced from the acknowledged leader in space to following behind Russia and China, and the prospects look like it will get even worse. It is ridiculous that we have so quickly been reduced to having to pay Russia to put our astronauts into space.

What is supposed to be an educational program that teaches students to think has become mostly an indoctrination program geared to make good socialists out of otherwise good students, and this has been done in such a way that students don't realize that they have been trained to think the thoughts they are told to think. Returning to a good educational system will be difficult, but it can and must be done.

Many millions of people have been completely fooled by Obama as he presented himself as a nice guy, but was really in the process of diminishing this nation to be on the level of third-world countries. Enough people have seen behind this façade to understand that, every chance he got, he was stabbing us in the back to make us what he wanted us to be. Many people accept things on face value, but there are others who have the ability to ask the question, "Why is this being done?" The answer they found was not in keeping with the Constitution of the United States and the Bill of Rights.

Many Americans have read neither the Constitution nor the Bill of Rights. If you have not read them, it is recommended that you do so. You would do well to read them both. Following is a part of the Bill of Rights:

"The Unanimous Declaration of the thirteen United States of America,

When in the Course of human events, it becomes necessary for one people to dissolve the political

Bands which have connected them with another, and to assume the powers of the earth, the separate and equal station to which the Laws of Nature and of Nature's Go entitle them, a decent respect to the opinions of mankind requires that they should declare the causes that impel them to the separation.

We hold these truths to be self-evident, that all men are created equal, that they are endowed by their Creator with certain unalienable Rights, that among these are Life, Liberty and the pursuit of Happiness – That to secure these rights, Governments are instituted among Men, deriving their just powers from the consent of the governed – That whenever any Form of Government becomes destructive of these ends, it is the Right of the People to alter or to abolish it, and to institute new Government, laying its foundation on such principles and organizing powers in such form, as to them shall seem most likely to effect their Safety and Happiness. Prudence, indeed, will dictate that Governments long established should not be changed for light and transient causes; and accordingly all experience hath shewn, that mankind are more disposed to suffer, while evils are sufferable, than to right themselves by abolishing the forms to which they are accustomed. But when a long train of abuses and usurpations, pursuing invariable the same Object evinces a design to reduce them under absolute Despotism, it is their right, it is their duty, to throw off such Government, and to provide new Guards for their future security."

Those who claim the vote for Trump was out of anger are completely wrong. A large number of Americans were familiar enough with both the Constitution and Bill of Rights to understand where the liberals were taking us, which was none other than abolishment of government under our Constitution. It was the duty of Americans to change a form of government the liberals were trying to create. Replacing the Constitution and Bill of Rights with socialism was not acceptable.

Bottom line: No, the vote for Donald Trump was not generated by uncontrolled anger, although there were many reasons to be angry. As Americans thought seriously about the damage to our country done by democrats/socialists, there was only one way we could have voted. That way was to save our form of constitutional government.

CHAPTER 8

NO SAVIOR FOR THE AMERICAN PEOPLE

There is no political savior for the American people. There never has been, and there never will be. With each election, however, we allow people with personal magic to charm and convince us that they will bring us into the land of nirvana where we will be saved from all that discomforts us.

Finding ourselves in the throes of incompleteness, we want to believe that some elected official can help us avoid being responsible for our own condition, and we are easily fooled because we want to be fooled. We like to believe that our redemption lies in the hands of those who wield power in Washington, and never stop to realize that we are the masters of our own fate.

We do not need to look outside ourselves for the power to correct what is wrong in our lives; what we need is already within us. By focusing our attention on receiving something from the hands of those we put into political offices, we keep ourselves blinded to the vast potential within to take care of our own selves. By not using the power within, we miss the chance to redeem ourselves. Yes, redeem ourselves! We want politicians to fix us, but we are the only ones who can fix ourselves.

We became a great nation because people were provided the environment in which they could make their own way and take care of themselves. Those who now want the government to be their caretakers fail to understand that this is a road to weakness.

For those who are not sure what they want in Washington, give careful attention to the politicians who understand that our nation's strength is not centered in what politicians do, but in what we citizens individually do as we make our way in this world.

CHAPTER 9

SINKING INTO MEDIOCRITY

S inking into mediocrity should never be a consideration for good Americans, but it seems to be the goal of many who haven't figured out how their uniqueness should be directed toward building lives of value.

Each of us is unique. There is not another person, in all the billions who inhabit the earth, exactly like you, and there never will be. You may have potential within to do some truly amazing things no-one else has or ever will have done. We've seen individuals throughout history rise and do something to meet the needs of their times.

One of the things of which we need to be aware is that contributions to making life better don't come accidentally. They come after preparation through either training or education, and sometimes both. To find one's uniqueness and how development of that uniqueness can bring blessings to others is one of the most exciting things that can happen to us. Sometimes the rewards of this come in the form of money, but what is the most meaningful payoff is the great sense of having done something that is good for others. To feel good about oneself may be the best reward we can receive.

We cannot be mediocre and make our potential contributions. However, we now face in this country an onslaught of efforts to make people mediocre. This is being done by people who are trying to drag us from a constitutional republic where people are individually responsible for what they do to a form of government, socialism, where individuals become what politicians want them to become, and outstanding individual accomplishment is diminished to meet the desires of politicians. Outstanding individual accomplishment that makes an individual stand out is frowned upon by people who want to control what each person does with his/her life.

CHAPTER 10

THINGS THAT HAVE DIMINISHED
THIS COUNTRY

Well, where shall we start? There are many things that have been made worse by people who think their ideas are superior to the framers of our Constitution. Only a few of these will be mentioned.

1. First, how about the military? There has been an erosion in both personnel and the things with which to defend ourselves. When Obama pulled our troops out of Iraq, it opened the door for the growth of ISIS

2. Then, there's our educational programs, which should be teaching students to think for themselves, but which have been turned into a system of producing clones who regurgitate what they have been taught, and they have been taught that group-think is far better than individual thinking and accomplishment. The very idea of colleges providing crying rooms for students to cry together over the election of Trump indicates not only gross immaturity on the part of students, but, also, a philosophy of teaching

students they don't have to grow up and meet the world as adults.

3. What about our borders? We have been told that we should let anyone wanting to come to this country to be allowed to cross our borders whenever they wished. Among those who have walked freely across are criminals, among whom are people intent on destroying this nation, and Obama refuses to keep these people out.

4. Then there is religion, where our president has become the best missionary to American the Muslims have ever had. His attacks on Christianity have been completely inappropriate and out of place for a president. This is one of many indications that he does not understand what his job is.

5. Then there are the laws of this land that many newcomers think they should not follow. They want to bring their own laws and disregard the ones we have. Our government is letting them do this.

6. There have been attacks on many things:
   a. "Political correctness" has replaced freedom of speech.
   b. Freedom of religion is no longer deemed appropriate. The Oval Office has projected Christianity as a bad religion.
   c. Attacks on ownership of guns are frequent by people who do not understand the real human problem. This exposes failure in addressing things which caused the real problem.
   d. Criminals have been given a pass by our president, and this has opened the door for many law enforcement personnel to be murdered.
   e. Free money from Washington has been given to people for doing nothing, a certain way to make dependents out of otherwise good people.

f. The housing market collapsed when "everyone should have a house" became the shout from Congress. This has caused many good Americans significant losses in the value of their property, and it led to people again failing because they could not pay notes.

g. The welfare system has made unproductive beggars out of millions of otherwise good people. Why should anyone get a job when free money from Washington can be had. Also, why not have another baby so the government will give you more money. A colleague tells about overhearing a conversation his mildly retarded daughter had with a friend. She said, "I need more money. I don't have enough." The friend said, "Have another baby and the government will give you another check." Sadly, women are definitely having more babies so they can get more money. This should never be a reason to have a baby.

h. Give-away programs that cost taxpayers loads of money have proliferated. The girl who bragged about having 30 free phones comes to mind.

i. Continuing some type of school only for the purpose of receiving government money has become popular with some students who have no interest in what they are "studying." An acquaintance of my wife quit her job because students let her know they would never get a job doing what they were preparing for.

j. Because of Obama, males can now go into women's rest rooms, and vice versa, and this opens the door for exploitation by sexual perverts.

7. Obama had an opportunity to help bring healing in racial relationships, something every president should be interested in, but he was interested in doing the opposite. He has done much in an attempt to elevate black people

while attacking white people. He has even given a pass to the criminal activity of some blacks, as mentioned above, and has contributed to the killing of law enforcement personnel. In the eyes of this writer, he has become "The Great Divider" by pitting people against each other.

8. Obama has planted thousands of Muslims in many places in the U. S., people who have no intention, whatsoever, of following our laws or assimilating into this country. If a person cannot follow our laws, that person should not be allowed to remain in this country. Citizens need to pay attention to this. Obama told us he wanted to change this country, and this is one of the ways he is doing it while portraying himself as a good American. I once heard a CEO of a large hospital say, regarding his Board of Directors, "Tell them what they want to hear, and you can do anything you want to do." Obama has done a lot of this, and gotten away with many things that should never have been done by a President of the United States.

These are but a few of the things that have been done in the last several decades to change this country from a nation where politicians serve people to one where people serve politicians. It took a long time for Americans to understand where politicians have been leading us, but, when they understood this, they voted to not let it happen. Correcting the damage that has been done will be difficult, and it will take time, but correction must be done.

CHAPTER 11

A DIFFERENT QUALITY OF PEOPLE

The United States was originally settled by people coming here to make a better life for themselves. They came because of the freedom offered to do anything they wished, and earn the rewards that come from working hard. They were allowed (and expected) to stand on their own feet, and live the kind of life they made for themselves. They were industrious people who relied only on themselves, not the government, to make it in this world.

This is not the kind of people who are now immigrating here. What we now have are those who are coming to receive a handout of money from the government. Many of them have no intention of working hard. They just want to live off the labor and earnings of other people.

This morning (12/02/16), the news caught my attention by referencing thousands of immigrants coming to the U. S. because they had been rejected by Australia. Our government will probably give them a welcome hand, giving them money so they can make a go of it. Question! Are we accepting people who do not meet the standards of other nations? This points to us becoming the dumping grounds for any kind of person wishing to come here. Where have our standards gone? Will we accept just anybody? That seems to be where we are going with Obama opening our borders to anyone who wishes to walk across.

We already know Obama has welcomed thousands of people who have no intention of assimilating and following our laws, and they have been planted in various parts of this country with our money given freely to them. We will pay dearly for this as they repeat the kind of lives they came from. Anyone fleeing another country should not live the life here they fled from there.

Making us become like the rest of the world may have been the goal of democrats all along. They chose a man for president who has made giant strides toward making this happen, and then they chose Hillary Clinton, who committed herself to follow in his footsteps.

Hopefully, Trump and his people will put a stop to this. If they don't, we will become a third-world country.

CHAPTER 12

THE GREATEST DAMAGE

The greatest damage done to the United States in the past 80 years was not the Great Depression or the Second World War. It was not the Korean War, the Vietnam War or any other conflict we have been in. It has not been any economic disaster or any disease that has hit us.

The greatest damage done to this country has been the things done on Capitol Hill and in the Oval Office. It has been done by people who often had good intentions, but actually screwed things up. Some, however, intended to do the wrong things, and accomplished what they set out to do.

The Depression and the wars we fought, and many other things, were disasters, but they brought the emergence of the great potential within the American people. These things showed what was on the inside of us: the possibility of doing great things. We saw great potential in people from all backgrounds. It did not matter if they were rich or poor, white, black or other. The only thing that mattered was the willingness to prepare for whatever the task was. Sometimes the obstacles were enormous, and these confronted black people more than others, but they dug down and showed what many people thought they did not have: people like the Tuskegee Airmen, Willie Mays and others showed us that color was no barrier to achievement. We have seen potential realized in the lives of men like Thomas Sowell and Dr. Ben Carson. We saw Martin Luther King, Jr. and his followers earn things long denied them, and they positioned themselves to do great things in the future.

But, the politicians stepped in and said, "Whoa, let us do the lifting for you," to both black people and poor white people. "Let us do for you what you need done," and they began passing such things as the Great Society programs and all the other welfare/entitlement programs which followed.

Some of the Civil Rights legislation was needed, but the politicians went far beyond need and did things which should never have been done. This resulted in both blacks and poor white people losing the desire to accomplish things for themselves. There was no need for them to make their own way, and the great potential in each of them was buried under the stream of dollars from Washington. Rather than building their lives on what was on the inside of them and opening a limitless future, they built their lives on how much money politicians could lift from successful people and give to them. This is why so many of them wound up in ghettos and other substandard environments, including jails and prisons. They allowed their future to be circumscribed by politicians, and stagnation and even retreat followed.

Had black people remained on the road they had begun traveling before these legislators took the initiative from them, it would have been only a matter of time until they caught up with white people. They have been and are as innately capable as any race on the face of the earth. They, too, when born mentally and physically healthy, have an equal 100 billion brain cells other people have, and, if developed and used, can accomplish things equal to any other peoples.

Having met and listened to Martin Luther King, Jr., he would not have put up with the politicians, through their legislation, relegating black people to the sidelines, telling them they could go home, do nothing, and the government would take care of them. He had the people moving, and they would have continued moving if his kind of leadership had endured. It was an insult to black people to tell them they were not capable of providing for themselves and needed politicians to take care of them. This was a powerful statement of the inequality of blacks, but millions of people did not understand.

What kind of great scientists would have emerged in black people who sat down, did nothing, and waited on the government check? How many great scholars, authors, statesmen, explorers, teachers, business men and women would have emerged by those challenged to use the minds God gave them?

Yes, the greatest damage done to the United States in the last 80 years has been all those things done by politicians in Washington to take care of people who should have been taking care of themselves. The result of their effort has put millions of good people on the sidelines of life, burying their talents, and leading them to believe their future was better in the hands of politicians than in their own hands. This has turned out to be devastating to their efforts to take their place as equals among the people of the United States.

The beneficiaries of these welfare/entitlement programs have not been black people or poor white people. The real beneficiaries have been the liberal politicians themselves because it created a system whereby black people and poor whites felt they had no other choice but to vote for people who would keep the largess coming from Washington. In the therapists' office, this is called a co-dependent relationship, and is one of the unhealthiest relationships that can exist between people. Not developing their own talents and abilities to compete with the best minds in this country left millions of them with the inability to meet the demands of a productive life, and they had no choice but to let the politicians keep the free money coming.

We all are losers because some potentially great people have been led to sit down, do nothing, and wait on handouts from Washington…and it has greatly diminished what productive people could have accomplished had their money remained in their own hands.

Yes, the greatest damage done to the American people in the past 80 years has been done by the politicians in Washington.

CHAPTER 13

THUMBING THEIR NOSES AT THE AMERICAN PEOPLE

I f the American people will look carefully and honestly at what Obama and his democratic supporters in Congress have done to degrade the United States, they will clearly see and understand that they have been thumbing their noses at the American people. They have moved ahead with their agenda in the face of overwhelming objection by our citizens.

Democrats have essentially abandoned the guidelines of the Constitution, and have empowered one man to do whatever he wants to do. This is clear rejection of their responsibility to serve the American people. They now are serving the wishes of a president who does not like the United States, has not liked it, and he never will. He has been removing our freedoms and building what he wants.

This has made it quite clear that the democrats have rejected the Constitution, and have chosen to allow one man to determine what our nation will become. If another democrat is elected president, the deterioration of this nation will continue. Democrats are in Obama's hip pocket, which means the direction he has set will continue if their candidate for president, whoever that might be, is elected to occupy the Oval Office.

(This was written before Hillary Clinton became the democratic nominee for president.)

CHAPTER 14

WHY WOULD THE BEST WANT TO BECOME LIKE THE REST ANYWAY?

In all areas of life, most people want to be the best performers, and they dedicate themselves to preparation and hard work. Most of the time, we cheer them on. We pack stadiums to see the best baseball teams, the best football teams, the best basketball teams, etc. We do this because we want to see and be associated with winners. We pay big bucks to people like Michael Jordan, Tom Brady, Mat Ryan, and many others because we simply are looking for the best performers we can find.

In the business world, we pay big bucks to the CEO who can add greatly to the profit of a company, astounding amounts of money to an entertainer we enjoy. Someone in the crowd today spoke of wanting to attend the concert of one of the outstanding singers, but the tickets were $400 apiece.

We go to restaurants where we can find the best food, willing to pay much more for an outstanding meal than the low prices to be found in a "greasy spoon." We avoid the restaurant that gets a score of 50 from the Health Department because we want the best food we can get.

It is easy to find a list of the best colleges on the internet, and we send our students to the best colleges we can find and afford. We pay outstanding professors big bucks because they can lead us to be better prepared to enter the business world.

We want to fly in the best airplanes, ride on cruise ships that have good reputations. We train the men and women who fly and steer these vessels, and pay them big bucks. We care not to ride on cattle ships or in freight cars.

But, then, we come to politics and there find a different story. We have been told, primarily by democrats, that excellence as a nation is not important. "We must become like the rest of the world. We do not need to stand above the accomplishments of other peoples. We should all be alike, walking on the same level with them. What the United Nations wants for the people of the world is good enough for us, so we don't need to struggle to be the best. The New World Order is what we should adopt. We must not do things that make us appear better than others. That is what is best for us because it will put us on the same level with others, and they will not feel bad toward us."

This is a bunch of hogwash being spewed by democrats, but it has attracted millions of people who think leveling the playing field is best for everyone. Something like this would never work on the athletic field, in business and industry, in academia. Fact is, it will not work best anywhere, even in politics and building a country. Why? Because it takes a person handing control of his/her life over to people who do not understand the importance of individual effort and performance in an environment of freedom, which our Constitution offers. In order to usher in "The New World Order," the American Constitution would have to be confined only to the history books, never to be used again.

No, reducing the United States to become like the rest of the world would be a tragic mistake because it would remove from the individual the great opportunities now available to anyone who wishes to make something of themselves.

The best should never desire to be like the rest because that can never be as rewarding as what we now have.

CHAPTER 15

THEY STOPPED DREAMING AND MARCHING

One of the greatest movements in American history was recently celebrated as thousands gathered in Washington to remember what Martin Luther King, Jr. had led black people to accomplish 50 years ago. It was well-worth celebrating because blacks had lifted themselves where no others could have lifted them. They did the heavy lifting that had to be done, and they took some giant steps.

But, tragically, they stopped dreaming and marching, turning their progress over to others. They turned over this progress to predominantly liberal politicians in Washington and the race baiters like Jessie Jackson and Al Sharpton who really snookered them with the message, "You can't take care of yourselves, but the government will." The politicians developed the entitlement programs, and the race baiters ratcheted up the message, "You need us and the government handouts to make it." Many black people accepted this as truth, and shut down any effort to develop their talents and abilities so they could be successful on their own. They were getting free money while having to do nothing to receive it. Then, to the surprise of no-one, millions of poor white people jumped on the bandwagon with them, and they all forgot about their responsibilities to make something of themselves.

The real beneficiaries of the entitlement programs were not the poor people. No, it was the politicians trapping them in a system that guaranteed votes at the next election. For the race-baiters it meant a flow of money to keep alive the message, "Poor people need the government handouts if they are to make it." A state of dependency developed whereby politicians had to keep the free money flowing in order to get votes, and poor people had to keep voting for these politicians in order for the money to keep coming.

PERMANENT INEQUALITY: What the entitlement programs did, however, was to lift poor people to a level of permanent inferiority and inequality. It made them dependent on the government taking money from productive people and giving to them. There can never be equality, something Martin Luther King, Jr. died trying to bring about, when another person has to work for you to eat. You will always be inferior and unequal to the person who makes money so you can live.

Robbing blacks and poor white people of the need to care for themselves has probably done far more damage than it has helped. The great potential blacks had begun to show ended when they turned their progress over to politicians and the race baiters. Many good things that could have happened did not happen because they stopped doing the things only they could do.

If a person wants to see the devastating effects of entitlement programs, all that has to be done is make a trip into inner-city jails and prisons and observe who is there or go to Wal-Mart and see people too obese to do any kind of productive work. Go to the poor neighborhoods and see young people and children wandering the streets in the evenings and at night rather than plowing through books to learn and do well for themselves.

A huge amount of potential that was on the verge of exploding under King's leadership was put to sleep by the gifts from Washington. Had this free money not come, poor people would have had to rely on themselves, depending on their own ingenuity, creativity, study and preparation to gain equality rather than on what the politicians could do for them. The free money put millions to sleep, to awaken only when it was time to vote again for politicians who would give them more.

There were, however, multitudes of poor people who did not accept the free stuff, and they now walk in equality alongside those who are successful. These are the people who chose to put their heads into books to learn and train, and they achieved equality, now occupying the middle and upper classes, enjoying many more things money can buy than is possible with handouts from Washington.

There should be more people developing what is on the inside of them, people like Dr. Ben Carson, who emerged from being the dumbest kid in the fifth grade and living on welfare to become the pre-eminent pediatric neurosurgeon in the entire world. He did this because he relied on himself, using and developing what he was born with. Had he kept relying on the government for his money, he would have remained on the government dole, accomplishing very little in life. This should have happened thousands and millions of times in the black and poor white communities, but the money from Washington put an end to personal achievement.

Witnessing so many natural talents and abilities being swept under the rug with free money from Washington is sad to see. Not making one's own way, but allowing others to determine what you will receive, only results in a life far inferior to what you could have made for yourself. Each person could have used the 100 billion brain cells we all came equipped with, but too often these brain cells have been put to sleep by the choices made.

Politicians in Washington bought off poor white people and those who were marching under MLK, Jr., and they and the entire nation are poorer for this having happened. Blacks stopped dreaming and marching, and poor whites sat down on the sidelines with them, and all who did so have not come nearly as far as they could have propelled themselves under their own power.

Black people should take up their dreaming and marching again, and they should be joined by poor whites. They can give themselves far more using their own abilities and power than can be given them by the Washington crowd. Everyone needs to march to his own tune, not to the tune that is determined under the Capitol Dome.

CHAPTER 16

THE WORK OF THE GREAT DIVIDER

What we are now seeing in this country are the results of eight years of The Great Divider. From the very beginning, he spewed words of division even as he was capturing the imagination of millions of people. Many saw him as their savior, one who would take them to the Promised Land.

He was and is a good-looking man with a winsome personality, and he said words that fascinated many, leading them to believe he could indeed take us to The Promised Land. Without asking what these words meant, which few people did, he captured the imagination and hearts of a crowd who quickly jumped on board, ready to go with him anywhere. People should have been asking "What is the meaning of his words?" but their fascination with him clouded out such a question. The answer was there, but the question was not asked.

He suggested that he would correct the wrongs of a country that is flawed. People believed him, and flocked to quickly follow him without trying to find out what his words really meant. They jumped on a train headed toward deep division, without any clue regarding its destination.

Shortly after capturing the imagination of people and winning election, he went abroad and quickly began attacking our country. Many people liked hearing him drag our dirty linen out for the world to see as he attacked our military, diminishing it significantly, creating a vacuum quickly filled by ISIS. He attacked our religion, indicating it was a bad religion, inferior to the Muslim faith. He attacked our Constitution and Bill of Rights, our law enforcement organizations. He opened our borders to good and bad people, and criminals came in by the scores. He set the races against each other, creating the worst racial divisions of the last 60 years. He made it possible for men to enter women's rest rooms, and no-one was to ask anything about it. He did many other things, and the list is long. He even fooled those who award Nobel prizes, and they bestowed one on him when he had done absolutely nothing to deserve it. The world became agog over an individual who kept his past shrouded, a man who had no track record of accomplishing anything worthwhile. He could mesmerize with his words, and that was all that counted.

He practiced well the art of "Divide and Conquer," and, what we see now in the many demonstrations against president-elect Trump, are the results of his planned divisions of this country. We have moved closer to becoming another third-world country, which is where he wanted to take us. People have become victims of what he has done, and have no clue about their victimhood.

This does not speak well for the ability of people to understand what a Constitutional Republic really is, a place where people are free to be what they wish to be.

A good leader, regardless of an organization's problems, tries to make it better, solving problems, bringing healing and unity, making things work better for all the people. He does not go about exposing its dirty linen, but tries to solve problems that led to this dirty linen. He did the reverse, and people, so mesmerized by his persona, failed to detect what he was doing. No good leader tries to destroy what he leads, but, that's what he did. Our Constitution and Bill of Rights became one of his favorite targets, and political correctness made people reluctant to open their mouths about anything less they be attacked.

People are now doing what this Great Divider prepared them to do. He wants to eliminate constitutional government, and many people have been prepped to assist with this – and they don't know he has done this to them.

CHAPTER 17

THE INABILITY TO UNDERSTAND

The present-day inability of college students and many of their professors to deal with the American people choosing Trump over Clinton does not surprise me. Professors do not teach and students do not learn the skill of thinking about things. Students are taught what to accept, and they must learn to regurgitate in order to make good grades. What is supposed to be a higher educational system has been turned into a system of indoctrination where it is the purpose of professors and college administrations to produce clones rather than educated people who have the ability to seriously think about anything.

Graduates of educational institutions in other countries, particularly those in the Orient, are running rings around students from American schools when it comes to quality education. This should be an embarrassment to American colleges, but they go on with an indoctrination program rather than one that teaches students to think.

This writer had the distinct privilege of being CEO of four small hospitals, and VP of one 500 bed big city hospital, as well as working in two colleges. It was surprising to me to learn that individuals with advanced college degrees many times lack the ability to think seriously about an issue. They will go along with the person who is an expert in a subject.

True education teaches students to think, to weigh the pros and cons of a given subject, and then decide personally on what they believe. It is not a matter of going along with a dominant personality, but, rather, it is establishing one's own beliefs.

We would still be living in caves if someone had not dreamed about something better, making decisions to do something about a given situation. Without questioning things as they are, and making personal decisions, we cannot find a way that is ours and not that of someone else. We must live our lives as we see fit. The dreams of other people cannot be our dreams. We must dream our own dreams.

The dreams of one man excited and drew the following of 96 percent of Germans in the 1930's, and we are all familiar with the results of this: World War II and the deaths of 60 million people. The best educated people in the world at that time failed to ask what Hitler meant with his words, and followed him into unbelievable horrors. This kind of story has been repeated throughout history as people have placed their thinking in neutral and followed the man with a golden tongue and the promise to take them to the Promised Land.

The Promised Land cannot be given by other people. It can come only through personal effort as each individual makes his life what he/she wants it to be. Development of what is on the inside is the secret to finding the life that is best for us.

It is the inability of individuals to think about things that brings attractions of the dreams of others, and leads to so much heartache in the world. Think your own thoughts and dream your dreams is the platform from which a good life begins. It doesn't come by jumping onto the bandwagon of someone else, which is at the heart of the disappointment of so many people re Donald Trump winning the presidential election. If ever there was proof that brainwashing does not deliver the desires of people, it is the election of Trump. Liberal politicians and professors circled their wagons, thinking they had a clear road to ascendency of socialism over constitutional government, but their thinking was all wrong because the American citizens decided that destruction of the greatest nation in the history of the world would not be accepted.

CHAPTER 18

WHERE WE HAVE COME FROM

The author of this book was born in 1934, and has had the privilege of living through some of the worst times and some of the best times this nation has had. Born during the Great Depression, he remembers his mother and five children living on $25 per month, struggling just to get along. He followed the progress of World War Two by looking at the maps printed in the paper showing where the battle lines were. He saw parents and grandparents agonize over the welfare of their soldier-boys. He read about the horrors in Europe and the island war in the Pacific.

He remembers seeing a brother, home just before shipping out to join the war in the Pacific, but the war ended one day before he was to ship out. The price Americans and the world paid for one man (Hitler) wanting to rule the world was staggering, with a death toll of 60 million people.

When the war was over, the soldiers, called by Tom Brokaw "The Greatest Generation," came home and, with the help of people on the home front who had supplied them with all the materials needed to win the war, helped build the greatest nation the world has ever seen.

The author remembers picking cotton for one-half cent per pound. He remembers his first public job off the farm was being a water boy at a tobacco warehouse in Douglas, Georgia, where he earned 50 cents for the whole day. He was glad to get the fifty cents: it was more than he had that morning.

Living in the South, he agonized over the racial conflicts that were enflamed by misguided politicians. The hatred spilled forth as evidenced by the assassination of Martin Luther King, Jr. Then he witnessed politicians stepping in and saying to black people, "Here, let us help you get what you are after. We will take care of you if you will vote for us." Then came an explosion of governmental programs aimed at taking care of poor people, both black and white, getting free this and free that. The programs took blacks off the march toward equality MLK, Jr. had them on, and their thrust toward earning their own way was curtailed, with many becoming no more than wards of the government. These programs were a guarantee that blacks would not move to a level of equality with white people, but many have not understood this.

These free programs were the wrong things. The words that should have been listened to were the words of Frederick Douglass, who said, in response to the question, "What shall you do with the negro?...Our answer is do nothing with them... Your doing with them is the greatest misfortune. They have been undone by your doings, and all they now ask...is just to let them alone undone by your doings, and all they now ask, and really have need of at your hands, is just to let them alone. They suffer by (your) interference, and succeed best by being let alone."

Black people would have been better off if liberals and others had not tried to lift them out of poverty. They would have done better if they had lifted themselves their own way rather than the way arranged by white politicians in Congress.

Making a life is not something someone else can do for you. It involves a personal journey an individual has to decide for self, not a journey decided by the occupants of Capitol Hill.

Politicians have messed up life for a lot of people, mistakenly believing their jobs are to lift Americans to a better life. That is not the case. Their job is to provide the environment where people can make their own way the way they wish.

This country, under its Constitution, offered the author an opportunity to build his life as he chose. This gave unlimited possibilities for him to build life as he desired, and politicians had nothing to do with it. Being extremely poor with parents who could not pay for college, the author worked, scratched, earned scholarships, did without and borrowed money that enabled him to wind up with thirteen years of education and training beyond high school.

He knows what possibilities people have within themselves if they once decide to make a good life. He has worked in an auto plant, in an aircraft plant, has been a laborer toting bricks and making mud for brick-layers, worked in admissions in two colleges, one where he was Director of Admissions, has been pastor of three small churches, Vice President in a 500 bed Atlanta hospital, Chief Executive Officer (CEO) in four small hospitals, is a Certified Pastoral Counselor, a Certified Clinical Evaluator and Certified Treatment Provider, Facilitator for Domestic Violence classes, Facilitator for Alcohol and Drug classes, an Individual, Marriage & Family Counselor, is a licensed nursing home administrator, and is author of several books. Plus, he played major college baseball and basketball, then transferring to a small college, played baseball and basketball and was captain of his basketball team his senior year. He said, "Some of this was tough, but I wouldn't change it for anything in the world."

THIS LIFE WOULD NOT HAVE BEEN POSSIBLE IF A GOVERNMENT PROGRAM HAD BEEN IN PLACE TO GIVE MONEY TO POOR PEOPLE. HIS FAMILY QUALIFIED AS POOR PEOPLE, AND HE SAID, "FREE MONEY WOULD HAVE BEEN OF GREAT HELP, BUT I AM GLAD IT WAS NOT AVAILABLE."

CHAPTER 19

WHAT HAS HAPPENED TO US?

During the last 60 years, we have experienced a decline in what has made the United States the GREATEST NATION IN THE HISTORY OF THE WORLD. This decline has been orchestrated by people who wish for us to become like other nations of the world where mediocrity or being average is the order of the day.

Americans put up with this too long, allowing those who wanted us to become like other nations to do things that brought decline in the ability of people to stand on their own two feet. This led us to having to make a choice between a presidential candidate who wanted to continue this decline and a candidate who wanted us to again stand up and become the best we can become. Those who finally understood how much we have declined in the last 60 years went to the polls and said, "Whoa, this has gone too far."

The onslaught of this decline was led by people who wanted us to follow the lead of other countries where "Be the best you can be" gave way to being average. This brought a serious decline in people being interested in making something of themselves. Outstanding performance gave way to average performance where the goal was to bring everyone to the same level. In the athletic world for kids, this meant giving the rewards of team participation to kids who sometimes never showed up to play. In the educational world, it led to passing students from one grade to the next unable to do the academic work traditionally required. In some places, earning a grade of "A" was never given because it would make the "C" or "D" or "F" student feel bad, so everyone got "P," a passing grade, including those who were not prepared to move on to a higher grade.

The goal was to reduce people to a common denominator where everyone received the rewards of accomplishment without accomplishing anything. This is why raising the minimum wage to $15 an hour became popular. What many people turn a blind eye to is the fact that $15 an hour and more has been available for a long time to anyone who would prepare through training and education, but millions of people wanted the reward without doing anything to earn it.

One of the things that has made America great is the opportunity to prepare, achieve above others, and be paid for performance and accomplishment. This has not been understood by many, as made plain by the pro athletes who have demonstrated by sitting while the national anthem has been played. They are great examples of individuals who have prepared, sometimes busting their butts, to perform better. By doing what was necessary, they have earned the big bucks. They could not have done it without the effort and sweat they were willing to endure. They should have said to the fans, "This is the way you make it in America," but they did not understand.

In our history, we have seen the unbelievable performance of persons who would not sit down and let their situation in life determine their future. One of the things that has led people to doing nothing with their talent is the availability of free money to the disabled. But, then, I look at Stephen Hawking and see an individual who appears to be incapable of any kind of performance, but he has risen to be one of the most outstanding people in knowledge about the universe. Although his body is terribly deformed, he has developed his brain to the genius level – and he has been paid well for what he has accomplished. This should shame anyone who asks to be paid $15 an hour when they have made no preparation to earn it.

What has made America great is the offer to everyone to work hard, and prepare through training and education for a chosen task. Anyone who champions rewards to everyone, regardless of preparation, does not understand the ingredients that bring greatness. If we ever lose the rewards of preparation and performance, we will assuredly become like other nations, the goal of those who have done so many things in the last 50 years to take care of people regardless of performance.

Eight years ago, we saw the champion of making us like the world occupy the White House. The people who put him there thought they had their champion who would complete our journey toward becoming mediocre like other nations, and this was to be followed by a candidate for presidency in 2016 who would put the crowning seal on the deal. Who are these people? Simply put, they are the liberal democrats who have little to no understanding regarding the true nature of a nation that became the greatest in the history of the world.

This book presents a series of articles written over the past ten plus years that address some of the decline toward mediocrity that has been orchestrated by people who want us all to be on the same level with other nations.

If you are satisfied with being mediocre, you may wish to read no further.

CHAPTER 20

FAILURE IN WHAT WE HAVE DONE

The things we have been doing in this country during the past 70 to 80 years have not been working. We should have become a better and stronger people, but that has not happened. Our mental health and strength of character are far less than they used to be. We have never been perfect, but we are further from it now than we were then. We have been powerfully reminded of this with the killings at Sandy Hook and other places.

We must make changes in what we are doing. A mentally healthy person with a gun in hand is not a dangerous person, but a mentally unhealthy person with a gun in hand will do horrible things. We must deal with the reasons we are producing so many mentally unhealthy people. It is not one thing which has led us to where we are now. It is a multiple of things, and we must take time to consider them all. A kneejerk reaction is not what we need at this time. We need good people to step up and identify where we have gone wrong, and each of us must search our own souls to determine if we are guilty, and be willing to do our part in correcting what needs to be corrected.

The path we will need to travel will not be easy, and there will be many who refuse to consider what must be considered. We must look at the failure which results from discrimination and the damage it does. We must look at the failure of religious organizations to teach and live the message of love they proclaim. We have abandoned a faith which at its very center says, "You shall love your neighbor as you love yourself." We must again learn the truth of this.

We must look at developing a better mental health system to identify and respond early to the needs that are so many. We must take a close look at legislation produced by politicians that divide us and removes from people their sense of dignity and worth, and there is much which must be looked at in this area. We must look at an educational system which seeks to clone a way of life that denies freedom of thought to students. We must challenge students to use their 100 billion brain cells in making their own way in the world, a way that does not take advantage of and degrade other people. We must look at our own individual belief systems and way of life which are often absent concern for other people. We must abandon striving to sit at the top of the totem pole by pushing other people down.

We must carefully examine an entertainment industry which glorifies sex and violence. We must be aware that all people are products of where they come from, and the more dysfunctional their backgrounds, the more dysfunctional they will be. We must look at the failure to prepare for marriage, and the failure to bring children into a loving and nurturing environment.

We must pull together good people to look at and consider the many things that must be considered. Politicians will tend to believe they can solve all our problems, but history has shown they often make things worse. We have many people with good minds capable of evaluating the multitude of problems we have, and what we must do to get back on the road toward health, freedom and equality for all. We have taken steps backward regarding this in my lifetime. Let's summon up the courage to identify where we have gone wrong, and get busy becoming better people who understand that good mental health is a prerequisite to building a better nation.

We have a lot of work to do. May we realize the work belongs to each of us.

CHAPTER 21

NEEDED: MORE RICH PEOPLE

What this country needs is more rich people. We do not need more poor people; we have enough of them already.

Rich people are the ones who produce wealth, and pay most of the taxes taken in by government to give to poor people. The top 50 percent pay 97% of all taxes, and the bottom 50% pay only three percent; many pay no taxes at all.

Eliminate rich people and the taxes they pay, and some poor people would starve to death because many of them are unable to take care of themselves. Poor people do not design and develop buildings; that is done by rich people. Poor people do not design and develop companies which produce televisions, computers, cars, trains, airplanes and rockets; that is done by rich people. It takes money, and lots of it, to generate economic growth, and this money is provided by rich people.

A favorite game played by liberals in this country is one we might call "The Mind-Poisoning Game," in which poor people are led to disparage rich people for their wealth. There are many examples of this, with the current one being that of berating companies for their "corporate jets." This is being used by the Oval Office to poison the minds of poor people against the wealthy. But, let's face it: the quicker rich people get from one place to the next, the quicker can they produce more wealth. Slow them down and wealth-building is slowed down, which means less taxes paid for the government to give away. And, we need to be aware that elimination of these jets would eliminate jobs of those who design, build and maintain them. This would be a certain way of increasing unemployment.

Why are poor people led to hate rich people? They are made to do this because it produces votes for the liberals. If poor people could ever figure out that the intent of liberals is to keep them dumb and poor, they would rebel and take their votes elsewhere. So, in order for liberals to stay in office, they must play this mind-poisoning game.

What the government (every politicians) needs to do is encourage and support people in their quest to become rich. In this way, more tax money would pour into IRS, and the more things this country could do. Instead of leading poor people to despise the rich, government should be helping them learn how to become rich themselves and contribute to the wealth of our nation. There are many minds in the heads of poor people which, if developed, would result in a lot of them becoming wealthy.

Yes, we need more rich people.

CHAPTER 22

THE WILL OF THE PEOPLE

One of the great strengths of the United States has been the "Will Of The People." It is the thing that, more than once, has brought us from things that would destroy our nation to a better life. The best example of this is the Civil War, which, had it not been fought, would have resulted with a divided nation that could never have accomplished the things that have made us the greatest nation in the history of the world.

What many people do not realize is that we have had, in the last several decades, liberal politicians moving us away from the things that have made us great. They have been slowly, but surely, moving us away from the Will of The People to a form of government where decisions are made by a select few people without regard to what citizens might want. We have seen in the last several decades, particularly in the last one, what can happen when politicians disregard the will of the people.

The strong statement that was made by the voters in the recent presidential election is, "We will not allow this to happen. You will not be allowed to degrade us from a constitutional government where you serve us to a form where we serve you, which, if that were to happen, would completely destroy our Constitution. We were slow getting to this point, but we finally were able to see the downgrading of our nation that has been taking place through programs that disregarded what is best for our nation. We will not allow you to continue your assault on our freedoms, and move us toward becoming a third world nation."

We are not a perfect nation, far from it, never will be, and we sometimes allow a strong personality to take us to places that are not good for us, but, give us time, and We the People correct our mistakes. We have begun to do that with our recent votes in the presidential election. The man who has been elected is not perfect, and he will make mistakes, as do all presidents, but one thing he will not destroy is our Constitution, which would have been done had we allowed continued assault on what has made us great.

Many people are expressing their anger through demonstrations and signing of requests for the Electoral College to undo the election. During the previous two elections, millions of Americans were angry at the election of Obama, and could have demonstrated and caused all kinds of trouble. But, we respected the Will of The People then and restrained our desire to cancel the election. We have found that controlling our anger is far better than turning it loose to lead us into all kinds of trouble.

Many nations still live on the level where one person or group of people take the position, "my way or the highway," but that cannot be a part of a great nation. We bide our time and wait to express our will when appropriate, and we did this in the election. The will of the people has been expressed. This is one of the ways in which we can maintain and continue a constitutional government for our nation.

If we ever lose the constitutional guidelines for "The Will of the People," we will be subject to the whims of the slick talker who can best convince us that he, and only he, can make us whole.

CHAPTER 23

SO MANY THINGS TO DO

We have too many things to do in this country for people, who are capable of taking care of themselves not to be doing so, choosing, rather, to be on the government dole. Foundations are overwhelmed with requests for assistance; charities cannot meet the needs of all the people who come to them asking for help. Churches cannot do all they could do if they had more money and more manpower. Homeless people can be seen in cities of any size, many of them with serious mental issues.

Dr. Stephen Hinshaw, professor of Psychology at the University of California, Berkeley, wrote in his book, "Origins of The Human Mind,""…it appears that ¼ of the world's population is afflicted with moderate to severe forms of mental illness in any given one-year period." We need many more people trained to work with the mentally ill, but too few are equipped to help.

The teacher told of the boy who said he and four other children living with their grandmother had been informed they would be kicked out of their apartment on Christmas Eve because the rent was not paid. She and others got busy and raised enough to pay the rent for two months. Many people are caretakers just struggling to get along without assistance they could use.

The casualties from drugs and alcohol are many, leaving families without someone with a job. A friend told of working with kids in a troubled Atlanta neighborhood where 75 percent lived with neither parent, and the other 25 percent lived with only one parent. Too many kids are brought into the world and no-one cares for them. Many of these, without proper rearing, wind up in our prisons.

This only scratches the surface of the human need that causes many to struggle. The men and women now living on free government money need to get a job and pay taxes to help with all this. In addition, many of them need to contribute time to help meet the needs of those mentioned earlier in this article.

One of the tragedies in our country is that our government gives free money to people, and, as a consequence, they do nothing to be of help to their fellow human beings. There are many things to do. We have enough people living in this country to do the things needed, but many sense no need to make themselves available to help, and just live off government money.

If everyone physically and mentally capable of working would prepare themselves to work, we could take care of all the human needs in this country as well as all the other things around us we see undone on a daily basis.

CHAPTER 24

ABANDONING THE CONSTITUTION

The Constitution of the United States was written to protect citizens from the kind of politicians now in Washington. Those who wrote the Constitution were good students of history and were aware that political leaders without constraints would take away freedoms and do things that are harmful to people.

From the current president to many of our legislators and now the Supreme Court, we have people who are disregarding constitutional guidelines, and the result is the removal of some of our freedoms. History shows that, once people's freedoms begin to be taken away, it is only a matter of time until more and more are gone.

Some of our politicians in the past have flirted with ignoring the Constitution, but there have been those who have called their hand, and constitutional government remained in place.

Over the past few years we have experienced what can happen when politicians have decided that they are better able to govern on their limited wisdom rather than on the Constitution. The result is a nation that no longer gives freedom to citizens to make their own decisions, but, rather, who are forced to accept what politicians in Washington decide is best for them. The

United States is no longer the bastion of freedom it once was. We no longer lead the world in exercise of freedom, and it is getting worse from day to day.

With the administration, members of Congress, and the Supreme Court moving away from constitutional guidelines, we find our nation rapidly falling apart economically (debt that is totally absurd), militarily, in international relationships, respect for each other, citizenship, religious freedom, and other things that have made us the envy of the world.

If we citizens do not make the corrections needed in our next election, we will be subjects of those in Washington who think they know what is best for each and every one of us. Thomas Sowell, political philosopher and senior fellow of the Hoover Institute, Stanford University, recently wrote, "When any branch of government can exercise powers not authorized by either statutes or the Constitution, 'we the people' are no longer free citizens but subjects, and our 'public servants' are really our public masters."

It is no accident that under the Constitution, we became the greatest nation in the history of the world. William Gladstone, four-time Prime Minister of England, said of our Constitution, ..."it is the most wonderful work ever struck off at a given time by the brain and purpose of man." Although we have often struggled with making freedom available to all our citizens, we, none-the-less, have been a nation superior to all others.

Current politicians in Washington are abandoning the guidelines of the Constitution, and the loss of freedoms we are now experiencing is only a taste of what is ahead for us if we citizens don't elect politicians who understand that the Constitution, although it is not perfect, is far better than any other governance document that has sprung from the mind of men.

(Written in 2015)

SECTION TWO

Changing the Greatest Nation

CHAPTER 25

THINKING ABOUT THINGS

One of the things that is a problem for many people is to do their own thinking. "You should not think like that" is the constant message many hear, first from their families and then from many others.

In the alcohol and drugs classes, this can be heard: "Yes, the reason I buy my date beer is so I can get her in bed with me." Things go like this: He buys her one beer; she drinks it, he gets fresh, and she says, "Don't; stop; don't do that." He buys her another beer, she drinks it; he gets fresh, and she says, "Stop, don't; stop!" He buys her another beer; she drinks it; he gets fresh, and she says, "Don't stop."

The man in counseling said, "Can't you see I'm stupid and can't do anything right?" When questioned why he thought that, he said, "When I was growing up, my father used to say that to me over and over."

These two things tell us that human beings are vulnerable to being manipulated by people who wish to control them. We should become aware that we need to learn to stand on our own two feet, and make decisions based on our own thinking, and not the thinking of others. If we don't do that, we become easy victims of those who wish to control us.

Political parties thrive on this. If they can get enough people thinking things they want them to think, they can get a majority vote and take over control of whatever they wish to control. History is full of disasters which follow good people allowing others to control their thinking.

As you read further, make certain your reaction to what is written is based on your own thinking, and not that of others who want you to think their thoughts.

CHAPTER 26

THE DESTRUCTION OF AMERICA

The destruction of America started a long time ago. We became a great nation because people clamored to get here so they could live as they chose and not as others planned. The freedom to build life on the basis of personal decisions was an attraction never before so completely offered by any other nation.

We became the greatest nation, but, as is always true, individuals with the need to control others were ever present. Coming out of WW II, we began to see more and more people believing they could rescue the world from its problems: we could live in a world where everyone had everything they needed. Many were attracted to the lure of communism, but communism proved to be a failure when seen against the backdrop of freedom. When this was understood, there developed an interest in socialism. Many people believed and still believe the playing field could be leveled with all wealth distributed evenly. One big problem with this is that vast numbers of people would become moochers, who are glad to let others labor and give money to them.

The United States is fast becoming a nation of moochers, and the cheerleaders out in front are those who have been developing a multitude of give-away programs under what we generally refer to as welfare programs. These are none other than liberal democrats, who believe the government should take care of people rather than people taking care of themselves.

The result of this is a completely different kind of people migrating here. We became the greatest nation by offering people an opportunity to stretch their wings, work hard and achieve as they were able. Now we are attracting people who are looking for a free check from the government. And, of course, millions of people who have been here have jumped at the chance to receive free government money that requires no personal responsibility to get a job, and they are not working as they used to.

At the entrance to the grocery store, this writer heard a lady say, "I could still be working, but I learned if I did not have a job, I could get government help." Upon hearing this, I stopped to listen, and she continued, "I managed to lose my job, and now I am getting almost as much money from the government as I was making, and I don't have to go to work."

This lady, and many people like her, are not the kinds of people who built America, and they fail to realize this is leading to the destruction of our nation.

Enough people became aware of how much weaker we have become because of all the give-away programs to go to the polls and reject the kind of leadership responsible for this. Real Americans could see that making government dependents out of people would drag us down to be on the level of third-world nations.

We should be doing everything we can do to make this a better nation so more and more people take advantage of the opportunity to build their however they wish. Great accomplishments never come from people who sit down and do nothing.

People voted for Trump because they did not want to see our continued destruction at the hands of liberal democrats.

CHAPTER 27

DISTRAUGHT OVER TRUMP'S ELECTION

For those of you who are suffering following the election of Donald Trump, I suggest you ask yourself this question: "How could I be enthusiastic about the destruction of this country?"

Whether you realize it or not, no matter how much education you have or the degrees that hang on your wall, you have been used by those who want to destroy this constitutional republic. You have not done your own thinking, and have become victims of liberals, who relish the thought of you being included in group-think. You have allowed yourself to be manipulated by someone and others who have no use for the freedoms we have enjoyed. You did not realize that continuation of what has come out of Washington during recent years was geared to replace our way of life with socialism, a form of government that has always failed and will fail in the future.

Ask how you could allow yourself to become a victim of people who have no use for freedom of the individual. Fortunately, as Abraham Lincoln once said, "…..you can't fool all the people all the time." The chatter coming out of Washington during the past few years has captured the minds of many, but people with their heads on straight saw and understood what was going on (the destruction of this country), and would not vote to continue it.

You have had plenty of company as you have been on the road to destroying this country. There was the news media who twisted the truth, there were entertainers who are good at entertaining you, but poor at thinking. There were the recipients of free money from Washington who do not understand the word "integrity." There were the colleges, the administrations, and the faculty who lapsed into thinking their job was to produce clones who would do whatever they were trained to do.

But, there were enough good Americans to see through the lies emanating from Washington to call a halt to the dismantling of what has made us great. We would not agree to destroy our nation and make us into a third-world country, so we spoke with our vote.

One thing we need to remember is that the thinking person does not fall for the banter of one who thinks he knows a better way for everyone. Whatever a big talker claims needs the scrutiny of questions regarding what he means by what he says.

CHAPTER 28

CRYING COLLEGE STUDENTS

Reports are coming in that college students are having significant problems adjusting to Donald Trump being elected President of the United States. College presidents, in an attempt to help students deal with this, are giving them the option of taking tests or not taking them. In some cases, tests are being canceled. In several, a crying room is being provided where students can gather and cry together. One president is even providing playdough so students can work off their disappointment and frustration.

This is utterly amazing and tragic, for it points to an extreme misunderstanding regarding the growth and development of human beings. Even six-year-old children are generally more mature than students who have to be coddled this way. It speaks loud and clear regarding the level to which college education has sunk. Baby-sitting of 17 to 22-year-old students should never be a part of college campus life.

Life brings its disappointments. This cannot be escaped. One of our jobs as adults, if we ourselves are mature, is to help prepare our children to cope with not only the successes and good things in life, but, also, to learn how to react to things that don't go our way. If we fail in this, we cripple our children to live in the real world.

One parent put on the internet that their child went to bed after Trump was elected, and was fearful of what the world would be like when she awakened the morning after. What this parent fails to understand is that this child is simply verbalizing the fears she and her husband have expressed. It's the old story of children being the products of where they come from. They must have been terribly surprised the next morning when life was okay.

This is a basic problem we now have in our colleges. Students are being prepared by both professors and administrators to be emotional infants who are unable to get through the simple disappointments of life. So much for graduating students prepared to deal with what they will find upon graduation. They are being prepared for emotional failure, which makes them easy targets for control by others who offer to take care of them.

CHAPTER 29

NOT UNDERSTANDING WHAT HAPPENED

Many democrats are expressing astonishment that Donald Trump won the presidential election. They are astonished because they do not understand what they have been doing to this country for the past 50 years, but the voters did, and called their hand on it.

Socialism has been the mantra of the democrats for decades, and they believed they had gotten Americans to the point where their "take from the rich and give to the poor" programs were preferred by citizens. But, there still are enough people to believe the Constitution's call for every person, both male and female, to stand on their own two feet is the way this country should function.

Democrats want citizens to serve the whims of political leaders in Washington, but a majority of Americans still believe, which is the message of the Constitution, that both Congress and the President should serve citizens. The many give-away programs, i.e., The Great Society Program and other welfare programs, are geared to make citizens subservient to politicians in Washington, and a majority of the citizens understand this, and don't want it.

For a long time, Democrats have been on a program of replacing the Constitution of the United States as the foundation document of this country. What they have wanted to replace it with is socialism, a form of government that allows them to take from the successful and give to the unsuccessful. In other words, they do not believe that every able-bodied person should stand on his/her own two feet, but should benefit from the labor of others. They wish to make dependents out of as many people as possible because making dependents would guarantee them votes. This is not what made the United States the greatest nation in the history of the world. It is far better for able-bodied people to be prepare themselves for a job and then get one, thus making a positive contribution to the welfare of this country rather than having them receive a check for doing nothing.

Democrats have known for a long time that, if they could make dependents out of enough people, they could guarantee enough votes to be elected and sent back to Washington to live off productive Americans. In other words, they were doing this in order to guarantee good-paying jobs for themselves in Washington.

A majority of the American people want all able-bodied people to be contributors to making this country great. That's what made this country the envy of the world because it placed the future of each individual in the hands of each individual, and not in the hands of politicians.

Constitutional government is far superior to any other form of government that has appeared anywhere in the world, and this is what the voters were protecting. It would be good if people could understand this.

CHAPTER 30

BANKRUPT, BUT WON'T FACE THE FACT

The United States is bankrupt, but no-one wants to face this fact, especially the politicians in Washington who have caused this bankruptcy. They give no semblance of understanding the difficult financial future they have built for us. Trump, with his business experience, is light years ahead of them in grasping the importance of sound financial management, something sorely missing in both Congress and the Oval Office.

On 11/16/16, at 9:57 a.m., our national debt totaled $19,821,919,183,300. That's a staggering 19 trillion dollars and counting, adding approximately $1,000,000 to our debt every 75 seconds. The politicians in Congress don't understand what they have done to us. This translates into every living person in this country, man, woman, and child owing $61,008 or $165,006 per taxpayer, and it gets worse every minute.

Eight years ago, our national debt totaled approximately $10 billion. This means that, in the past eight years, we have almost doubled our debt. This is unbelievable, to think that the politicians have no idea what they have been doing to the American people. No thinking individual would ever knowingly create this kind of problem for himself/herself, but the politicians have done this to every living American and for all who will be born in the foreseeable future.

Our printing presses are spewing out ridiculous sums of money, and politicians have their heads in the sand regarding what this is doing to us citizens. The standard of living for a majority of Americans is being lowered because of their irresponsibility.

Any administration in Washington, whether it be the new one in January or any other, will have their work seriously affected by the irresponsibility of the ones who have caused this debt. No-one knows what will happen when we can no longer print enough money to placate everyone.

Much of this unbelievable growth in our debt has been caused by liberal politicians who think it is their job to make people's lives better by giving them free money even though it increases our debt. What these politicians do not understand is that, sooner or later, financial collapse of our entire nation will take place.

When you can print more and more money, as the politicians are now doing, it is easy to disregard what this is causing, but, at some point in the future, politicians will have to face the reality that no-one is to blame for our total financial collapse "...but we ourselves. We are the ones who have brought financial ruin to this great nation."

People born in the last 50 years have grown up as the give-away programs of liberal politicians have exploded, and give little concern to what this has been causing. And, as long as they receive their free gifts, they could care less about its affect.

For a long time, this nation will be seriously affected because of this incredible-and-unbelievable debt politicians have placed on us. The ability of the Trump administration to deal effectively with this debt will be difficult, and it may have to become even worse before it can be made better.

This has been the work of liberal democrats moving us toward socialism.

CHAPTER 31

AWAKENING THE SLEEPING GIANT

There is a sleeping giant among us, and it needs to be awakened. Sadly, there are many who wish it to remain asleep, and even sleep more soundly.

The sleeping giant is the millions of people who have had their innovation and productivity removed by the free check from Washington.

Who knows what great brain power and its development has been idled in the entitlement society? The minds of potential scientists, authors, teachers, physicians, mathematicians, space explorers, and many others who could contribute great things to the world – there awaiting development? But, put to sleep to never emerge and bring untold blessings to the world.

If those who receive free handouts from politicians could catch a vision of who they were made to be, contributors to a better life for untold millions, they would shake off their inactivity and pursue education and training that would open up their talents and bring wholeness to many.

The free gifts from Washington have served to anesthetize many from their early years, and the effect has been to completely remove them as of value to this nation. They have remained asleep to what their gifts developed could mean in a world crying out for a better life.

Those who have authored the free gifts don't want this sleeping giant awakened, for their kingdom would come crashing down as people caught on to the fact that they had been used to support a system of uselessness for many otherwise good people.

Catching a glimpse of this potential put to sleep can be seen most everywhere in our society as people remain in the throes of lower income and rail at those who receive the rewards that come from preparation and usefulness.

Shaking off the free money from Washington will be essential if this sleeping giant is to awaken and help make this a better nation and world in which to live.

CHAPTER 32

THE RESULTS OF BRAINWASHING

It is easy to see the results of the brainwashing that has taken place in this country as our educational system has been dumbed down. The ability to think seriously about what being an American really means does not seem to be a part of the curriculum in our institutions of higher(?) learning. Rather, it appears professors have been busy marketing socialism to students rather than teaching them to think.

The process of teaching students to think, and think seriously, which should be at the core of a college educational system, has been replaced with a program that is geared to indoctrinate students to believe socialism is the sunum bonum of education, meaning it is superior to a constitutional republic or anything else. Professors have made up their minds, and students are supposed to adopt their thinking. This is not education; it is training to think what one is told to think.

We have seen the results of this as students have gathered in many places to protest the election of Donald Trump as president. They are revealing what they have been taught plus their inability to seriously examine what has happened in the presidential election.

Individual responsibility is at the heart of what has made America great. As a result of this, individuals have done some amazing things. We have led the world in development of many things, and it is because of the individual freedom and responsibility we have enjoyed. We have been free to think our own thoughts, be and do what we wish to be and do. This is a major reason the world has envied us, and why millions have clamored to become a part of us.

At no place in the world has socialism achieved what has been achieved in the United States. It never has and it never will. That's because socialism places responsibility for the life of all citizens in the hands of politicians, some of whom lack the ability to think seriously about anything, sometimes being led around by the nose by the strongest voice in the crowd, who, themselves, lack the ability to think seriously about anything. On the other hand, a constitutional republic calls for individual accountability on the part of each individual. Do your own thinking and make your own decisions: this is the best that life can offer to you.

Brainwashing led us to the brink of destroying the Constitution, but the American people, who understand its value, took the position that this would not happen. To keep our Constitution from being relegated only to the history books, there was no final choice but to vote for Trump. Had he not won, the decades-old deterioration of this country and our Constitution would have continued until we became a part of third-world countries, with all the chaos attendant there.

The task each of us has is to think seriously about what life is all about. It is not about believing and doing what other people want us to believe and do, as is true in socialism, which has created calamity after calamity throughout history. It is about standing on our own two feet, and doing what we think is individually best for us, not following a system that removes individual responsibility from us. What we do individually with the talents and abilities we have is a personal decision that each of us confronts. We need to free ourselves from the dominance of others, and make our own decisions. This is where life really becomes meaningful for us.

There can be no better life for you than the one where you stand on your own feet and make your own decisions. Socialism does not allow this. Our Constitution makes it available for you, and it is in choosing to be your own person that you make the best choice you can make.

CHAPTER 33

MAJORING ON THE BAD STUFF

Colin Kaepernick has majored on the bad stuff. In doing so, he has joined millions of people who miss the good stuff. Many people are this way and end up with a distorted view of whatever they are considering.

Majoring on the bad stuff always gives a corrupted view of anything. Even marriage can be viewed as bad if a person fails to recognize what true marriage is all about. This is true of religion, politics, business, sports, education, or what have you.

The reason anything can be seen as bad is because it is people who run all things, and there has never been a perfect person. Sooner or later everyone is going to make a mistake and cause an organization to look bad. To base an opinion on this bad stuff is a mistake, and it speaks of a failure to properly evaluate something. As an example, if you consider only the mechanical problems of cars and the number of people killed in them each year, you would never purchase a car or perhaps never ride in one.

The problems of the United States come because it is made up of imperfect people, and, as such, will never be perfect, just like all other countries and all other religions. If we happen to look, however, at the accomplishments of the United States, this country stands head and shoulders above other nations in the world because we have done a lot of things right. People clamor to migrate here more than to any other country in the world, and this should speak volumes to us all.

In a way, Kaepernick has lived a rich life that has never been possible in any other country, and he does not seem to understand this. Contrary to what he is suggesting with his action of sitting during the national anthem, he has been far more privileged than most people in this country or any other country, and it did not matter that one of his parents was black. What mattered was performance, and he was highly rewarded for that. What he does not realize is that this kind of reward has been available for years only in the United States, and, if you go to the trouble of looking at the rosters of many teams in the pro leagues, you will find more blacks than whites on many of them.

Education, training and effort present a pathway to success for anyone, white, black, yellow, red or any other color, to build a good life and a good job. Many of the people in my classes grew up with only one parent and they quit school, leaving them without skills to earn a good living. A pathway to success has been available to them and others, regardless of color, over the past five or six decades, but they did not take advantage of what was available. A black lady across the street finished her master's degree this year, and she runs her own business. Something like this has been available to anyone in the Unites States for over a half century, but many lack the courage to set out on the journey to success.

My success in life does not depend on what others do for me. My success depends on me and what I can do for myself. Contrary to what Kaepernick is suggesting, this has been true for decades for everyone in the United States, regardless of color. Holding on to and majoring on the deficits of life where you are will always cloud your view of what is available for you to accomplish.

If you will accept the fact that everyone around you is imperfect, and so are you, perhaps you can then turn your attention to your future and prepare to meet it with success. Complaining about the bad stuff in life always detracts from dealing successfully with the present and the future.

Perhaps it would do us all a little good to remember the story of the little train engine that could. Faced with the hills to limb, it said, "I think I can, I think I can, I think I can." Setting his mind to it, he did it – he had success.

Whatever the struggles regarding the failures of other people in this country, take your eyes off their failures and concentrate on doing the things that bring you success. Your future is in your hands, not in the hands of other people.

The United States presents more opportunities for individual success than any other country in the world. Take advantage of that, regardless of the color of your skin, do what success requires you to do, and you will be surprised at the outcome. The days of other people limiting your success are past. Turn your eyes to the future and see that, in the United States, your future is what you make it.

CHAPTER 34

BIG DIFFERENCE BETWEEN SOCIALISM & CONSTITUTIONAL GOVERNMENT

There is a huge difference between what your life will be under socialism and what it will be under the Constitution of the United States, and this is something everyone needs to think about.

Under socialism, your life will be what politicians make of it. Under the Constitution, your life will be what you make it to be.

One of the many problems our younger generations face is that much of what is supposed to be our educational system has become a system of indoctrination in which they are not taught to think. People have received the teaching that it is the responsibility of government to take care of its citizens, and many believe this. Under the Constitution, you are given the freedom to take care of yourself as you choose, and the government will step in only when you are not capable of caring for yourself, i.e. when you are physically or mentally unable to care for yourself.

This puts the onus for control and development of your life on you. Under this, you are given the responsibility to get an education that teaches you to think for yourself or to get training that prepares you for some specific job. Either of these ways offers you the opportunity to be successful. You have to choose to make your life what you want it to be. You do not depend on politicians to take care of you.

The rewards that come from taking care of yourself can be significant because there is no limit on your ability to create income. That depends on the endeavor which you enter. The result of depending on the government to take care of you means a limitation in the amount of money you can receive, which is determined by the politicians who are taking from the successful and giving to you. There will always be a limit on how much they can take from the successful, but there is no limit on what you can do for yourself.

Politicians will always set the limits in income in socialism. In a constitutional government, Individuals will always set the limits of their income by the professions they choose.

Satisfaction in life is much better when you are the master of your own fate.

CHAPTER 35

FAILURE TO ASK QUESTIONS

Failure to ask questions is at the center of many of our problems. We turn our heads and think, "This is not going to create problems for us. It is just a flash in the sky, and will soon be gone." In the past, we have ignored ideas and movements which seem to attract, and, ignoring, have played the fool by not asking questions about them.

Slavery was a thing ignored for centuries, but then a question was raised about it, and we suffered through a Civil War, followed by a wrenching of our minds and lives which resulted from the cruel treatment of fellow human beings.

When Hitler stepped onto the scene and convinced 96 percent of the Germans that he could take them to the Promised Land, they lined up in lock-step behind him, and the result was 60 million deaths in WW II.

There are always people with a new idea that will usher in Nirvana, and, without thinking, millions believe a new way has been found to this ever-desired Promised Land. Putting their brains in neutral, they line up in support of the one who dreams of unlimited bliss.

In the last few years, we have been presented with the idea of "The New World Order," and people have been marching with this new idea. The United Nations has developed this, and wishes it to be followed by all nations.

We don't need to accept this without giving our best thought to it. It is an idea that we dare not fail to question. If we look closely at it, we will realize that its goal is the same goal as that of The Third Reich under Hitler: development of a system of government where a small group of people, headed up by a leader, makes decisions regarding the kind of life all people will have. Living life as one wishes to live has no place in The New World Order. What life becomes is what the leaders decide.

Such thinking can never be compatible with freedom of the individual, one of the great gifts of life in the United States under our Constitution. Freedom to decide for oneself is recognition of the dignity and worth of individuals in making life what we want it to be.

Any system that herds people into basing their lives on the proscription of others will always place limitations on what life should and can be. We are all individuals with our own unique abilities and possibilities, and we need to live in an environment offering the freedom to live our lives as we desire, not as someone else desires.

Whether it be "The Third Reich" or the "New World Order," individuals must give up their sovereignty to life determined by others.

We were made to be who and what we are, not who and what other people want us to be. We need to give serious thought to this.

CHAPTER 36

MOSTLY SELF-INFLICTED

It is time for black people to face the fact that most of their current problems are self-inflicted. This writer is aware that this is the wrong thing to say in today's world of political correctness, but it must be said by someone.

During the past 60 years, black people have had access to training and education, which would prepare them to compete with anybody in the world, but many have chosen to believe the government, rather than themselves, will give them everything they need to have a good life. A large number of blacks, however, having learned the value of education, now enjoy the income and prestige that comes through achievement, having achieved the American Dream. But, this is not a majority of black people.

Too many blacks have chosen to believe they should be given a free ride when it comes to being responsible for what they do. "After all, white people enslaved some of my ancestors, and the white people of today ought to pay for what they did to us." This is nothing but a bunch of non-sense perpetrated by people who prefer to live by self-inflicted ignorance or are too lazy to carry their own load. Add to that the educated black person being attacked as trying to be white: "Whut you tryin to do talkin like dat? You tryin to be white?" Yes, this is often said. I hear it in my classes. Education, however, has nothing to do with the color of one's skin; it is color neutral. Making such an excuse is nothing short of trying to justify one's deep ignorance, which seems to be the preference of too many people, black and white.

This writer has worked with black people on the farms in South Georgia, in educational settings, in hospitals, and other places, and has learned that educated black people can hold their own with educated white people, but that the uneducated black or white person is unable to compete.

What a lot of people do not realize is that many of the programs coming out of Washington, although presented as high and mighty for black people, have actually hurt them. Democrats have peddled, promoted and passed the Great Society legislation and many give-away programs they said were for the purpose of helping blacks rise above their limitations. What has happened, however, is that blacks have looked to these programs as substitutes for their own effort, and have huddled in their poor enclaves to mull over how unfair life is to them. Democrats knew this would happen, and that it would guarantee votes in future elections. They are pleased that government assistance programs keep poor black and white people poor, and, while they are poor, they will vote democratic.

CHAPTER 37

A CLEAR DIFFERENCE BETWEEN REPUBLICANS & DEMOCRATS

Facing a critical presidential election between two people with problem backgrounds, we may need to look at the basic philosophy of the parties they represent and the basic thrust of each.

First, the democrat's basic message to people is, "Let the government do it for you. We will do for you what you need done. If you will vote for us, we will see that all your basic needs will be met."

The republican message is, "You are responsible for taking care of yourselves. Go and get training or education in order to prepare for the future. If you will do this, you will be prepared to earn more than the government can ever give you. We will assist you as you learn to take care of yourselves. Your life will be much better if you learn to stand on your own two feet."

People have a distinct choice re who will take care of themselves. With the democrats, the government will take care of you; you will be in their hands. With the republicans, you will take care of yourself; your future will be in your own hands. That is a huge difference. Vote democratic and your future will be what the politicians in Washington make it. Vote republican, and your future will be in your own hands, and the politicians in Washington will serve you. This will make all the difference in the world to you.

Your life will always better in your own hands.

CHAPTER 38

BECAUSE OF WHO I AM

It is easily seen. In the domestic violence classes, it goes something like this: "if she had not done what she did, I would not have hit her," or many things like this. In the alcohol and drug classes, it goes like this, "I was not going to drink this time, but they are my friends, and they don't want me with them unless I do what they do."

This is the age-old and familiar effort of trying to escape being responsible for what we do, and often we feel good about blaming our failures on somebody else. "It's not my fault; it's their fault; I'm really a good person." And, with this, people buy into thinking they are better than they really are, and that's the way we want it, anyway.

There is great difficulty with this because, deep down, we know the truth. We know this is a reflection on the kind of person we really are. We simply lack the ability to do things because of who we are. We lack the ability to stand on our own two feet, and we don't feel good about this.

We see the criminal in prison, and we hear the sociologist explain that he was reared in poor circumstances with a drunken father and a mother who ran around with other men, leaving him to fend for himself, even at supper time. But, then, we know this fellow with a similar background who overcame his neglect, graduated from college and holds down a well-paying job.

What's the problem with this? One makes it and one does not.

Perhaps we all need to consider what we have on our hands when we give birth. A baby is not a thing to have because it will get us another check from the government, and it is not a thing to neglect and believe we are not the key to him/her becoming a responsible human being. Eighty to 100 billion brain cells come with each baby, and those brain cells will not get their kick-start unless we do our part. Waiting for kindergarten for our child to begin is placing them behind those who got their kick-start almost on the first day they entered the world.

Yes, people grow up to be responsible for what they do, whether we believe this or not. Society would end in chaos if it was not this way. But, we parents, with our zipper problems and all the other things we allow to distort our lives, give a poor road map to our children, making good decisions difficult for them.

One of the best things people can learn is that we are each responsible for ourselves. On the final analysis, no matter how much we point our fingers at others, and say, "It's their fault," the truth is that we are what we make ourselves to be, no more, no less. The man who drinks too much must finally say, "I opened my mouth and drank that stuff. Nobody held me down and poured into me." And that is what we must all say, "I did it. It was my decision.'

If we accepted the fact that we are who we make ourselves to be, then we could begin to do what we know, deep down, is ours to do. This would force us to do our own thinking, and it might just result in changing many of the things we do.

CHAPTER 39

IF BLACK PEOPLE EVER FIGURE IT OUT

If black people ever figure out what the democrats have done to them, they will leave the Democratic Party in droves.

Martin Luther King, Jr. had black people marching toward equality with white people, and, had he survived, they would now stand shoulder to shoulder with white people. He would have had them training and educating themselves to compete equally with white people, and they would have earned equality. But, he was assassinated, and the direction in which they were headed came to an abrupt halt. It came to an abrupt halt because of what the democrats did.

In the 1950's and 1960's, large numbers of well-prepared black students were entering prestigious schools, and the numbers were increasing as they began to realize they had the potential to achieve just the same as whites. This would have continued but for the work of democrats.

What happened? Democrats destroyed many black families, and made it possible for blacks to get along without having to get jobs. What they did was work on and expand the welfare state, offering blacks ever-increasing government handouts. An example of the effect of this is seen in the increase of black children being raised by single parents who had no intention of marrying the fathers. In the 1950's, only 22 percent of black children were in homes of single parents. At the present time, over 70 percent of black children are in single parent homes. How did this change? It changed when the government started giving money to women who had children, but who did not live with the fathers. Financially, it became better for fathers not to be in the home. Women, therefore, had children for the sole purpose of getting more money from the government, a bad reason to have children.

Educational programs were changed so that black children could be promoted without having to meet the standards required of white students. Preference was given to them for admission to colleges without being academically prepared. Many white students with better grades have not been admitted to colleges because a quota required admission of blacks even though they had poorer academic backgrounds.

The change in rules of conduct for blacks has resulted in such things as what happened in Ferguson, Mo., where criminal activity has received a pass and sometimes held up as okay if done by a black person.

These are just a few of the many things democrats have done to present themselves as saviors of black people. The ever-expanding welfare state they brought has allowed them to present themselves as protectors, and this has captured the imagination of untold millions of blacks.

Did the democrats understand what they were doing in development of the welfare state? Yes, they did. And, why did they do it? They did it to capture the black vote, and it has worked as millions of black people have flocked to the polls to vote for democrats, who promise to give them more.

One of the major problems with this is that the government money will never be as much as blacks could have earned if they trained and educated themselves to earn their own living. To a great extent, the ghettos and lower class neighborhoods where many blacks now live would not exist if the welfare programs had never developed beyond what they were in the 1950's. Multitudes more blacks would have educated and worked themselves out of these neighborhoods.

Although democrats present themselves as the good guys who have done marvelous things for black people, the reality is that their action, geared to win votes, has been one of the worst things that could have happened. Many blacks are now much worse off than they would have been had they only continued the march on which they had started under MLK, Jr.

Frederick Douglas, black American abolitionist and social reformer, once said, "Everybody has asked the question, 'What shall we do with the Negro?' I have had but one answer from the beginning. Do nothing with us! Your doing with us has already played the mischief with us."

The programs developed by the democrats in Washington have played the mischief with many black people over the past 50 years.

If blacks ever figure this out, the Democratic Party will become a thing of the past.

CHAPTER 40

THE HARM OF DOING FOR OTHERS

There comes a time when people are unable to care for themselves, and that is when good Americans respond and give needed help. This is a part of being a good country.

But, doing for others what they can and should do for themselves is one of the worst things that can be done. We see this all the time, and, perhaps, the worst perpetrator of all may be our federal government with all its give-away programs.

We might be able to best understand this by reference to a football player in the NFL. It would be a tragedy for the head coach to say to his tackle, "Here, you go sit on the bench, and I will do the struggle for you in getting your body in shape. I will lift your weights; I will do your wind-sprints; I will knock heads with opposing players on the scrimmage line. It is not necessary for you to work hard when I can do it for you." Of course, if this was to be done, the player would in no way be prepared to play in a game.

So, it is in living the life that is ours to live. We can't be prepared unless we prepare, and no-one can do our preparation for us. They may say, "Here, let me do it for you," but, if we allow them to do our heavy lifting, we can never grow the muscles we need to make our contribution in the world, and we all have a contribution to make if we understand what life is all about.

Liberal politicians in this country have been attempting for decades to convince people to let them do their work for them. "Here, we'll make certain you have what is necessary to live. Sit down, give us your vote, and we will do all that is necessary for you to get along and have a good life." And so, we have the proliferation of programs resulting in the loss of skills development, which is necessary for people to receive the best in life. These liberals consider themselves to be the good guys, but, in reality, they are bringing great harm by rescuing people from the task of being responsible for selves.

The result of this is tremendous loss of what these people could contribute to this country, to their families and to themselves if only they would do the heavy lifting that is necessary for them to build good lives. Accepting free gifts from the government to avoid personal responsibility will never be a good substitute for development of inborn talents.

CHAPTER 41

LOOKING AT THE DARK SIDE

When you look only at the dark side of something, you can quickly decide that is what is true about the whole thing. The problem with this is that just about everything has both a dark side and a bright side.

If there is one thing we know for certain, it is that all organizations are made up of both good and bad people. This is true of the best organizations, even religious ones.

If we choose to make comments about something, we many times paint a wrong picture of what that something really is, and, in the process, reveal our lack of a true understanding, and of our need to learn more.

We see this happening all the time. It is quite apparent in the political scene where each paints the other as evil. We see it in philosophical differences and in theological circles.

To paint something as dark and evil often points to failure to know what is really true, and to rouse the ire of people by withholding truth from them is wrong.

Many people around the world are now painting Christianity as evil, and many are cheering them on. What they are doing is playing on the ignorance of people about the good in Christianity.

Yes, bad Christians have done many bad things: we can name the Crusades, support for slavery, the Inquisitions, and many other things that belie what Christianity really is. Only looking at such bad things gives people a wrong picture.

Christianity is about loving your brother (this means everyone), and seeking his/her higher good. There is no room for the dark side in real Christianity. Those who get Christianity right (where the bright side is) serve human kind in many ways. It doesn't matter who your brother is. We see people like Albert Schweitzer, Mother Theresa, and others, who gave themselves to improve life for others. The list could be long as we see those who have started colleges and universities to develop the minds of people. We see those who have led in the medical field; we see many who have led in feeding the hungry, clothing the naked, attempting to make life better for others at great sacrifice to themselves. The story of the Good Samaritan is the story of untold multitudes of Christians who seek no recognition for what they do.

What draws the attention of people are the bad Christians who do bad things. These people make the news and give a wrong picture of what Christianity really is. Such things as providing housing for the homeless in my community do not make the news. Delivering food to the shut-ins is never in the local newspapers. Neither is the collection of money for the medically needy.

When people see and discuss only the bad in Christianity, they are there-in making it known that they are ill-informed. People having the wrong view about something join the forces throughout history that have set development of the human race backward. It usually is the genesis of discrimination and persecution, and, as we are now seeing, even death delivered by ISIS.

To those who see only the dark side of Christianity, take another look. Do not concentrate on the dark side by looking at the negative news stories. Go where the bright side is dispelling a lot of darkness in the lives of countless millions of people. If you will take a look at the bright side, you will understand that this is what you will be talking and writing about. There is no room for darkness where the light of Christianity shines.

CHAPTER 42

BLACK LIVES MATTER....REALLY???

If black lives matter, you can't tell it by looking at the black community. What you see there is black on black crime where over 70 per cent of black homicides are at the hands of black people. Somewhere along the way, the value of each human being has not been a part of the black community.

My class members report being shot at and of shooting at others, and some have witnessed the shooting deaths of friends. This does not have to be, but the lure of staying where you are born seems to cloud the desire to be done with dangerous communities.

People don't have to stay where they are easy victims. They can move on to safer environments, which includes both physical relocation, and, also, a change in mind-set. That mindset includes a determination to avoid settings where people have little appreciation for the value of each human being.

A lot of anger toward police has developed, and police are being killed because of this. The reality is, however, more white guys than black guys are being killed by police, but we don't hear anything about that. One of the reasons is because our president has, from the beginning, been trying to bring as much division between people as possible. He had an opportunity to help heal the racial divide in this country, but he chose to make it worse. He has succeeded quite well in this.

CHAPTER 43

NEEDED IN WASHINGTON: A NEW KIND OF POLITICIAN

Politicians in Washington have ruined this great country. They have deliberately changed their job from what the Constitution requires it to be to one that gives them freedom to do whatever they decide to do.

The Constitution is clear in that it requires elected officials to serve the citizens of this country. They have changed this to one in which they see their job to be that of having citizens to serve them. They do not seem to be concerned about this, and continue to develop and pass legislation that increases their control of all aspects of our lives. They believe they are doing well, making life better for citizens, but they are really making life worse for the majority of citizens.

The net result of this is an erosion of what has made this the greatest nation in the history of the world. They have managed to create an environment in which millions of citizens believe it is okay to live off the labor of others, and they are doing so. They have destroyed within people the need to develop and use the many talents hidden within. They have created the greatest divisions between citizens that have ever existed, supporting a president who has earned the title of "The Great Divider" by the things he has said and done. He has elevated to a fine art the "divide and conquer" theory that brought so much trouble to our world, and people have clamored to support him, lured by the belief that he has their interest at heart. In reality, they are being used by him to diminish life in the United States.

It will take time for many to realize how much he has harmed this country. The lives of the majority of citizens are far worse now than they were a few years ago because he has been our president.

Many other things have been done by the politicians in Washington to damage this nation, and the checks and balances called for in the Constitution have been ignored. Even the politicians who on paper are the loyal opposition have failed to take care us citizens, letting The Great Divider and his followers have their way with this country. They need to be replaced because of their failure to follow the Constitution, letting happen what has happened, uttering only wimpy objections. less we return to Constitutional government, this nation will recede into the milieu of all the other also-ran-countries where citizens build their lives based on what political leaders want for them instead of building lives based on their own talents and abilities, becoming what they want to become.

CHAPTER 44

A NATION OF WIMPS

We are fast becoming a nation of wimps. We could say many things about this, but it boils down to people being unable to take care of themselves. This is the legacy of socialism, where people are directed to let the government take care of them. This has been the thrust of the Democratic Party since before the 1960's when MLK, Jr. was assassinated, and it has been done in such a way that unthinking people are not aware of what has been happening to them.

The Democratic Party does not attract thinkers because thinkers can see through their lie that people can't take care of themselves, and need the government to send them money. If people did not believe this lie, they would get busy doing whatever was necessary to make a living.

Apparently, if you look at the number of Americans on the government dole, many can claim this lie.

CHAPTER 45

FAILURE TO UNDERSTAND

Poor people, both white and black, do not understand how they have been used to degrade "government of the people, by the people and for the people." This is what our Constitution calls for, and it is what Abraham Lincoln held high as he led a nation in preserving our constitutional government. Struggle is always a part of preserving freedom because there are people waiting in the wings to tell us how to live.

Liberal democrats have led us into government by a handful of people who think they are qualified to replace the Constitution with ideas that have no semblance of freedom.

⊷⊶

For those who love freedom, our constitutional government is light years ahead of socialism.

⊷⊶

CHAPTER 46

THE LAST TIME I CHECKED

The last time I checked, it was possible for an individual with training/education and the drive to succeed to actually be successful in the United States. The door has been shut for no-one willing to pay the price of success during the last 60 years. This is one of the things making the United States a great nation.

Perhaps the best way for us to understand this is to point toward athletics. In the tenth grade, Michael Jordan was cut from his basketball team: not good enough to make the team. He did not accept this as his future in basketball. He went to work doing what he needed to do, and became the best NBA player in his time, perhaps for all time.

After Michael completed his fabulous career, a man speaking about his achievements and the possibilities inherent in people who are willing to pay the price for success, made the following comment: "There is probably a thousand other basketball players with equal talent who are driving trucks, but they do not have the drive to develop their talent."

This is the very reason so many millions of people do very little with the talents they have. They simply don't have the drive to be successful. Unfortunately, they still wish to receive the rewards of being successful.

Anyone born with a good brain in the United States during the last 60 years has been given an opportunity to get an education and/or training to be successful. Many people have turned down this opportunity, but still want to be given the rewards of success.

Sometimes working hard and being successful in school is frowned upon. Multiple individuals, both black and white, in my alcohol and drug classes say that other students make fun of them if they make good grades. This is nothing other than being told, "Come and be dumb with me." But, these people still want to be paid well for whatever they do. Being dumb is not a good thing, and never will be.

The reason so many people are still living below the poverty line points to their lack of achievement. Some of these people are victims of circumstances they cannot control, and we should maintain systems to help them. I think here of the people in my classes who are victims of severe abuse when they grow up. Some of them need our help, but some of them, through grit and determination, achieve in spite of their abuse. This points to the fact that we have a reservoir of strength deep within if we will only go to the trouble of finding it.

Complaining or crying about not enjoying what others in this country enjoy is a sure sign of lack of achievement, which normally points to not taking advantages of opportunities available.

We don't need to make excuses for ourselves and each other, a popular activity in our time. We need to quit talking about other people giving us things, and concentrate on doing those things that we have to individually do to bring the rewards of success. These rewards are and have been available to each of us willing to pay the price for success.

A successful life in the United States is available to all who are willing to pay the price for success. It is not available to those who do very little with the talents they have. Michael Jordan found this out, and does not complain about what others do not receive. Anyone today who develops talents and abilities will experience the same thing.

CHAPTER 47

DRAMATIC CHANGE NEEDED IN WASHINGTON

When we look at the disappointing decline in the lives of Americans over the past several decades, it becomes quite obvious that the American people have not caused this decline. It has come from the actions of our congress and presidents in Washington, who have been dismantling the Constitution by trying to change the way we live. They have been in the process of trying to take care of citizens rather than doing things to assist people as they take care of themselves. People who learn to take care of selves have made America great. Struggle is always a component in the emergence of great people, but now people are being paid to sit down and do nothing.

Politicians have developed the mistaken idea that the future viability of our country rests on the decisions coming out of congress. However, citizens, not politicians in Washington, have been the backbone of this country, and this is where our greatness has originated.

Some of the results of their actions follow:

1. Fewer fulltime workers now than several years ago, during a time when the population has increased.

2. Welfare, the EBT card, and other forms of free money from Washington have replaced the necessity of learning to take care of selves. When I grew up in the forties and fifties, no capable person ever desired to be idle with no income from personal labor. Now people take great pride in doing nothing as the newly printed money arrives.

3. Politicians have replaced freedom of speech, a hallmark of American life, with political correctness, which is an element of people-control.

4. Politicians have eliminated freedom of religion as we have seen one religion praised and another strongly condemned, the genesis of this being in Washington.

5. Politicians thought they were responsible for providing housing for all people, passing legislation that allowed people to borrow 100 % to 105% mortgage money while having no jobs. In my neighborhood, once the best in the county, we now have multiple empty houses, trashed by people with low income, and by some squatters, resulting in the decline in value of over 50%. This has been a royal screw-up by politicians.

6. In the past few years, our national debt has more than doubled, thanks exclusively to politicians in Washington, who seem to lack any understanding whatsoever of basic economics. They do not understand that spending more money than you take in always leads to bankruptcy.

7. Their lack of ability to use their brains for thinking purposes is shown dramatically in many wanting to eliminate the Second Amendment. This would take guns away from law-abiding citizens, but not from the Mafia and common criminals. They should hear my mechanic, who grew up in Germany and heard the bombs fall during WWII say, "When they took away our guns, we could do nothing." Removal of guns from citizens were projects in both China and Russia that led to the deaths of millions by Mao and Stalin.

One of the things we need to ask is something politicians do not want us to ask. Each of us should ask the question, "What does life require of me?" Asking this question will lead us away from asking, "What can the

Government do for me?" which seems to be the question politicians in Washington want us to ask. if we are to salvage this country, we must have a new kind of politician in Washington, the kind who understands they must not try to lift us above where we are, but to support us as we lift ourselves.

CHAPTER 48

WHAT ABOUT FAIR SHARE?

We have been hearing a lot in the last few years about rich people paying their fair share of taxes, and now Hillary Clinton has been saying that one of the things she will do when she becomes president is make those rich people pay their fair share.

Whether we think this is good or bad, the truth is that we should, on the contrary, be talking about fair share of effort. This is where the field can be leveled by anyone. We don't have to wait for others to share their wealth with us. We can enjoy it for ourselves regardless of what others do. We do this by sharing in the effort to make money.

People who are rich today were once little children like the rest of us. Their brains were formed the same way as were ours. The difference was that they did something to develop those brains so they could make money, and sometimes a lot of it. Each of us could have done the same thing.

What is required for this is study and training, and all of us had the opportunity to do the things that would prepare us to make money. We understand preparation and training when it comes to sports, and most people have little trouble accepting the fact that athletes deserve the money they make. This is pure competition, and, when an athlete excels in his/her skills, we have no trouble with the big bucks. We think of Michael Jordan as an excellent example of this, and we do not ask him to share what he has made with us

This is the same way we should look at the business person who makes a lot of money: just pay them and let them enjoy what they earn. There are many examples of people who are able to lift themselves out of poor circumstances through study and effort, and, believe it or not, this has been possible with each of us, regardless of the circumstances in which we were born or the color of our skin. Reference to Dr. Ben Carson is appropriate at this time. He developed and used what was inside his brain, and excelled in what he did. He became the outstanding pediatric neurosurgeon in the world. This could have been a similar story for millions of people who sat down and waited on their fair share to be taken from others and given to them.

There is no better nation than the United States in the world to reward people who prepare themselves to make and enjoy a lot of money. Each of us could do this. Our country gave us the opportunity, but many turned it down. The reason we didn't do this is quite simple. We didn't give equal effort.

We need to change the subject and start talking about everyone **DOING** their fair share. A lot of people are not interested in doing this, but it would level the playing field, and then we would all be receiving the rewards of our effort. There would be none of us waiting for someone else to share their fair share with us because we would then be earning our own share. This happens to be the only way that living with each other makes sense.

There is no sensible reason why one able-bodied person should sit down, do nothing and wait on another able-bodied person to give them money. This is discrimination of the highest order, and it has become a central part of the democratic platform.

People should be able to pick up their own load and carry it, and millions more in this country would be doing just that if they made the effort to study and prepare to make money. This country is amazing in that it offers so much to the person who is willing to work for it. Any form of government not offering this opportunity is inferior to the Constitutional Republic we have had.

Get busy preparing to make excellent money, and you will be surprised at what can happen to you. You would never have to ask people to share their earnings with you because you would then be earning your own fair share. That's amazing, isn't it?

CHAPTER 49

THE GREATEST DAMAGE TO POOR PEOPLE

If poor black and white people ever figure out what the democrats have done to them, they will abandon the Democratic Party in droves.

A good question being asked today is, "Why are there so many poor people still living in substandard housing, some of it being ghetto housing?" Well, that's the way democrats wanted it.

It is no accident that there are so many people, both black and white, still in substandard housing in the United States. It is no accident that millions have dropped out of the labor market, choosing rather to sign up for government help. It is no accident that over 70 percent of black births are now to unwed mothers, whereas, prior to The Great Society Program, this figure was less than ten percent. It is no accident that the vast majority of prisoners in jail in Atlanta are blacks.

Why are these things no accident? The short answer to this question is: that's the way liberal democrats wanted things. They knew that anyone who gets good training and/or education would be able to take care of themselves, and would not be candidates for government help, choosing rather to become productive individuals. Liberal democrats devised programs that would suck people into dependency on free government money. Thus, the Great Society Program, and all the other free money available in a multitude of other "give away" government programs. The democrats have been quite successful in luring poor people into their trap.

The major problem with these free money programs is that they result in removing millions of people from the education and labor markets, but this money given is not enough to get people out of the ghettos. Therefore, these programs are a guarantee that people will be stuck in ghettos dependent on liberals doing more things for thcm, which produces the votes liberals depend on. Thus, the promise liberals make to poor people: "Vote for us and we will keep the free money coming." Liberals have little to offer other than being a conduit for money taken from successful people and given to unsuccessful people.

If poor people could become aware of these liberal programs having been designed to keep them poor, perhaps they would decide to pursue training and education to become productive people. Sucking people into dependency on the government has been the thrust of democratic programs during the last fifty years. When MLK, Jr. died, there was no leader to step up and continue the march toward equality he had begun, and the liberals stepped in with their offer to make free money available. Many black people could not turn this down, and, therefore, became government dependents, something that was less than they could have done for themselves. The result: continued life in substandard housing and residents at the bottom of the social ladder.

This great damage to poor people, both black and white, and thus to our nation, has been done without them realizing that it was done. A ten-year-old boy phrased it well when he was asked, "How are you going to earn money when you grow up?" He replied, "I am going to live off the gov-ment check." That reply indicates what the free money from Washington has done to people. It has resulted in the loss of self for millions of people, and they are not even aware this has happened to them. Liberal democrats have led them to believe it is better to live off the earnings of other people than off their own earnings.

Money given without it being earned has led millions of poor people to abandon their responsibility to develop their talents and abilities through education and training. Many of them have seen this freedom from responsibility as a great gift, but it has been one of the worst things that could have happened to them.

Not only has this led people to abandon their responsibility to make the best life possible for themselves, but it has denied this country the contributions that only they could make. Developing the self is one of the essentials to building a good, mature, useful life. Our country needs every citizen contributing to making this a better nation, but many now sit, making no contribution whatsoever, just living off government help.

It is not a good thing to be rescued from the responsibility of developing one's talents and abilities through education and training, but many people have been led to believe it is. An idle and wasted life is nothing to be proud of, but the free money from Washington has made it happen. Liberals, by doing this, have brought great harm to people and to this nation.

Unprepared people are easily led around by liberals who do not want them to succeed and do well. Keeping them subservient to their wishes is what liberals are all about. It is the only way they can get elected.

Once someone wants to develop his/her talents and abilities, and succeeds in getting a job, learning to take care of selves, there is nothing liberals have to offer. The Democratic Party would not exist if everyone received education and/or training and was working and earning his/her own way.

Yes, the greatest harm done to this nation in the past 60 years has been done by liberals as their work has resulted in millions of poor people being able to do nothing as they live off the earnings of other people.

CHAPTER 50

THE POWER OF INDOCTRINATION

I ndoctrination is far more powerful than education. This is seen throughout history and it is seen in contemporary life. The only antidote to indoctrination is the ability to think for oneself. This is tough because political leaders normally want people to follow in lock-step with whatever they wish to do. Then it becomes doubly harmful when college professors have a goal of training students to think as they think. This seems to be what has happened on our college campuses. "Don't think your own thoughts, but think as I think," seems to be what is now heard coming from the mouths of college professors. Education is teaching students to think for themselves, not requiring them to think as their professors think.

Leaders who wish to gain a following usually never ask people to think for themselves, but to accept the agenda they are told is good for them. People with a poor history of building their own lives, unable to think for themselves, are easy prey for the leader with a golden tongue.

The leader who wishes subservience from the people always attacks a nation for its weaknesses, not its strengths. And, because there is no such thing as perfection, nations always have weaknesses, and people will complain because life is not what they want it to be. This is how Adolph Hitler was able, at one time, to attract 96 percent support from the German people.

Thinking for oneself, however, can often be dangerous, as many in Germany found out. There were a few who could think, and they understood what this great orator was doing. They were not fooled by the slick words of the Fuhrer. One of these people was Dietrich Bonhoeffer, who understood what Hitler was doing. He was put in prison and killed two weeks before he might have been rescued by the allied army.

There is a distinct difference between a leader who wishes to make a nation in his own image and one who supports people in becoming the best they can become. This has been made quite clear in the United States in the past seven years. We were the greatest nation in the history of the world, but, since 2008, we have been under a president who desires that we follow his agenda rather than the Constitution, which is the basis for us becoming the greatest nation. Obama's work has been a disaster for this nation.

He has been moving us away from freedom for each individual and into a system where political leaders determine what life will be like. A part of this has been bringing thousands of Muslims to this country who have no intention of following our laws. They wish to follow the laws of the countries from which they come, which have heavily relied on their religion. They and we should be aware that these countries have produced some of the worst violence in history, both in the past and in the contemporary world. If they are successful in planting their way of life in the United States, we will sink into the kind of chaos they have been experiencing for centuries. Their religion has helped them become failing nations, and that is where they will take us if their goals are realized. The kind of life those countries have had is far inferior to the freedoms we have enjoyed.

CHAPTER 51

GOOD PEOPLE: WHERE ARE THEY?

Listening to the news morning or night leads to wondering if the world has run out of good people. Where are they? What we hear and see are reports of shootings here, stabbings there, and bombings in other places: disaster after disaster. And then the lies that accompany reports are misleading. Reports of good people doing good things are crowded out by things bad people do. It's gotten to where I don't even want to turn on news channels morning or night. Other people tell me the same thing.

Upon reflection, though, I am aware that what is presented on TV is what people like to hear. It has been found that good news is not appealing to the average person, who relishes seeing what bad people do and not what good people do.

When I get to thinking about this, however, and the people I know and read about, It becomes quite clear that there are many more good people in the world than bad people. Good people just don't make much noise about what they do. Most people I know have jobs, work hard, go to church and share good things in their lives with people who are less fortunate than they are. We hear too much about the takers in society, but very little about the givers.

If I were to list the good people I know, they would far out-number the bad people I know. This is probably true with most of us. We have not had the environment or brainwashing bad people have grown up in, and we appreciate the laws that help protect each of us.

It would be nice if our leaders in Washington were all good people, but they are not. Too many of them have an agenda that does not include what is best for the American people, only what will advance their personal welfare. Some of our leaders have difficulty telling the truth or understanding what their jobs are, and this has led to a great proliferation of laws and directives degrading the life we Americans had. Good leaders try to make things better for all the people, but many have carved out programs that are patently unfair, and then they seek to paint a picture that everything is alright.

Bad people in charge of our government have already diminished our nation. We need good leaders who attempt to lead us in becoming better people. If that were to happen, we would find more people trying to improve their lives rather than sitting at home, doing nothing, and waiting for the check from Washington that pays them to do nothing. Government doing for people things they are capable of doing for themselves often produces an environment where really good people are hard to find.

CHAPTER 52

USED & ABUSED

A lot of people in this country, both white and black, have been used and abused, and they don't know it.

This started earlier, but, shortly after the assassination of MLK, Jr., who had started black people on a march toward equality with white people, it picked up speed.

MLK, Jr. presented blacks with the opportunity to stand shoulder to shoulder with white people, and many of them began doing just that. Those who did not like it saw this as a danger to what they wanted. These people are known as liberals. What they were interested in was a system where they could control what black and white people did.

One of the things necessary in getting people to support you is to make them believe you are trying to help them.

So, how did the liberals do this? They did it by telling people that, if they would follow them and vote for them, they would relieve them of the responsibility of getting a job: they would give them government money without them doing anything to get it.

It took strength of character to refuse free money, and get a real job. Apparently, strength of character has too few places to reside in many Americans. Once people sign up for free government money, they usually will do whatever the politicians want them to do.

CHAPTER 53

THE VALUE OF ONE HUMAN BEING

There is nothing as important as one human being. That is the crux of the matter when a person finally understands what freedom is all about. Arriving at this conclusion has been a difficult struggle for us human beings because we have a tendency to push our welfare and concerns above that of other people. This can be covered by the concept of sitting at the top of the totem pole: we just want to believe that we happen to be the only one who has put life all together, and all others are inferior to us. This is the road that is easiest to travel as we respond to the urges within. Unfortunately, this is how the world turns, and it is the reason for our inability to get along with each other.

Where does the work need to be done? It needs to be done by each individual human being as we begin to understand that life is not about accumulation of things or wealth or prestige. It is about helping each other become what we were made to be. It isn't about placing people in boxes determined by us. It is about freeing individuals to be whom they were made to be. This has been the lure of life in the United States. People just have a tendency to be in touch with those things within which compel us to be free to be the best we can be.

There will always be people who wish to force their way on us all, and that is where many of the great struggles of the world have originated, and that is where the current great struggle in the United States has arisen. Some people now in leadership have not developed their thinking to the point where the concept of freedom takes flight and ushers in the light toward which this country has been traveling. Release of freedom for people to become what they wish to become is never in the repertoire of those who misunderstand what they should be about in this world.

The vision of the founders of this nation enabled them to look beyond the chaos that accompanies the animosities that have resulted in our wish to control each other to the time when all humans could live as brothers. They knew from history that one person controlling what other people do and think always turns out to be a disaster, and they were able to place within their dreams a time when all humans could sit down as brothers. They knew the journey would be difficult, and they understood that, for this to be accomplished, each individual had to be free to make his/her own choices. The restraints we are now feeling are the result of failure to understand what our founders understood.

A good life is not about anyone controlling the future of others, regardless of where you might like to take them. That is a denial of freedom, and that is the great mistake of those who have been trying to take this country into socialism. Socialism never offers freedom to people because, at its heart, it is about controlling what others do.

The struggle towards freedom is never easy, but freedom is the great hunger of people. If we lose sight of this, we have lost the vision that compelled our founders to establish a nation where each individual has freedom to become.

The herding of people into pursuing the dreams of others always leads to chaos, and we now find chaos growing in great leaps and bounds in many places around the world. The thrust of removing our freedoms in the United States, the country that has raised the hopes of freedoms for others, is the legacy of our last several decades. It is no wonder the world is falling apart, as it seems to be. The light of the pursuit of freedom in this country has diminished, and the shadows that have resulted are taking their toll on the dreams of the remainder of the world.

The dousing of this light of freedom has consequences not only in this country, but around the world. The result has been the quick emergence and spread of ways of life that deny freedom to all, even to adherents, where life is determined by a head man or religion and not by each individual. There is not a great future to life when one's future is determined by others.

The United States has struggled with this concept of freedom, but it is what, even with our failures, has brought such great hope to a world bogged down so long in subservience to the whims of people who think they know how other people should live.

Return to our pursuit of freedom for all people beacons to us because we, as a nation, have allowed the dreams of others to become our dreams. A return of freedom for all to live their lives as they wish is much better than any life that is determined by others.

One human being learning to be and do individually what is desired is the best of dreams. We have been working on this, sometimes too slowly, but it is what has made America great, and it is what will return us to our greatness. One human being free to choose what life shall be is the best there is. All other ways of life are inferior to this.

CHAPTER 54

DISREGARDING THE CONSTITUTION

The framers of the Constitution were fully aware of historical figures who had mesmerized people and led them down paths that ended in chaos and destruction. They developed three branches of government as protection against those who wished to control the thought processes and the lives of people.

Until the last few decades the politicians in Washington have worked within the limits of the Constitution. No branch of government has been able to disregard the other branches. But now things have changed, and the executive branch has walked away from our guiding documents and sought to control all aspects of our lives. The result has been an erosion of our freedoms and elimination of the government serving the citizens of this country.

Now we have life in the United States being determined by mostly one man, and history powerfully teaches that this will end in calamity. In the beginning, words from the silver tongue replaced the thought processes of the non-thinking who follow this man without question. Sooner or later, their world will come tumbling down.

Those who wrote the Constitution understood that the lust for power was too great for one person to be given permission to do his own thing, but, in the last few years, we have seen this danger actually become a reality as Obama has completely disregarded his job of serving the wishes of the people and pushed his dreams to dominance.

What may lie ahead for freedom-loving Americans is anything but freedom. We have been brought deliberately to the point where one individual could possibly bring our nation completely down. Others have projected how a good nation could be destroyed. We need to recognize that some people currently in our government have been well-schooled re how to do it. Following are some of those things:

1. Government takes control of healthcare: already true in the U.S.
2. Increase the poverty level: almost 50% of our population currently receives government assistance.
3. Increase the debt to where it can never be paid off: already done.
4. Government takes control of guns: efforts seriously under way now.
5. Welfare (Income, housing, etc.) takes control of people's lives: extremely high already.
6. Control education: much of this already accomplished.
7. Religion: attack all aspects of religion: the assault is well under way.
8. Create class warfare: we now see signs of this every day.

All these things were suggested by a man named Saul Alinsky, under whose writings our president has been well-schooled.

In a country where the nation was dramatically changed, Russia, one of the things that made this possible was, as one man described them, "useful idiots." Many people in this country are now taking advantage of the support of our own "useful idiots," and have brought us to the brink of destruction as the best nation in history.

CHAPTER 55

THE DEVASTATING WORK OF LIBERALS

This nation is nowhere close to being the great nation it used to be. For 184 years, our government moved from our tenuous beginnings to the pinnacle of being the greatest nation to ever appear on the earth. Yes, we had our ups and downs, some of which decried the freedoms our Constitution held up, but, through it all, we emerged as a true bastion of freedom.

Martin Luther King, Jr. helped bring us closer to understanding that all men are created equal. We were on the verge of achieving his vision of black people standing on the same level as white people. But, then something happened to arrest our progress. In the 1960's, liberal politicians decided there was a better way, and that way was to use the taxation system to remove money from the pockets of productive people and give it to poor people. As a result, they began the Great Society Program, and convinced poor people that their lives would be better with money from Washington. Other "Entitlement" programs were added, and people who were fully capable of taking care of themselves gave up their responsibility to do so, becoming wards of government.

What many people fail to realize is that this "free money" had a huge cost to it, and that cost was giving up their responsibility to become productive citizens. Many capable people sat down and performed no valuable work, becoming useless in making this a better nation and world.

Another cost of this free money was loss of freedom to vote for people who are interested in things that bring additional improvement to this nation. They had no choice but to vote for other liberals who would keep free money coming from Washington, who, in turn, had no choice but to keep the money flowing. This is a program guaranteed to keep voters voting for liberals, and liberals keeping money flowing so people will vote for them.

Then the biggest supporter of free money to the poor became president in 2008, and presses at the mint churned out more and more dollars to the point where, in just a few short years, our national debt was doubled to twice it had been. And the liberals celebrated.

Not only do we now have our huge debt we can never pay off, but we have lost much of what it means to be an American. Because of the leadership of liberals, and the current president they have given us, we are no longer the envy of the world, leaving a vacuum where we once stood. As we have made dependents of millions of our citizens, printed unbelievable amounts money to lift "poor" people, brought in thousands of people who want to change us to a form of government that has never worked.

Liberals have no interest in our Constitution, the document that has kept us moving forward, and they have pushed us toward socialism, in which people walk to the beat of others rather than themselves, and which has never worked anywhere as well as our Constitutional Republic. And, because of the free money being received from Washington, they will continue liberal in their current work of destroying this nation.

CHAPTER 56

THE NEED TO REPLACE THE POLITICIANS IN WASHINGTON

They offered $135,000 for the well-kept four bed room, three complete baths, all brick home with approximately 3200 square feet. In 2006, this home was worth $275,000, in a community where this was average.

The year was 2006 when Congress made the decision to lift poor people into better housing. What they did was to pass legislation that allowed people to show no proof of ability to repay a mortgage when they borrowed 100 % to 105% of the purchase price of a home. This brought a stream of people into our neighborhood, once the nicest neighborhood in the county. A lady, having no job, with two daughters moved across the street, and lived there six years. When she moved out, she told a neighbor she had never made a house payment.

A home to the left of that one was purchased by a family who had multiple people living with them (we never knew how many). It was not unusual to hear them making drug deals on the phone in their front yard. One time my wife saw nine narcotics agents, with drawn pistols, surrounding the house. The occupants moved out in about seven years, having made only a few mortgage payments. The house stayed empty, and then some squatters moved in and trashed it. After squatters trashed that house and the one further to the left of it, then abandoned them, both houses sold for $40,000 each.

This is the story of politicians in Washington trying to lift poor people to a housing level equal to the middle class, and it indicates the incompetence of the politicians who sit in the seats of power. They simply don't know what they are doing. They tried to help one class of people by hurting many of us. They are not smart enough to realize that people have to lift themselves, that, when you try to do something for people they should do for themselves, you always make a mistake.

These politicians also don't understand that their task is to serve all the American people, doing what they can to help all people have a better life. They are failing miserably with this. It should be no surprise to us that for as long as the past six decades, liberals in congress have been fixed on taking tax money from wage earners and giving to people, capable of caring for themselves, who do no kind of productive work.

The budget of the United States, with our debt now in excess of 19 trillion dollars, is a stark reminder of their lack of understanding that continued spending of more money than you take in always results in bankruptcy. They have had no understanding of this whatsoever.

There are many indications of the fact that many of our politicians, perhaps a majority of them, do not understand our Constitution. If they did, our country would not now be on the brink of collapse from the debt they have accumulated for us.

The only way for us to have intelligent politicians in Washington who understand their jobs is for the American people to vote to send them there. We must remove from those seats of power anyone who does not understand that the Constitution calls for elected officials to serve the people, not for the people to serve the elected officials. We have an excellent opportunity to do this in the election in November.

CHAPTER 57

IDENTIFICATION OF THE NON-PRODUCTIVE

It isn't difficult identifying the non-productive people in this country. They stick out like a sore thumb, being those who have time to march and demonstrate. Those who have jobs and are contributing to the welfare of this country don't have time to do such things. They are busy earning a living for their families.

The non-productive claim they should be treated like other people without them getting education/training and holding down jobs like other people. They want to stand equal with those who contribute to the well-being of this country, but that's impossible, because equality is something that is not given. It is earned. Just as a person sitting in the baseball stands cannot claim equality with the player who hits home runs, so the person sitting on the sidelines of work cannot claim to be equal to the one who actually works. Failure to learn, train and get a job leaves a person far below those who have pursued better things for themselves.

Inferior people are those who vote for politicians who will keep them inferior by giving them money to stay inferior.

CHAPTER 58

INFERIORITY GUARANTEED

No-one likes to feel inferior, or, so that is what people say. Many people, however, without being aware of what is happening, allow themselves to be put into that position. This has been done by politicians who have learned how to subtly do it as they have gained experience in the art of fooling people.

What they have done is tell them they care about them, and, to prove it, they have put government money into their hands without them having to do anything to earn it.

One of the best ways to prove your inferiority is to accept without question this gift of money taken from productive Americans through the tax system. This is failure to develop and put to use the 100 billion brain cells each of us brings into the world. Proper use of those brain cells leads people to realize that they have just as much responsibility to prepare and earn a living as anyone else. But, many people are looking for ways to avoid responsibility for themselves, and jump right on the offer of free government money.

In the art of fooling people, liberals have been able to replace our educational system with a system of indoctrination by teachers and professors who do not understand that a mentally healthy individual always wants to stand on his/her own legs and not be a burden to others, which is right the opposite in socialism. Indoctrination has slowly and effectively replaced real education in our colleges and universities, and is spilling even into earlier grades. Students are not being trained to use their 100 billion brain cells in learning to think for themselves. Training them to accept what others tell them to accept and believe is cheating them of development into becoming responsible adults.

The risk in this is slowly losing the ability to live as one wishes to live, but rather to live as others want them to live. With indoctrination into "think like we want you to think," which begins as early as kindergarten, people can easily be led to do and become what their superiors desire. When this happens, leaders can lead people into believing they can't do for themselves and get along in life. This is the basis on which socialism and communism are being crammed into this country.

The reason socialism has become so popular in the United States is because our so-called educational system has trained people to believe they can't get along without government money funneled to them by liberal politicians in Washington. And, so, we have in place in Washington a system that removes money from working people through taxes and gives it to people without these people having to do anything to receive it. These are the people who have entered into a life of inferiority and are not aware of where they have been taken by these liberal politicians.

Productive and mentally healthy people come into this world wanting to take care of themselves by doing for themselves, earning what they receive. The little four-year-old boy said it well when his shoes became untied. His mother said, "Here, let me tie your shoe laces." He said, "No, I tie them." He struggled to tie them, and his mother again said, "Let me tie them." Very emphatically, the little boy said, "I tie them!!!." He verbalized what is on the inside of each of us unless we are trained to let others do for us, which is at the heart of socialism.

If you are capable of caring for yourself, but are receiving government assistance, you are inferior to people who are making the money you receive, having become a victim of socialism, and you will never rise to equality with them.

CHAPTER 59

MAKE THEM THINK WHAT WE WANT THEM TO THINK

Liberalism/socialism gives answers before we know what the questions are. This is accomplished through indoctrination, in which People are taught to cancel their thinking mechanism, which is none other than the brain. It has been popular throughout history as leaders and would-be leaders have found out that the average person has no interest in doing his/her own thinking, simply looking for someone to tell them what to do and/or believe.

Leaders sweeten the pot, making susceptibility easy for those they wish to control. Offering money and/or other things renders many people immediate followers because they lack the ability to think for themselves.

This brings us to what should be an educational program in the United States, but which, in reality, has become a system of indoctrination which runs the gamut from pre-school activities to even the Supreme Court, where men and women have begun to change law rather than interpret it. This, of course, means that their indoctrination has been effective. It is good that there still are some justices who have not cancelled their thinking mechanism and insist that law rather than corruption of law should

145

guide their decisions. Helping someone rule this country is not permissible under our Constitution, but that is what we now face in the president and liberal members of Congress.

Disregard of the Constitution has been a hallmark of Obama, and Hillary Clinton has promised to preserve his legacy, which means she will, also, disregard the Constitution and do whatever pleases her. Already knowing of her lack of respect for the law, she will be free to do anything that pleases her. The American people will be sitting ducks without ability to protect themselves.

SECTION THREE

More Things to Consider

CHAPTER 60

A GREAT OPPORTUNITY MISSED

When Obama became president of the United States, he had an opportunity to follow in the footsteps of Martin Luther King, Jr. and help bring healing to our nation. He did not do that. Instead, he has allowed the indoctrination of his growing-up years to poison how he looks at the United States and generate his desire to harm our country.

Someday black people will realize that Obama has done more to hurt them than to help them. They will realize the government money he gave them was his way of buying their loyalty so he could guide them in joining his hatred of America.

A good example of what Obama has done to gain the following he now has was seen in Ferguson, Missouri. A common criminal, having just robbed a store, attacked a police officer and was killed. Instead of dealing with things as they were, Obama used it as an occasion to vilify the white officer and white people in general, honor and praise for this criminal and, thus, hatred of white people. This was followed by blacks rioting, destroying property, and the president gave them a pass for what they had done, in effect approving of their lawless activity.

His reaction to the killing of five policemen in Dallas, the daily/nightly demonstrations we are now seeing, the occupying, take-over and shut-down of I-75/I-85 in Atlanta, and many other things all point to his work of inspiring a racially polarized society, clearly show the results of what he has done. His disparaging of the United States on the world scene just after becoming president gave indication of a poisoned past. He has been anything but a healer of relationships in this country.

We are now seeing almost daily/nightly demonstrations in many cities where people have been inspired by the failure of Obama to support law enforcement. In certain cases, criticism is appropriate, but he many times takes aim at officers when they do what is right. He has been anything but a healer of relationships in this country. This writer has heard him referred to as "The Great Divider-In-Chief," and that seems to be what he has become. Even though he now says some people have gone too far, he needs to realize they would not be headed where they are now going had he not begun and encouraged the journey. He should be fully aware that when mobs get started, they have a way of getting entirely out of control. His background involves being well-schooled in the art of revolution, and he knows the results of crowds being stirred up.

He has been well-versed in how to build a following. Anytime you give people money when they do nothing to earn it, you do them an injustice, but they will follow you most anywhere you wish to take them. The process of doing this has had the desired effect. He has bought their allegiance, and this has made committed followers of millions of them, with many now poised to do anything he desires.

This is not the first time in history a leader has done this, and it certainly will not be the last time it will be done.

What he has done is similar to what happened in Germany last century, as their leader, Adolph Hitler, gave the people things that resulted in 96 percent support. He did things that led them to believe he was their great and needed savior. He enhanced their lives, and, in the process, bought their support, and, with this support, was able to round up Jews and send them to concentration camps where many were put to death. Many Germans were more than happy to vilify the Jews because he gave them permission to do so. We are now in different times with different people, but the approach to gain a following is basically the same.

A president's job should be to make life better for all citizens, but Obama has made things worse for both blacks and whites. From the very beginning, he has attacked Republicans, cops and white people, poisoning the minds of many people along the way. Someday all of us will understand what this man in the oval office has done to make life in the United States more tenuous and troublesome than it has been for decades.

White people are not the enemy of black people, and it is time for the president to stop turning blacks against whites, assisting all of us in learning to play, work, and live together. He could have done this, but it would have required a fundamental change in the brainwashing that made him what he is.

One of the sad things through this, perhaps the saddest, is that he botched his opportunity to go down in history as one who was able to overcome his background and do things to help fulfill the "Dream" of Martin Luther King, Jr., a time when "all God's children" could stand shoulder to shoulder as brothers. He seems to be enjoying the many divisions he has nurtured among the citizens of this country.

A lot of people to this date have no idea regarding what he has done, but someday they will learn that they have been used by a man who hates this country.

CHAPTER 61

BEING USED AND UNAWARE OF IT

Leaders throughout history have sucked eager, but unsuspecting followers into supporting programs that sound good, but ultimately are destructive for them. At one time, Adolph Hitler had 96 percent support from the German people. Some of the most gifted intellectuals in Germany were talked into using their brainpower to advance things that sounded good, but which they did not understand.

The leaders in Japan were able to accomplish the same thing. The "Banzai charge" is an excellent example of this. Life was not as valuable as honor, a belief that permeated the charge into death by Japanese soldiers.

When there is a contest between intelligence and enthusiasm for an idea, intelligence is often the casualty. People building support for their causes know this, and cleverly present their programs in such a manner that intelligence is forsaken. Leaders know this, and cleverly prepare people for anything they wish to do, and, when people fail to think about things, the leader can take people into all sorts of disaster.

This has been happening in the United States for quite some time. The idea that it is okay, even mandatory, for one person to work hard and give part of what is earned to another has been presented in such a way that millions of Americans embrace it. This is totally contrary of where MLK, Jr. was trying to get us all to go.

Some of our leaders in Washington have been preparing Americans to reject the Constitution and Bill of Rights in favor of things that sound appealing, but cannot stand up to reason. The "Second Amendment" is being attacked as dangerous to our country, but guns in the hands of good people never are harmful. They become harmful only when bad people have them.

There is solid history about what happens when leaders successfully remove guns from private ownership. My mechanic of 49 years was born and reared in Germany, and his words could be prophetic about what could happen in the United States if our leaders take away our guns. He said, "When they removed our guns, we could do nothing." If our leaders, now identified as wanting to remove our guns, actually get them removed, their total control of our entire nation will happen. This is the time that the "change," which has been talked about a lot will hasten the destruction of this nation.

People are being used to bring about the death of this great nation, and they do not know they are being used.

CHAPTER 62

THE FAILURE OF MONEY

Quite often, members of my alcohol and drug classes are there because they have been arrested and jailed because of drug-dealing. Without exception, they speak of selling drugs because they can make more money doing that than getting a legal job and going to work.

One woman showed me a picture of a table on which she had put many stacks of money, and told me that was a picture of $100,000. It looked like it very well could have been that much money. She had been doing this for years and had become a key individual in distributing drugs from Chicago to Boston. When she was finally arrested, she was sentenced to several years in prison.

Asked if she would do this again, she emphatically said, "No!!!" For several years, her children had grown up without her, and this was definitely not acceptable.

Many people think money will answer all their needs and make them happy, but being arrested and spending time in jail never gives them what they are looking for. Happiness never comes from the amount of money one has, even though many people place making money ahead of everything else. We see this in many areas of life.

Working as an administrator in several hospitals introduced me to brilliant physicians who were making unbelievable amounts of money, but just as miserable as they could be. Some of the happiest people I have known were poor when compared with many others, but they had found that genuine happiness comes from what is on the inside of us, and never on the basis of what is on the outside.

The best thing each of us has is the gift of our own uniqueness. There is not another person in all the world exactly like you, and it is that person we need to develop.

CHAPTER 63

IT'S TIME TO THINK ABOUT THINGS

It is time for the American people to step back, pause and think about what has happened to this country during the past 50 years, and especially during the last 10 years. Fifty years ago we were on the threshold of making real progress in our relationships with each other.

We were recipients of the great contributions made by Dr. Martin Luther King, Jr., and were poised to make significant progress in relationships between blacks and whites. There was great hope that we were learning to live together as both black and white people responded to King's challenge to stand shoulder to shoulder as equals.

Great progress was inevitable had the "Dream" been realized, but it was not. What stopped it was the decision by liberals to lift blacks through entitlement programs. Thus, we had the beginnings of The Great Society Program, and all the other entitlement programs. Instead of blacks lifting themselves to equality, liberals offered them something quite inferior: money without effort.

What too many people do not realize is that taking money from working people and giving it to capable, but non-working people will never elevate anyone to equality with these workers.

The entitlement programs were a certain way to relegate people to an inferior life.

Liberals understood the effect of entitlement programs, and buried the "Dream" of MLK, Jr. As millions of people began to depend on government money to get along instead of on personal effort, votes at the ballot box were assured. There were reports of seminars being provided for black people to learn how to get more money from the federal government. Why was this done by liberals? It was done because liberals knew that people who learned to depend on themselves would not vote for democratic candidates, so the free money was to assure votes for liberals at election times. And so, the great damage liberals have done to black people, perhaps more damage to blacks than anything else we have had in this country in the last 100 years. And, when poor whites caught onto the flow of free money, they quit trying to earn their way through personal effort, and, also, turned to this free money from Washington. This is entirely wrong for people and for our entire nation, resulting in us being less than we should or could be.

The end result of this has been job security in Washington for liberal politicians, and permanent inferiority for poor blacks and whites. The words used by liberals to present these programs have been such that poor people have heard them as liberals doing them a great favor. What has happened, in reality, is just the opposite. Great damage has been done to poor people because the government money has placed millions of them in a state of permanent inferiority when compared to those who earn their way through development of individual talents and abilities in training and educational programs. Standing shoulder to shoulder with those who earn their way, both blacks and whites, is not possible for people who live on entitlements.

We need to review and dismantle programs that lead to permanent inferiority, replacing them with programs that facilitate and prepare people to get jobs and take care of themselves.

Human beings can never be fully human until they earn their way. If people would learn to care for themselves, the liberals would be put out of business, and we could enhance our position as the greatest nation in the history of the world.

Our current administration in Washington has bankrupted this country by ratcheting up entitlements to the highest level ever, and citizens are now experiencing the pain that is the aftermath of a leader pursuing his promise that "change is coming." The change has made things worse for most Americans.

We need people who can think through this and the many other things politicians do to guarantee their future. Our Constitution states unequivocally that politicians are to serve the citizens of this country, but too many of them have twisted things to the point where they do things for their own benefit. The worst thing they have done during the past 60 years is probably their action to guarantee votes for themselves, and, in the process, guarantee permanent inferiority for untold millions of Americans.

CHAPTER 64

TIME TO HIT THE "RESTORE" BUTTON

For a long time, liberal politicians have been hitting the "delete" button regarding the things that have made America a great nation. It is now time for real Americans to start hitting the "restore" button, and bring back the freedoms we have lost.

The "delete" button in the hands of liberals has been used effectively to eliminate much of our distinctiveness, making us more like a third-world nation. Some of the things they have been eliminating are:

1. Freedom of speech. They have been pushing us toward "political correctness," with liberals making decisions regarding what we can and cannot say.
2. Freedom of religion. We are no longer free to express our religion without being attacked by people who have little understanding re what freedom is all about. At the same time people who hate Christianity are being given a free pass to publicly gather for their prayers and worship.
3. Liberals are doing their best to take away our right to bear arms: the second amendment. Their kneejerk reaction comes because they do not understand how to handle the

deficits in the lives of those who pull the triggers. Gun control does not address the real issues here.

Liberals do not understand the ramifications of taking guns from freedom-loving people. My mechanic grew up in Germany in the 1930's and 1940's, and said, "When they took away our guns, we could do nothing." Hitler took the guns, seizing control of Germany, and World War Two followed. We know the result of this: 60 million people killed. Free people without the ability to take care of themselves are easy prey for the would-be dictator, who always seems ready to pounce when given the opportunity. Right now we have politicians in Washington ready to pounce and take control of everything citizens do.

4. The Constitution itself is being attacked as irrelevant and in need of confining to the history books. The people working to do this have little understanding of this powerful document and the freedoms possible under it.

5. We have lost freedom to protect our borders, made wide open by a president and followers who are giving easy access to people who wish to destroy us.

6. Liberals have supported the president in his dismantling of the greatest military the world has ever known. We may now lack the ability to successfully defend ourselves against those who wish to attack and conquer us. We need to remember that Japanese leaders said the reason they did not attack our mainland was because citizens had so many guns.

This is only a partial list of things done to harm our nation, and American citizens are coming to a better understanding re what politicians in Washington have been doing to us. Without our consent, they have ignored the Constitution as they have been trying to change us into their image of what we should be. They have done this by taking away first one freedom and then another, and we are rapidly finding out this is completely unacceptable.

This nation has been built on the freedoms offered under our Constitution, and the attempt by liberals to destroy this document is something good Americans cannot accept.

If this nation is to return to being a bastion of freedom, it will be done by us citizens, not by politicians. We understand freedom, but they are doing things to eliminate these freedoms in order to control us. They want to determine what we will be, but our Constitution and Bill of Rights give us this privilege.

Not only have liberals rejected the Constitution, but they have, also, rejected the words of President Kennedy, "Ask not what your country can do for you, but ask what you can do for your country." Liberals have given free money to millions of people and they have turned their backs on our great Constitution and their responsibility to get a job and help make this a better nation.

Those of us who understand what the Constitution is will have to do what we know we must do, and that is take control of this nation out of the hands of liberals who are trying to destroy our way of life, and put it back in our hands. That will have to be done by our courage to remain free and to use the ballot box to send to Washington only those politicians who value the Constitution and our freedoms. We must realize that those citizens who have been bought by free money will work to keep liberals there who will continue their gravy train, so our action is vitally important.

Those of us who understand and value the Constitution and the freedoms it offers are the only ones left to salvage this great nation. That is why we must act at the ballot box, making sure that liberals and not the Constitution is what passes into the history books.

Who are the liberals? Most call themselves democrats, but a few others who understand neither the Constitution nor the freedoms we have call themselves by different designations.

American citizens who love our freedoms and our Constitution are the only ones who will hit the "restore" button, and we must do it now if we are to preserve our status as the greatest nation in the history of the world.

CHAPTER 64

THE ART OF PRODUCING WORTHLESS PEOPLE

The inability of the American people to not understand where liberals have taken this country is astounding. The government in Washington, once a champion of people doing for themselves through education, training and hard work, has now developed programs whereby individuals can easily get by without lifting a finger to help themselves.

Money taken from taxpayers and funneled to the "poor" has replaced "roll up your sleeves, get to work, and make something of yourselves." Thus, we have almost fifty percent of capable workers living off the labor of other people. This is a travesty perpetrated by liberals who want to replace our Constitutional government with a watered-down version of socialism. This is none other than a major sign that liberals fail to understand that people come into the world with 100 billion brain cells poised to be developed and used to make life better for themselves and others.

The programs developed in Washington during the past 60 years have trapped millions of people into thinking there is no need to develop the best thing about them – their brains. There is a world of potential residing in the brains of people who have been lulled to sleep by the free money from Washington. Had this money not been available, millions of people, now virtually asleep, would have had to make their own way, gotten an education and/or training and made their own contributions to this becoming a better nation for themselves and everyone else. There is no way of determining what brains put to sleep would have accomplished, but it has to include some great things.

It is easy to see the results of people not having to get busy doing for themselves by looking at the TV news in Atlanta or any other big city, and seeing evening and morning reports of shootings, robberies, and other crimes perpetrated by people who have enough time on their hands to plan to supplement the government money they receive by doing all kinds of unlawful things. If people had to work for a living rather than use the EBT card and other things provided by liberals, they would not have time for much of their criminal activity. We can also see the effects of people not having to do for themselves in the numbers of people too fat to hold down any job.

Liberals will deny that programs out of Washington have led to deterioration in the quality of life that we all experience, and will blame other things for this, but anytime you do something for someone else that someone else should do for themselves, you do them a great wrong. Many of the programs that have come from Congress and the presidents have led directly to this deterioration.

There are indeed individuals needing a helping hand from others, and we should respond positively to them, but we do not need to rescue any capable people from their responsibility to care for themselves.

All of us should take a lesson from the successful athlete. A good athlete is successful if he/she practices over and over, doing what is necessary to become good. It doesn't come without effort. A successful life also does not come without effort, and liberals sending money for people to get along without effort should be considered a crime, but they walk about wanting to get pats on their backs and votes that will return them to Washington for what they have done. Liberals have mastered the art of producing worthless people.

Correcting what liberals have done to this country will be difficult, but it must be done if we are to regain the status we had as the best and greatest country the world has ever seen.

CHAPTER 65

BECOMING LIKE THE WORLD

The administration in Washington and liberal politicians are trying their best to make the United States become like the world.

Obama has been trying to change us from being Americans to something less than we have been. The people he has brought here have no intention of becoming Americans, but wish to change us to be like they are. If we don't, they think it is okay to kill us. This is not why people have come here historically, and it is not acceptable for anyone to try and make us like the world.

In the past, people have migrated here because this nation has stood head and shoulders above the rest of the world. People wanted to be a part of us. In being aware of our history, we recognize our imperfections, but realize that, in spite of them, we still stand taller than other nations.

In the coming election in November, we face an alternative that is new to all of us. One candidate for president, Hillary Clinton, wishes to preserve the legacy of Obama, which is none other than continuing to make us like the world. She does not understand what freedom to choose is all about. The other candidate, Donald Trump, wishes to take us back toward being a nation where people have the opportunity to become what they wish to become. In other words, the democrat wishes to make us like the world. The republican wishes for us to return to the freedom to decide what we will be and do. This is a stark difference, and is the first time in our history we have had such an obvious choice. During the time he was campaigning to become president, Obama hedged his message in words that fooled millions of people, and he did it again when he was re-elected.

We do not need to be less than what we have been. We need to hone the qualities that have led us to being the envy of the world, where freedom has been our choice. We need to be more than what we have been.

To those who wish to make us like the world, hunters have a saying that is appropriate, "This dog won't hunt." There is no way the American people should have interest in becoming like the world. We should make our "specialness" even more special as we resume our march toward extending freedom and opportunity for all.

As an American, I appreciate the opportunity to be what I choose to be, and don't want anyone trying to make me what they want me to be, our president or anyone else. It is a privilege to be an American.

We should repudiate those who wish to change us, and accept those who wish to make us great again. Becoming like the world is not possible if we follow our Constitution. It offers us the opportunity to rise above the achievements of other nations. Marching like an American is much better than walking in the footsteps of the world.

CHAPTER 66

POLITICIANS THEN, POLITICIANS NOW

In my 82 years of life, a lot of water has passed under the bridge. During this time, I have experienced the United States reaching the pinnacle of the greatest nation the world has ever known, becoming the envy of people everywhere. People clamored to come here for the opportunity to experience a new kind of freedom never before offered in any nation. The history books were and still are full of stories of men and women who sacrificed greatly for this nation to become what it became. It took real men and women to build what we became.

But, beginning in the 1960's, we saw the emergence of a new kind of leadership. We began to change from a nation offering freedom for people to build their own dreams to one where politicians in Washington would provide whatever people needed for their dreams. Over a period of time, it became not what people could do for themselves, but what politicians could do for people. President Kennedy's words, "Ask not what your country can do for you - ask what you can do for your country," have been rejected and replaced by signing up for the free check from government. Now, millions of people build their dreams on the largess of Washington, and no longer on themselves, courtesy of the Democratic Party.

Since that time, we have gone from a government helping people build their own dreams to one where politicians are in charge of the building. The result of this has been, since the 1960's, politicians tearing down this great nation by offering to do for people what people should be doing for themselves. It is no accident that leaders in Washington have damaged our nation so much. They have lost an understanding of what freedom and constitutional government really are, and have begun to see themselves as the key to the future of this nation. As the focus has shifted from government of the people, by the people, and for the people to one of government by politicians, there has been no alternative but for us to become less than we have been.

If we do not change the direction this country has been taking during the past 60 years, we will see this beacon of liberty fading away to be replaced by the weakness of the politicians in Washington. A nation built on the wisdom of politicians will never equal a nation built on the wisdom of its citizens. Our Founders understood this and were willing to die to give us freedom to build our lives and our country. In recent years, politicians in Washington have been taking power from the people and placing it in their hands. Thus, we have experienced a great loss in our standing as the greatest of all nations.

Failure for us to change where politicians have been taking us for several decades will result in our falling to be an also-ran country where politicians serve as the foundation of the nation and not the people. We need politicians in Washington who have read and understand our Constitution. Many today do not understand what it says or what it means. If they did, we would not have seen the erosion of our country that has taken place during my lifetime.

The politicians now occupying the seats of power in Washington need to be replaced by politicians who understand that our greatness has come from us citizens, and not from the largess they dole out. If we the people don't make changes in the politicians we are sending to Washington, our greatness will fade into the history books, and that will be a tragedy, not only for us, but for all peoples who dream of the freedoms we have offered.

CHAPTER 66

LEARNING *FROM* BRITAIN'S EU EXIT

Americans should learn something from the exit of Britain from the European Union. The British people wanted to start making their own decisions again. They had found that, when the power to make decisions was in the hands of non-British people, decisions would be made that were not good for Britain.

The American people have found the same thing is true when non-Americans make decisions for us: the decisions are often detrimental to us. To have non-Americans making decisions for us has already cost us some of our freedoms, and things will get worse if we allow it to continue. To become like the world will be to become less than we are.

Obama has been trying to change us to become more like the world. Many of the people he has brought here have been trying to make us like they are. Historically this is not why people have come here, and it is not acceptable for anyone or any people to try and make us like the world.

People have come here in the past to become a part of a freedom-loving nation, not to transform us into what they want us to be. It is clear that, if we do not become what they want us to be, some of them think it is okay to kill us. This is totally unacceptable.

No other nation has had the freedoms offered us by the Constitution, and, for that reason, do not have the same basis for decision-making as do we. Many people do not understand that the power of this nation has rested with us citizens, and that is where it should remain if we are to remain a nation that is a beacon of freedom to the world. Foreigners making decisions that should rightly be made by Americans will always create problems that are not good for us.

In the past, being an American has been something special. To become something less than special, which is what our president wants, should be unacceptable to good Americans. Hillary Clinton, the democrat running to replace him, wants to preserve his legacy. This indicates she neither understands our Constitution nor what he has done.

We should not be trying to change our "specialness." Rather, we should be trying to make this specialness better for all people who choose to be here, which means making more freedom and opportunities available for everyone.

As an American, I have the opportunity to be what I want to be, and do not wish for anyone to interfere with this, our president or anyone else. We have no place in our government for anyone who wants to make us like the world.

We should repudiate those who want to change us into something less than we are, and to respond positively to those who wish to return us to our "specialness." Marching like an American is much better than walking in the footsteps of the world.

CHAPTER 67

WHEN YOU DON'T KNOW WHAT TO DO, DO SOMETHING ANYWAY

The killings in Orlando present another opportunity for politicians who don't know what they are dong to do something anyway. Depraved minds and spirits lead people to harm others, and they are always able to do so, that is, unless someone stops them.

Removing ways for people to protect themselves always ratchets up danger, and, with no-one in the club having a gun for protection, the murder of all those people was as easy as a cake walk. One person with a handgun could have stopped the whole thing.

If the attempt to remove guns is made, they will never be taken from the Mafia or from criminals who have stolen and hidden them, and then the rest of us will be sitting ducks to become victims of those who have no respect for the law or the dignity and worth of every human being. This will, also, be a time when border security will vanish because people in other nations with guns will be able to quickly overpower whatever defense we have available at the borders. We should remember that the Japanese did not invade the United States at the start of World War Two because American citizens had too many guns and could use them against an invading army.

The killings represent a serious human problem that will be unaddressed if politicians busy themselves doing something they should not do. Current politicians in Washington have presented an environment that has invited people to express the worst that is in them, and we now have the most danger within this country we have faced. The administration has given a pass to criminals, thus increasing danger to our law enforcement personnel, and has knowingly released from prison people who have killed Americans (from Guantanamo). The administration has also brought thousands of people into this country who think only their way of life should be followed. Taking guns from Americans will increase our danger exponentially.

Killing others deliberately is a human, mental health problem that needs to be addressed, something completely misunderstood by politicians and, because of this, we have little effort being made to help people who come from backgrounds where life is devalued. Contributing to this is the way some religions approve of killing those who do not think the right thoughts, which is a product of the primitive mind that should have been discarded centuries ago. Minds given to primitive thinking will always present danger to us.

Politicians in Washington need to learn that their job is to make life better for all citizens, not make them worse. Taking guns away from good citizens will always increase their danger because guns will always be available to criminals.

Too many things in our lives have already been compromised because of the ineptness of congress and the presidents. Taking guns away will increase our dangers because it will leave us defenseless against those who, disregarding current laws, will continue to disregard them.

CHAPTER 68

PRIMITIVE MIND IN CONTROL

One of the things impeding the progress of humans is our failure to let go of primitive ideas. Holding on to ideas and beliefs that should have been discarded in days gone by has led to not only heartache, but deaths of many good people.

Those who keep primitive ideas alive prevent progress in many areas, severely limiting development of not only our minds, but of our ability to find a way to live in peace with each other.

The pages of history quickly reveal how primitive ideas have done so much damage. Primitive ideas led to the Crusades where soldiers, as they killed Muslims, shouted, "It is the will of God." This followed the speech by Pope Urban II, in which he shouted this slogan to be used as the soldiers did their killing.

Primitive ideas were alive and well during the Inquisitions as groups were sent out by the church to make certain people believe what they were supposed to believe, and, if they did not, to be punished, even killed, because they did not accept official church dogma.

Primitive ideas were alive during slavery days. Many people believed it was okay, even acceptable by God, to own slaves. After all, slavery had been accepted throughout history, and, for that reason, it should continue.

Galileo ran into rejection and house arrest for learning and saying the earth was not the center of the universe.

Hanging onto ideas and beliefs that should have been discarded centuries ago is a primary reason we have so much trouble in contemporary life. Many of us are fearful of not being accepted by others if we don't say we believe what they believe. Often, we accept, without question, what others tell us to believe, shutting down our own thinking mechanism because we don't want to be out of step with our peers.

Many people hang onto the idea that it is okay to harm or kill other people if they do not believe what they are told to believe. Radical Islam is the contemporary expression of this as people are poisoned with the primitive idea that people must be killed if they will not accept the Muslim faith. This is a primitive idea with which too many Muslims have been indoctrinated since birth. There is nothing more harmful in the present-day world than a religion that says it is okay to kill others who do not accept the correct faith.

The 100 billion brain cells each of us has been given were given for the purpose of thinking. We seem not to know this and accept without question what we are told to accept. If we will put these 100 billion brain cells to use and do our own thinking, we will never, in any way, seek the death of another human being. Primitive thinking is totally out of place in the contemporary world.

CHAPTER 69

TO BE OR NOT TO BE? STILL THE QUESTION

William Shakespeare had hamlet raise the question, "To be or not to be. That is the question - whether 'tis nobler in the mind to suffer the slings and arrows of outrageous fortune or to take arms against a sea of troubles, and, by opposing, end them?"

As Americans, we are confronted with the outrageous: people who have grown up in the midst of freedom and opportunities, receiving the rewards offered by only this country, now planning to replace what has made us great with socialism, a form of government that has never given people what our Constitutional Republic has given us. Democrats are on the march to change the nation and make people subservient to the politicians in Washington, something socialism will bring.

Some of the things that will happen if the oval office continues to be occupied by a democrat:

1. Full entrance into socialism.
2. As verbalized by Mrs. Clinton: maintaining the legacy of Obama.
3. Loss of our Second Amendment.

4. Continuing budgets that far exceed income, with eventual bankruptcy. Good minds don't do this.

5. Maintaining governmental programs that do more harm than good. As an example, our educational programs have deteriorated since the Department of Education was formed.

6. Continued dismantling of the greatest military in the history of the world.

7. Maintenance of programs that divide us, i.e. Obamacare, men in women's restrooms, et al.

8. Continued destruction of talents by giving free money to people who do nothing to earn it: the biggest waste of talent the world has ever known, which brings continued purchase of votes.

9. Continued loss of our freedoms.

10. Complete loss of The Constitution of the United States.

As Americans, we have the choice in November to return to a Constitutional Republic or continue the decline into socialism, a form of government that has failed wherever it has been tried.

When people who notoriously break our laws are elected to places of leadership, they will continue to do what they have done in the past. Getting away with lawless activity only encourages more lawless activity. That is in our future if a lawless person goes into the president's chair.

Yes, the question is, "To be or not to be? Will we remain a Constitutional Republic or will we choose to become a socialist country where life is never as good as we have had it in the United States?" We will answer this question in November as the choice is made between a democrat or a Republican president.

CHAPTER 70

PRODUCTS OF WHERE WE COME FROM

We are all products of where we come from...always, unless we make the decision to change and be different. People often struggle in the therapist's office as they attempt to leave a life that has been less than good. Some people are successful in this, but others decide that change is too difficult.

Relocating to a new country always calls for a decision regarding change. People who immigrate face this question: "Will I become a part of this new country or will I seek to repeat the kind of life I lived where I came from."

One of the great things about the United States is that each individual in presented with the opportunity to participate in freedom, which has offered the best life anyone can enjoy. In this country, you do not have to fit into anyone else's plan for your life. It will become what you make it unless you make the decision to turn your life over to those who want to make you in their image.

After the past several years, citizens in this country need to take a careful look at the efforts some of our leaders have made to change us to what they want us to become. They have been trying to build us in their image and take away our right to build our lives the way we wish to build them. Their strong efforts to convert us into a socialist country have already taken away some of our freedoms. They will remove more of these freedoms if given the opportunity to do so.

There is no question but that our quality of life has been diminished by those who wish to change us, and it will diminish even more if these people remain in office. If we are going to preserve our freedoms, we must replace those who have damaged our way of life so much.

We should not be surprised that our quality of life has diminished during the last six years. That was the intention of our new leadership: to change us from the greatest nation in history to one that fit into a third-world category. My family now lives in the most dangerous environment we have lived in, and the promise is that it will become even more dangerous. The lure of violence becomes attractive when we fail to understand what this nation is all about. The killings in Orlando we recently saw are a reflection of where we have been heading during the past few years.

People who don't like us are now being given unrestricted freedom to be here, many of them walking across our borders with the intention to do us harm. In addition, many have been given a free ride by our government to come here and repeat the kind of life they chose to leave, not with the intention to become one of us, but to make us what they wish us to be.

When leadership makes effort to change us from what we are to what they wish us to be, we should all strongly resist and not let it happen. Becoming a third world country should be of no interest to Americans, but it is amazing the kind of following and support a leader can build with some money placed in people's hands. The mushrooming money supply of the past several years given to people who have not earned it has been the catalyst to bring support for changing us to a more dangerous nation. People have been used by politicians to bring change, and these people have no clue regarding how they have been used to bring about the change we are now experiencing.

Our current leadership in Washington has been successful in diminishing the quality of life for most Americans. It is as was intended, and, if we continue our current slide into mediocrity as a nation, we will cease to be a beacon of liberty to the world. To continue the policies of the past few years, which is the intention of many leading politicians, will take us further into mediocrity as a nation.

The killings in Orlando? They are an expression of the direction we are heading. We must change the leadership in Washington if we are to reverse the slide of the United States into mediocrity, and such things as the killings in Orlando.

CHAPTER 71

LACK OF IDENTITY

One of the things troubling millions of Americans is lack of identity. They neither know where they are coming from nor where they are going. The result of this is lack of any idea regarding their purpose in life.

Being an American is a great privilege, and countless numbers of people are either coming here for a better life or wishing they could come.

Many people who come here try to bring an old way of life with them, and attempt to repeat it, trying to change what has made this country great. What they do not realize is that making life as it was in their old country replicates what they wanted to get away from, and does not answer the yearning they have deep within for something better.

A mistake many people make, including many Americans, is to suppose there is a perfect way of life that can be found somewhere. Thinking, "Nirvana is awaiting me if only I can find it," they look outside themselves to others for the secret to life. But, they never find it.

They never find it because finding Nirvana is a personal journey that takes place only from within. And...this points to that which makes America the country that is best of all in the world. We have the only environment where it is possible to pursue our own dreams rather than the dreams of our leaders/rulers.

Some people make the mistake of supposing this country simply should answer all their needs, but that is a pipe dream. The only way to have our deep needs met is to develop what is on the inside of us. This is a great freedom offered each of us. We can do or become whatever we want to do or be if we are willing to make the effort to get there. No-one relegates us to a certain level of attainment. We have the freedom to choose for ourselves; no-one determines the direction of our lives unless we allow them to do so.

Freedom to be and do as we choose is a great gift. Many people miss this gift when they turn their lives over to a leader who wants them to follow his/her dreams.

People who ask you to follow their dreams will always be among us. They rise to power only when we decide they have a better answer to life than do we, and we know from recent and past history the results of abandoning our own dreams and following another. Whether it be the false dreams of Hitler, the Crusaders, the slave holders or the recent promise to change America to someone's image, all such efforts come to naught when people finally realize that the one who promises to fulfill our dreams is a frail human being promising to do what cannot be done.

We grow a lot when we cease looking for happiness and success outside ourselves to realizing it is something that comes only from within. This is one of the many things that make America great: the best life for you can be determined only by you.

When we understand that life is what we make it, we can get to work doing our own thing. We are free individuals, free to decide what life will be for us. We have no need to follow the dreams of others, just our own dreams. When we do this individually, we establish identities as people who are free from the constraints other people or forms of government would force upon us. No other country in the world offers this to us.

The identity of personal freedom and responsibility in a free country needs to be preserved.

CHAPTER 72

USED AND ABUSED, BUT DON'T KNOW IT

The poor people in this country, both black and white, have been used and abused, but think things have gone well for them.

The first responsibility each person has is to take care of self. Anything that prevents us from doing this is keeping us from developing the talents and abilities we have, and it is wrong. This country became the greatest country in the history of the world because people were given the freedom to pursue their personal dreams, and they did just that.

During the last several decades, liberals have put a road-block in the path of people pursuing their dreams, and many Americans have chased something other than their own dreams, something that is far inferior to what they could have done for themselves.

Liberals have herded poor and lazy people into government give-away programs by offering them free money taken from hard-working Americans. This free money has been so attractive that millions have given up the task of making something of themselves. Money from the Great Society and welfare programs has killed the sense of personal responsibility that comes from being a healthy human being.

Liberals stepped forward and gave them something, but, in the process took something far more valuable from them. The money given to them was so attractive that it blinded them from seeing what was behind their gift, a form of slavery that herds a person into thinking the thoughts of other people. Healthy people who accept government money instead of working for it give up their responsibility to be a productive part of our country. When election time comes, poor people have no choice but to vote for those promising more and more free money. Any individual who says every able-bodied person should have a job has no chance with government free-loaders. Thus, the popularity of those who are taking us into socialism, a form of government far inferior to our Constitutional Republic.

The gift they received was free money through the welfare system. What was taken from them was their very dignity, dignity that comes from the inside of each person as talents and abilities are developed to do something worthwhile in this world. Each person has the responsibility of taking care of self, but the liberals stepped in and said, "You don't have to do that. We'll do it for you, that is, if you vote for us."

Many people, preferring to avoid the responsibility of taking care of self, jumped on board, and the checks started coming from Washington. Poor people liked this so much that, and, at the next election, they voted to let those politicians continue their craft of taking tax money from those who worked and give to them. The cost of this was great, but millions enjoyed getting something for nothing.

What was lost can be seen in a report, "The War On Poverty 50 Years Later: A Progress Report", published by The Council of Economic Advisers, January, 2014: "A measure of 'market poverty,' that reflects what the poverty rate would be without any tax credits or other benefits, rose from 27.0 percent to 28.7 percent between 1967 and 2012." People were receiving tax credits, but they were still unable to emerge from poverty.

This is an indication that free stuff does not change how people approach life. The assistance we make available to people should be tied to their participation in things that bring progress. Gifts given without corresponding responsibilities do not lift people out of poverty.

CHAPTER 73

TIME FOR BLACK LEADERS TO DO THEIR JOB

If you want to see how successful black leaders have been for the last five or six decades, go to the jails in Atlanta or watch the evening news on T.V. In both places, you will see a disproportionately large percentage of black inmates in the jails or committing crimes out in communities. This is not the way things should be, and the question must be asked, "Why?"

For the past five or six decades, black people have had access to education and/or training, but many have chosen another way. Martin Luther King, Jr. challenged blacks to stand shoulder to shoulder with white people by doing those things that would bring them to an equal level, and he died while doing this.

Black leaders had the opportunity to point the way and keep blacks marching toward equality, but they dropped the ball. Liberal politicians offered blacks an opportunity they could not turn down: free money from the government. Liberals communicated, "Vote for us, and we'll give you money for doing nothing," and black leaders began marching to the tune coming from Washington, and ended the march MLK, Jr. had started them on. These black leaders turned their people toward the free money from Washington, and millions ceased any effort to make their own way, and many whites joined them. Seminars to help people learn how to get money from the government became far more important than programs that would help people find jobs

What the liberal politicians did not tell people was that the free money would not be enough to give them the kind of life for which they were looking. It was enough, however, to kill their desire to train, study and learn, and, so, sitting down and waiting on the government check took the place of effort to make something of themselves.

Signing up for welfare, which brings in less money than they could earn with training and education and good jobs, left them with a lot of time on their hands, time enough to plan how to get additional money through crime. We see the results of this each time we turn on T.V. news.

No-one capable of supporting self, but who is supported by the earnings of another person, which is at the heart of government handouts, can ever claim to be equal to the one working and making that money.

Martin Luther King, Jr. Day is celebrated every year, but the meaning of the day is not what he died for or intended it be. He wanted black people to earn their way, but the free money from Washington put an end to that as black leaders led the procession to the government trough.

This writer knows black people who pursued education and training, and today enjoy equality with whites. They live in my community and enjoy achievement and the respect that comes from preparation and work. They have continued the march MLK, Jr. started, and the results are participation on an equal basis with whites. Many, also in my community, did not do that.

Black leaders have led millions of people into subservience to the liberals in Washington, with no chance that the money they receive could ever lift them shoulder to shoulder with whites. It has resulted in crowds of black people joining gangs, being in jails, and appearing on the evening news.

If black leaders do not again lead their people on the march MLK, Jr. started, there is no chance they will ever attain the status of equality with whites he dreamed about.

SECTION FOUR

Over and Beyond

CHAPTER 74

ANOTHER LOOK AT THIS POLITICAL MESS

M any people are wondering why we are having such political mess in the selection of presidential candidates. A woman many believe should already be in prison is the democratic nominee; a man often seeming out of control is the Republican nominee. Well, we have been building toward this for decades while people who should have been saying something about it have been quiet.

For several decades, Congress and presidents of the United States have been in the process of destroying our Constitutional Republic. Some things they have done are:

1. They have changed government from a Constitutional Republic to one moving rapidly toward socialism. This has moved us from being a great country to one of great mediocrity.
2. They have destroyed the need of people to make something of themselves to a bunch of beggars waiting for the free check from government.
3. They have destroyed MLK's dream of black people standing shoulder to shoulder with white people. Making black

people dependent on the earnings of white people never elevates them to equal status.

4. Seeking to be everything to everybody who will vote for them, they have put us into unacknowledged bankruptcy, with no way to ever repay our debt.

5. They have ruined good neighborhoods, making it possible for people with no jobs to borrow 100% of the cost of a house. Houses in my neighborhood that once sold for $250,000 TO $300,000 have been trashed and abandoned. Two recently sold for $40,000. This has produced the most dangerous neighborhoods in my 80 years of life.

6. They have elected as "President" a man who has acknowledged he hates the United States and has done what he could to degrade us.

7. Our military has been reduced to where it is now only a shadow of what it used to be.

8. Our borders have been opened for both good and bad people to stream unhindered into this country.

9. They have spent great sums of money working on problems that do not exist. When I grew up, guns were everywhere, and people did not kill with these guns. Now they want to take away our guns, doing nothing about the fact that this is a human problem, not a gun problem.

10. They have launched attacks on freedom of speech and freedom of religion.

11. They have rammed an unconstitutional healthcare program down our throats.

12. Government tyranny is well-illustrated in the transgender problem. Creating risk and danger to greater numbers of people in order to protect the feelings of a small group who feel "different" is not constitutional government. Accepting our differentness and learning to live with them is a mark of mental health. The art of "divide and conquer" has been used quite effectively.

This is a small sampling of what liberal "democrats" have done to this country. Behind this problem is an educational system that has changed from education to indoctrination. No longer do teachers and professors say, "Learn to think for yourselves," but, "Think like us and we will take care of you." This is abandonment of the educational process, and is producing clones rather than mature people.

Democrats have fully supported Obama because they believe he has been doing the right things. It is clear that the goal of democrats is to control every aspect of our lives.

These programs of control will pick up speed if a democrat is elected president. The American people have been slow realizing this, but now understand that many programs coming out of Washington are harmful to our nation. Many now feel their money and future are endangered by each piece of legislation Congress passes, and believe we must protect ourselves against Washington politicians. We do not feel they have any idea that the Constitution calls for them to serve us, not for us to serve them.

The anger toward Republicans is because they have kept their mouths shut when they should have been raising all kinds of resistance.

If a dramatic change is not made in Washington, many Americans believe this "beacon of freedom and liberty," THE UNITED STATES OF AMERICA, will cease to shine.

The politicians in Washington have botched their jobs. Many Americans now believe our nation is being destroyed by the very people we have elected to make us a better country. Many now feel they want no politicians in Washington who either think like, look like or smell like what we have had for the past several decades.

This is a primary reason Donald Trump has gained such popularity. In no way does he remind people of those who have done so much damage to our nation. They are thinking, "Anything is better than what we have had."

CHAPTER 75

ESCAPING THE PRIMITIVE MIND

In some ways, the human mind has progressed from what it once was, but, in other ways it has been stuck where it was thousands of years ago.

Humans should have left their primitive minds back in primitive times. However, the thinking of people thousands of years ago still serves as the guide in many people's lives today. It is seen especially in the way politicians herd their followers, and in the way religion uses what is termed "holy scripture" to control the thinking of followers. Politicians lure people by telling them, "We will take you to the Promised Land," but people never get there. Some people will say, "If it is in Holy Scripture, then it is absolutely true." This is the background for people claiming every word was dictated by God."

A quick look at history books and contemporary life makes it plain that neither politics nor religion has been successful in helping people live with each other.

We must understand that people are different, and that it is okay to be different. What we don't need to do is think, if someone disagrees with us, we have every right to harm that person. The position, "You think like me or you are history," has no place in our world. We need to understand that the process of working toward agreements or agreeing to disagree is far better than picking up a gun and shooting each other. Retrogression into barbaric ways does anyone any good.

If we could understand the value of each individual, regardless of culture or education, we would never seek to destroy each other. Lashing out because someone is different fits the primitive mind far better than the one we have in today's world.

CHAPTER 76

JUST DON'T THINK ABOUT IT

Our brains, all 80 to 100 billion brain cells between our ears, were given to us for thinking purposes. Many people do not know this, and allow others to do their thinking for them.

When people refuse to think for themselves or are unable to do so, they become easy prey to those who want us to think like they think. We see this in many areas: in politics, in religion, in education, in the crowd who wants us to take illegal drugs or drink too much booze, in those who want us to be politically correct, and in many other areas of life.

The basic message is: "Just don't think about it. Let us to the thinking for you. If you let us do the thinking, we'll make life better for you." If we are alert, we can see and hear this all around us. It is particularly true right now as we are building toward the election in November. Many people have already become subservient to one or more of the candidates, and have completely lost the ability to understand what is really being said.

During the last eight years, many people have put their thinking apparatus to sleep, and have stood quietly by as many of the people they have listened to have severely reduced the freedoms that have made us so great a nation, not a perfect nation, but one that is the best in all of history.

If people will do their own thinking, they will move out from under the control of those who wish to manipulate them. Those who wish to control others are quickly drawn to the political field because they know millions are out there looking for someone who will promise to take them to the Promised Land. As we have experienced in the past several years, in spite of the promise for Nirvana, it has not come because it can never be delivered by another person or group of people. It is something that can be delivered only by the person willing to do his/her own thinking.

The pages of history are full of the tragedies that come from the message, "Just don't think about it. Let us do your thinking for you."

Socrates drank the hemlock in 399 B.C. after he was found guilty of "contaminating the youth," telling them to decide personally what they would do with their lives, not what parents and relatives told them to do, plus he didn't worship the gods he was told to worship. The Inquisitions came about in an attempt to stamp out those who did not believe all they were told to believe by the Church. Slavery was the result of people thinking it was okay to subjugate others, disallowing them to build their own lives as they wished. World War Two was the result of people believing Hitler could give them what they wanted

Mind control is never good. As we think about the politicians now wanting us to allow them to tell us what to think, we need to be careful that we think our own thoughts and make our own decisions. Those who are asking us to continue stepping in their footprints may be leading us toward a dead end that will bring the demise of all our freedoms.

We all should be trying to do our own thinking, taking our places in making certain the freedoms we have enjoyed in this country are not diminished, but made stronger. Each of us is required to do our own thinking because, if we don't, our lives will become subservient to others rather than to what we build for ourselves.

CHAPTER 77

COMFORTABLE IN ONE'S OWN SKIN

If you believe people should think your thoughts and agree with you on things, then you are saying something about yourself, and this something is that you are insecure in what you believe. Being comfortable in one's own skin, determining life as you want it to be, and allowing others to do so, is a mark of good mental health. Clients come to the therapist's office for assistance in getting out from under the control of others. They come wanting to be what they want to be and not what others want them to be. Often, they are burdened with the demands and expectations of other people, and this is always troublesome, sometimes resulting in insecurities or some form of mental illness.

Those who demand that others walk to their beat are purveyors of illness. Demanding that someone become what I want them to be, a favorite ploy exercised by many in the last several years in the U. S., is a sign of not-knowing what life is all about. Life is not about fitting a pattern acceptable to others. It is about learning to express the unique, unrepeatable persons we are.

Building clones is a certain sign that people do not understand life as it ought to be, and that they, themselves, haven't figured out where they fit in this world. "Political correctness," a popular thing with the mentally unhealthy, is a clear display of not-knowing. In reality, you have no responsibility to think or be what others want you to be. Your responsibility is to be what you decide to be.

Some of the greatest tragedies in history are the result of people demanding that others fit a pre-determined pattern. The Crusades, the Inquisitions and slavery are great examples of what can happen when people are forced to be what they do not choose to be.

Where this country is going with the demands that others fall in lock-step with what they want them to be is a sure sign that we are not the citadel of freedom we once were. If we do not restore freedom for people to be what they want to be, we will fall further into thought control and eventually become pawns of those who take pleasure in pulling our chains. Thought control is one of the worst forms of slavery.

A nation is most healthy when people are given freedom to be whom and what they want to be. There will always be unhealthy people who do not understand this, and will seek to demand that each of us fit their pattern. We are currently seeing the results of those who are demanding we think and act as they wish, and, as many people are realizing, we are fast losing our status as a bastion of freedom and liberty. Freedom and liberty are always casualties of those who think they know better than me what I am supposed to think and do.

If I am going to be mentally healthy, it is important that I be whom I wish to be, and, equally, it is important that you be whom you wish to be. Anytime we do not give each other this freedom, it is a clear sign that we fail to understand who we are and what life is all about.

It is only when we are free that we can give others the freedom to be free.

CHAPTER 78

WHEN BRAINS DON'T WORK RIGHT

History and current life are full of examples when human brains have not worked the way they're supposed to work. Our brains are given for the purpose of developing things to enhance our lives and for learning how to live with each other. We often use them for other purposes, creating problems for each other. Used wrongly, we leave casualties along the way. We do things that are not reasonable, and we usually pay the price.

When our brains work right, we never knowingly and deliberately hurt anyone. We seek to do things that are good for, not only us, but, also, for others as well. We do not knowingly do things that place the welfare of others at risk.

At the present time, we are giving people who were born males, but who now feel like they are feminine, and vice-versa, the opportunity to enter female or male restrooms, whichever they prefer. This removes a lot of protection in that it makes it possible for sexual perverts to enjoy their perversion. Yes, there will be some of this, and not only adult women, but girls and boys will face the possibility of being molested. Allowing this to happen is beyond reason. It makes no logical sense.

Each of us was born as either male or female. Preferring to be the opposite of how we were made, does not allow us to escape that fact. Nature made us what we are, either male or female, and no mental gymnastics will change that.

This new gender-neutral restroom is now offending far more people than all the transgender people added together. If we are concerned about offending people, we should offend as few as possible, and end this idiotic open restroom for people who would rather be what they are not.

It's okay to be different, but it is not okay to impose our beliefs on others, particularly if what we want creates risks to others.

We need to start using our brains the way they are supposed to be used, for thinking purposes, not for others to control.

CHAPTER 79

HORNSWOGGLED AMERICANS

A lot of Americans have been hornswoggled. They don't know it, but it has not been too difficult for them to be hornswoggled. It reminds me of what happened in Germany in the 1930's. We could use the word "bamboozled;" it means basically the same thing.

Millions of Americans have bought into thought processes that, if not corrected, will result in the destruction of our nation. At first, the ideas of a new leader sound quite good, and many people think they have found a way to the Promised Land. They sense that someone other than themselves can give them what they have been looking for, and they pledge full allegiance. We now see life in the U. S. less grounded than it used to be as people are attacked for no other reason than for doing their own thinking and not being politically correct.

There was a time when we had freedom of speech, but that time has passed as we have to consider what is politically correct. Sure, I used to hear things that were contrary to my way of thinking, but so what? It didn't bother me if you said things I did not believe. But, now I must check the crowd I am in lest someone gets his/her feelings hurt.

We need to become aware that, when someone's speech becomes offensive to us, it usually means that we are the ones who have the problem. If we feel good about ourselves and what we believe, it really doesn't matter if people agree with us. We are all individual and it is okay not to think like others think.

Americans have fallen victims to "group-think," which is nothing other than becoming victims of those who wish to control us. We see much of this generated by the Washington political crowd, a crowd that has often led us in the wrong direction. We have seen emanating from Washington a steady effort to lead us away from what has made us a great nation. No longer is the emergence of individual rights to be seen as a good thing, but as something to be avoided.

When the wheels start to come off, as they are doing now in this nation, as seen in the growth of our insecurities and the way we are attacking each other, those who have led us down the wrong alley escalate their efforts at control. Thus, the unrest being created by those who are yelling that we must all be politically correct. This is nothing other than crowd control, and has no place in this great United States.

Those who have been hornswoggled, or bamboozled, need to find a way to feel good about themselves and what they believe. If they can get to this place, they will realize that it is okay for us to have the freedom not to think alike. There is no need to continue living someone else's dream. It's okay to live your own dream, and good mental health requires it. That is the only way to enjoy being persons with our own rights, a unique gift that has been one of the hallmarks of life in the United States.

CHAPTER 80

DYSFUNCTION IN OUR FACE

Never before in my 82 years of life have I seen such dysfunction lurking in the lives of people now running for the office of President of the United States. This is a symptom of the sad legacy politicians of the last half century have left us.

For a long time, members of Congress and the Presidents have not understood that they work for us, the citizens of this country. It is their responsibility to develop programs to help all citizens be successful in what they do. Instead of this, which is at the very heart of our Constitution, they have created programs to take from one group of Americans and give to another group. In the process, we now have untold millions of people physically and mentally capable of earning their own way doing absolutely nothing to earn the bread they eat.

Instead of helping people learn to stand on their own two feet, taking their places in making us a better country, they have generated dependency that leads to helplessness. The process has produced the "haves" and the "have-nots," and has led to great animosity of one group toward the other. Accepting the government check has become an aspiration for many people, but it should be seen as an admission of failure in life.

Now we have politicians promising pie-in-the sky that cannot be delivered, and even have some ranting about wanting to do more and more, even though it will add to our deficit.

Seeking government help when you can help yourself is an admission of failure, but it is a dysfunction that is well accepted by millions of people.

CHAPTER 81

TROUBLE IN AMERICA

The reason so many American citizens are upset and reacting so negatively during the campaign season is the behavior of politicians over the past several decades. Our nation has been built on constitutional government, which has produced the greatest nation the world has ever known. Now, for quite some time, politicians in Washington have been trying to turn us into a different form of government, one that seeks to have people serve government rather than government serve citizens.

Democrats have led in making citizens dependent on government rather than on themselves. Thus, their efforts to change us into a socialist nation, and the Republicans have stood back and let them get away with it.

The strength of this nation has always been in its citizens, not the government, and the change is creating a weaker people and nation. Whereas people used to flock to this nation for an opportunity to work and earn their way, they are now flocking here to receive a free check from the government. The quality of people coming here has deteriorated greatly from, "We will work hard and earn our way," to, "Where is the line I can get in to receive free government money?" This is a great change, and has done great damage to this country.

The founders of this nation would never support what politicians have made of this country, and the howl that is now coming from so many people is a reflection of how far we have moved from what has made us great.

The quality of the people now trying to become president of this country is a reflection on just how much we have deteriorated from what this nation once was. The democrats openly state they will take us further into socialism, and the "give me" crowds are flocking to them. For those familiar with socialism weighed against constitutional government, this is a retreat of the highest order. It completely flip-flops the thing that has made us great: from dependence on ourselves to dependence on government.

CHAPTER 82

LETTER TO A POLITICIAN

The following is a letter I wrote Senator Wicker in March, 2016. It says some of the things many people felt regarding the absence of good leadership in Washington. It points to one reason establishment Republicans were cast aside in favor of an individual who looks nothing like what we have had in the seats of power.

Doing things the way they have been done for the last several decades, particularly the last one, could be tolerated no longer by a majority of people. For that reason, we chose someone who is far different from what we have had.

March 19, 2016

Senator Roger F. Wicker
Chairman, NRSC
P. O. Box 97112
Washington, DC 20090-7112

Dear Senator Wicker:

You will find the enclosed Republication Party Area Assessment has not been filled out. The reason for this is, in my opinion, the Republican Party leadership has failed to pay attention to us voters for a long time, and you won't pay attention this time. You have done your own thing, and, in the process, have, for decades, allowed the democrats to move us rapidly toward becoming a socialist country. Republicans in Congress have allowed Obama, with the full support of the Democratic Party, to attack and dismantle some of our freedoms, and we now stand on the verge of the destruction of the greatest nation the world has ever known. In other words, I think Republican leadership has been a failure.

What you are now seeing in the disgusting presidential campaign is a reaction of people who, in effect, are saying, "Anything is better than the people who have been sitting in the seats of power in Washington for generations. They have failed to make the Constitution their guide in governing this country, and we don't want anyone who looks or smells like what we have had."

The Republican leadership has a decision to make: either to continue the failed policies they have followed for the past several decades or to let the American electorate know that they will fight tooth and nail to return this country to a Constitutional Republic.

I will support and vote for whoever runs for president on the Republican ticket. If a democrat wins, our Constitutional Republic is, in my opinion, gone forever. We need good people in Washington who will not let this happen, and I am not so sure the current Republican leadership can give us the good people needed.

Sincerely,

CHAPTER 83

INSULTED AND UNAWARE OF IT

One of the biggest insults a person can receive is to be told, "You can't do it. You don't have the ability to take care of yourself." When a person accepts this as being true, the result is giving up. Internalizing this as something that is true has led many people to give up. It is, in fact, a big put-down and insult.

The client who continued to get fired from every job said, "Can't you see that I'm stupid and can't do anything right?" When asked about this, he said, "My father used to tell me this all the time when I was growing up." He had come to fully believe his dad was right, and acted out his dad's opinion of him.

A lot of people in this country are acting out what the democrats have told them, "You don't have the ability to take care of yourselves, but, if you will let us, we will take care of you." Millions of people have accepted this as fact, and, as a result, have flocked to sign up for government assistance, and now live off taxes taken from people who actually work and take care of themselves.

Many of these people, if they will reconsider, will realize that this communication from democrats is really a put-down, a genuine insult. If Michael Jordan, in the tenth grade, had believed the opinion of the basketball coach that he was not good enough to make the team, and had quit trying, he never would have become the best basketball player of all time.

Countless people who have signed up for free government money are fully capable of getting a job and earning a living that is far better than the money democrats give them. But, they have settled for a life that is less than the one they would have if they refused government help and went to work taking care of themselves.

People need to realize that politicians are in the business of doing things that will capture enough votes to be re-elected, and they will promise and do all sorts of things to earn votes. Democrats have found that, if they tell people they are incapable of taking care of themselves, but, "We'll do it for you," these people will deliver the desired votes. This is an insult of the highest order, but not many people have yet figured this out.

CHAPTER 84

LIBERALISM'S WORST DAMAGE

The young lady in the Women's Domestic Violence class stated the major problem with socialism when she said: "Y'all are crazy to get a job and go to work when you can stay at home, do nothing and get free money from the government." The result of this is tremendous waste of human potential through huge waste of talents and abilities.

Some of the members in the class felt a responsibility to get a job and earn a living, but not this lady. She is representative of the millions of people who have accepted liberalism's offer of free money if they will but bury their talent, stay at home, accomplish nothing worthwhile, and allow other people to work and pay taxes so they can eat.

People fully capable of taking care of themselves, but choosing to accept liberalism's offer of free money for doing nothing, probably represent the worst things Americans can do. Failure to develop things on the inside of them robs this country of contributions that come only from disciplined lives, and robs them of a powerful sense of accomplishment. We will never know the great scientists, authors, statesmen/women, great teachers, mathematicians, engineers, astronomers, presidents, religious leaders, etc., etc., who might have risen from the millions now receiving government money to do nothing.

As the athlete accomplishes great feats only with disciplined, concentrated effort, spending time in dedicated training, so the emergence of a person's God-given talent comes only after the discipline of study and training. Einstein may never have made his great contributions had he lived in a nation where he could have gotten free money from his government.

We can never know the full damage done by free money given to people, but it has to be great. Liberalism may be the greatest waste of human potential produced by any form of government anywhere.

Additionally, we need to consider what might have happened with our ability to care for people who genuinely cannot care for themselves, not only in this country, but around the world. To accept money you do not deserve means this money is not going to people who genuinely need it. Some of these people live on our streets, and many of them can be seen in the worst slums in other parts of the world.

None of us is where we ought to be if, knowing we are capable of developing our minds and becoming productive citizens, we choose rather to let others work and take care of us.

The worst damage done by liberalism is easily seen in the words of the lady in the Domestic Violence Class.

CHAPTER 85

VICTIMS OF SOCIALISM

Victims of socialism are easy to spot. They're everywhere. All we have to do is just recognize what we see.

At the grocery store, the lady in front of me paid for her $100 plus groceries with an EBT card, and then pulled out a $100 bill to pay for her booze. With only two items to pay for, I got out to the parking lot in time to see her load her things into a new Escalade with the dealer tag still on it. She had learned that it was okay to cheat. Teaching people to cheat is at the heart of socialism.

Then there was the lady in the domestic violence class who said, when other members started talking about getting a job, "Anybody is crazy to get a job and work when they can sign up and get free money from the government." Burying talent is one of the significant results of liberalism: people just don't see the need to study and train, developing their talent so they can earn a living.

There was the lady who moved in across the street after Congress tried to elevate poor people by granting them 100 percent loans. In six years, she and two well-dressed daughters never had a job, and then were forced out because they never made a payment on the loan. Socialism has led them to believe it is okay to enjoy life without having to pay for it.

The house next to them was where six to nine people (we never knew how many) moved in, and, after eight or nine years, were kicked out because they, too, did not pay the mortgage. After about a year in the house, they figured the grass should be cut after it had gotten knee high, this after I had cut it when they first moved in. In the eight or nine years they lived there, the leaves were raked one time. They did have a business going: it was not unusual for us to hear one of the men standing in his front yard making drug deals over the phone. And, then one time my wife opened the garage door to go shopping, and called me to come see the nine narcotics agents with drawn pistols surrounding the house. The drug trafficking and the welfare checks kept them going.

Walking into the grocery store one day, two ladies got my interest when I heard one of them say, "I liked my job, but I was told if I got myself fired, I could draw unemployment. I arranged to get fired, and I am now receiving a check that is about what I was taking home from work. Now I can do anything I want to do.

Then there was a man at Gold's Gym I overheard say, "I could be working now. I was offered a job, but found out the government would continue to give me a check if I did not work. Right now, I can receive seven more months of checks from the government before I have to work again, so I'm not going to work"

Take a visit to the Fulton County jail in Atlanta, and you can see it crowded with a lot of people who have grown up in families receiving the government check.

The lady in my alcohol and drug class told about her sister, who happens to weigh a little over 300 pounds. This sister has two young children out of wedlock. She is receiving checks for her disability of obesity, but works part-time and receives cash for her work to hide it from the government; both her children are receiving checks. She is still not married and is pregnant with her third child, so will receive another check from the government when this child is born. This young lady has learned it is acceptable to cheat and live off the government check.

CHAPTER 86

REPLACE THE JUDGE: NOW OR LATER?

The fight is on. Should Obama's pick to replace Judge Scalia be accepted or delayed until the sitting of the next president? A lot of people will get upset at whichever is done.

The responsibility of the members of Congress is to do what they think is best for the American people, not what is popular at any given time. That is the only thing that matters right now. We already know our president is trying to change this country into a socialist state, and he has gotten the unwavering support of the democrats, who have been trying to do this for a long time. The Constitution is not a document to be followed only when you want to. It is to be the controlling document in all the operations of government. The collective wisdom of the politicians now in Washington pales in comparison to the wisdom contained in the Constitution, so setting it aside whenever it suits your fancy, and using it when it is convenient, cannot be acceptable.

It is not possible for a socialist state to exist under our Constitution, which calls for a government to serve the people. In a socialist state, the people serve the government. This makes socialism totally incompatible with our Constitution.

People who understand this, and the fact that our president already ignores the Constitution whenever he wishes, must do what they think is best in preserving the Constitution as our governing document. Had the Constitution been followed during the last few decades, we would not have lost our standing as the leader of the free world. Now people around the world laugh at us for throwing away what has made us great, which has been nothing other than the chance to pick up and carry our individual loads of personal responsibility in making life good, not only for ourselves, but, also, for others.

Socialism places control of people's lives in the hands of the politicians. Our Constitution places control of citizen's lives in the hands of citizens with politicians serving us. One of the worst problems people can face is that of their lives being under the control of someone else and not themselves. This is a problem often brought into the therapist's office as clients desperately seek to find the mental health that comes from learning to stand on their own two feet.

Those who have the responsibility to either reject or deny Obama's pick are dealing with the future of our country: will we be a constitutional republic or will we slide further into being a socialist state? What they will really be doing is making a decision as to the United States again claiming its greatness as a nation or sliding further into being an also-ran nation.

CHAPTER 87

WHEN VOTING: USE EMOTION OR REASON?

Several months from now, we will be electing a new president. Will we choose someone on the basis of our emotions or on our ability to think and reason? We can do either, and, if done carefully, we will recognize that emotion has often led to wrong choices. Emotion doesn't need or want reason as a companion.

Emotions are fickle, and we all have them. The ability to think and reason is a different matter. It is easy to ratchet up people's feelings when we use certain rhetoric, but feelings tend to take a back seat when reason and thought are used. Reason and thought will teach us that emotions are indeed fickle, and can be turned every which way by a skilled speaker.

It is easy to spot historical figures who have won great following through the use of emotions. The Germans responded emotionally to the verbal skills of Hitler (at one time 96 percent of the people supported Hitler), and were plunged into the worst war the world has ever known. Radical Muslims live on emotion, and kill as if life means nothing. Slavery cannot stand up under the scrutiny of reason. There is no room for thought and reason to the person addicted to alcohol or drugs. Allowing other people to work and take care of us is never done on the basis of reason. It comes from the false lie of one who does not understand the responsibility each of us has to make our own way by developing the good things each of us has been given at birth.

Reason is kicked out of consideration by the person who promises to take from the worker and give to those who choose not to work. If we cannot learn from the destruction of nations by leaders who promised the impossible, we need only look at the results of the past two elections in this country: we now have almost as many people not working as are working. The soundness of our country is the casualty of the government check going to those fully capable of working and making their own way, but choosing to live off someone else's labor.

Our last two elections were decided on the basis of our emotions. If we choose not to use reason and thought this next November, we will have effectively eliminated the things that have made the United States the greatest nation in the history of the world. We have been great because people responded positively to the offer to work hard and enjoy the fruits of their labor, and they have done things no other nation has been able to do. If we choose to continue to move further into socialism, something that encourages people to sit and do nothing, we will move further toward being an also-ran country where too many people become absolutely worthless.

The 100 billion brain cells given each of us at birth were given for the purpose of use. Socialism proclaims you do not need to develop and use these brain cells. A nation built on our constitutional form of government leads us to need everyone using these brain cells to make life better.

Those who desire to have a country where millions live off the labor of others will vote for those who promise to give them more things. Those who believe in a constitutional form of government where people are expected to amount to something by carrying their own load will vote for those who expect them to make something of themselves. Voting through emotion will be for those who make up the "give me" generation. Using thought and reason leaves room only for those who believe each of us should be responsible for doing our part in making life the best it can be.

The next person to occupy the president's chair will be placed there either by the "give me" crowd, which requires no individual effort, or by the people who feel each of us should use our gift of 100 billion brain cells to learn to take care of ourselves and do what we can to make this a better nation.

CHAPTER 88

NEVER SHOULD A MAN ABANDON HIMSELF

We had just gotten onto the Belle of Louisville for an evening's excursion on the river. A couple with a four- year-old boy had gotten on just before us. One of the boy's shoe laces had come untied, and he bent down to try and re-tie it. His mother saw it had come untied, and said to him, "Here, let me tie it." He said, "No. I tie it." He struggled to tie it, and, his mother, seeing this, again said, "Let me tie it." Very emphatically, he said, "No, I tie it!" He was learning, and did not want any help.

Humans come into the world poised to do things and achieve for themselves. They are ready to begin the process of accomplishing things, but often, all too often, they never get a kickstart. I remember the speaker saying he grew up in a rich family with servants to do everything, and, when he was age 18, he didn't know how to zip his pants. People from all levels of society don't learn if they are not challenged

A child needs parents, both parents, if he/she is to make a good start. A child never gets started without help, and, if help is not there, the start is delayed.

One of the things we need to remember is that our brain is one fine muscle, and it needs to be exercised in order to develop. That is one of the things wrong with socialism. It proposes to do for people what they should be doing for themselves. Ineptness is the reason many people do not get a kick-start in life, and find themselves unable to take care of themselves and their responsibilities.

A person should never turn over what they are to let others determine what they will be. In government, this is only possible where freedom to become is given to each individual.

CHAPTER 89

MARTIN LUTHER KING, JR'S. "DREAM": ABANDONED

Each year Americans celebrate one of the greatest citizens we have had in our entire history. His amazing life inspired not only Americans, but many people around the world.

In his, "I have a dream" speech, he gave a vision of what life could be when "all God's children" could stand side by side as brothers. He looked forward to a time when people would be treated on the basis of "content of character" and not color of skin, a time when we could all stand shoulder to shoulder as equals. Many people responded to the challenge and pursued education and training to prepare for jobs, and they achieved this dream, earning a good living, and building good lives. Some of my neighbors are among those who stand shoulder to shoulder with anyone, having to take a back seat to no-one.

Unfortunately, however, liberals did not want blacks and poor white people to earn equality, and they stepped in and derailed the movement dreamed about by MLK, Jr. They put roadblocks in the way of pursuing this "Dream," and countless millions gave up any hope of making their own way. They were led to believe personal effort was not essential in standing shoulder to shoulder with others.

What happened was that liberal politicians, fully aware that people who take care of themselves do not need others to care for them, decided they could not let that happen because they would lose much of the reason for their programs. Liberals thrive on keeping people dependent on them. They desire that people base their future on the gifts and work of liberals.

What did liberals do? They proposed and passed legislation to give money to poor people. They got the votes needed to give free tax money to people without requiring them to do anything to earn it. Thus: the welfare state.

What does free money do? It makes victims of the people receiving the money. It frees them from having to do what is necessary to make their own way in this world. As the free money has rolled in over the past several decades, how much talent has gone to waste? How many people have not pursued development of what is on the inside of them? How many scientists, authors, statesmen, inventors, mathematicians, teachers, doctors, lawyers, theologians, space travelers, etc. would have emerged if welfare people had been required to develop the talents deep inside them? As the lady in the domestic violence class, said, responding to a discussion about getting a job, "People are crazy to work when they can stay home and get free money from the government." People with a lot of potential become lazy when they receive free money.

History makes clear that accomplishment comes through personal effort and struggle. The great advancements of history never took place in the lives of people who sat down and did nothing. The things that make life good and comfortable are the products of people doing something with the stuff that is on the inside of them just waiting to be developed. It never comes from those who sit and do nothing, something that is all too evident in the lives of those who receive free government money.

No-one will ever know how much damage the welfare system has done to us in the loss of undeveloped talent, things deep within us that are stirred into life only by education and/or training plus struggle, but we can be assured the talent kept hidden by free government money could have brought us many good things. It would not be surprising to learn that these gifts of free money from liberals have done more damage to our future than most anything that can be mentioned. We would be a much greater nation now if everyone had rolled up their sleeves and gone to work contributing whatever talent they have to offer.

This writer knows no-one who thinks people truly in need should not be helped. But, he knows countless numbers who believe capable people should stand on their own two feet, being responsible for taking care of themselves.

MLK Jr.'s "Dream" can never be achieved by a person fully capable of taking care of self who signs up for the government check. Signing up to receive this check is abandonment of MLK's "Dream". Capable, but dependent people who don't support themselves will always be looked on as inferior by those who must work so they can eat. The "Dream" will only be realized when we all learn to do our part, take care of ourselves, and try to make this a better world.

CHAPTER 90

THE COSTS OF INDOCTRINATION/ BRAIN-WASHING

If you just look, it is easy to see the costs of indoctrination and brain-washing. Look at contemporary life or thumb through the pages of history, and the results stare us in the face. Listen to the words of politicians, and they are leading the charge to form people in their image with the result that they follow without question. Right now, Washington is full of those who claim to have arrived at the place where they know life for others can be had only by heeding their words.

A banter being shouted out loud and clear is, "Share the wealth." This is where the less fortunate economically can rise to the level of others, and, if you follow those who proclaim this false rainbow, all your basic financial needs will be met and life will be good. They don't talk about the rewards of personal achievement.

What these purveyors of "sharing everything with everybody" do not say is that the sharing of wealth has been available to people all the time. It's called "PREPARATION": defined as getting an education and/or training. After that, you roll up your sleeves and go to work. Those who have done this have shared in the wealth of this great country. Those who have not prepared have not shared.

Learning to take care of self is a hallmark of good mental health, something that does not come by placing your welfare in the hands of another person. No-one ever comes to the therapist's office asking how to become dependent on others. What clients normally state is something like this, "Help me get out from under the control of this other person." The journey to becoming a person in one's own right is an exciting journey as self care is learned.

What the "Share the wealth" crowd is really doing is leading people to become totally dependent on others for their well-being. The costs of doing this are heavy, for it means people give up their responsibility to do something with the potential talent and abilities they have deep within, and which can be developed only with struggle and determination.

The government's welfare system has sucked millions of people into its program of paying them to do nothing, and, in the process, has taken away from our country and the world the many contributions that could come only if these people had rolled up their sleeves, studied and/or trained, and gone to work making something of themselves. The true, great cost to mankind of burying so much talent and potential ability under government money can never be known. Who can put a price on the value of the person who would have been a great chemist, professor, mathematician, scientist, author, entrepreneur, inventor, economist, explorer, etc.? No, the full cost of the government check given to those who do nothing can never be estimated, but it is great.

CHAPTER 91

WHEN YOU DON'T KNOW WHAT TO DO, DO SOMETHING ANYWAY (ONE MORE LOOK)

H ere we go again: a politician who doesn't know what to do, but feeling he must do something anyway. This is happening too much in Washington as politicians don't know what to do, but still think they must do something. Nancy Pelosi characterized the political brain power of her fellow politicians when she said, regarding Obamacare, "Let's pass it so we can learn what is inside it." This is one of the stupidest comments ever made by a politician in all of history, but it clearly reveals what kind of mentality the current politicians in Washington really have. And they passed it.

Now it's on to gun control, and Obama is continuing to chip away at our freedoms. Obamacare is already proving to be a mistake, but not knowing is no hindrance to politicians who believe they alone can determine what is best for everyone. This is another case of the blind leading the blind, but many will eagerly jump onto the bandwagon.

It would be good for politicians to educate themselves: pay attention to historical facts, but facts usually have little to no meaning to those who charge blindly ahead with an unproven idea.

One of the ways to evaluate anything is to look the lessons of history: has it ever been tried, and what were the results? History, treated honestly and fairly, never lies to us.

Here are some homicide facts of history that should be considered:

Before Gun Control	Legislation	After Gun Control
Great Britain: 10.9 to 13 per million	1996	18.03 per million in 2003
Ireland: 0.1 to 0.6 per 100,000 people	1972	1.6 per 100,000 people

Perhaps the best place for us to look is where gun control legislation resulted in guns actually being taken away. Germany comes to mind. On 11/11/38, "Regulations Against Jews' Possession of Weapons" was passed in Germany" (Wikipedia). We know the results of this: six million Jews died at the hands of Hitler. Although not a Jew, my mechanic, remembering the bombs as they fell on Germany, said, "When they took away our guns, we could do nothing." Then WW II followed with total deaths being approximately 60 million.

We do not need to forget Mao Tse Dung, who said, "All power comes from the barrel of a gun." In 1949 he took guns away from the Chinese, and this was followed by the slaughter of 20 million.

Then there was Joseph Stalin and his gun control, which was followed by the deaths of tens of millions of Russians.

Cambodia, where Poll Pot killed 25 percent of the population, up to three million people.

Gun control is a tyrant's tool.

There are always people in every nation who would like to take over and run things. The United States is no different. Removing guns from law-abiding people sets the stage for the would-be tyrant/dictator to flex his muscles.

Where we as a nation really need to work is in the area of growing good, sound people. This is true of every nation. Good people do not gun down others. Rather, they involve themselves in making life better for others, beginning with family. If we could ever get to the place where we grow good people, not only gun violence, but other forms of crime, would be significantly reduced. This is an area where the politicians in Washington are clueless.

Politicians are interested in growing their voter base, and much of their legislation is geared to do just that.

The real problem we face in the United States and in other nations is a cultural problem. Helping people learn how to live well and get along together is where the real work needs to be done, and this is an area where politicians are helpless, not having a clue regarding how to develop programs that will assist us in learning how to live with each other.

Any program that will help people learn how to treat each other demands a new kind of thinking where all people are taught to stand on their own two feet, assuming individual responsibility for contributing positively to this nation. Too long, Washington politicians, with the programs they have enacted have pitted one group against another group, and taught us how to take advantage of each other.

History has shown that gun control legislation does not reduce the murder rate. Why don't we develop programs that do? This demands a new kind of thinking that does not seem to be existent in Washington politicians. Relying on things that have never worked and often makes things worse must be abandoned.

CHAPTER 92

HYPOCRISY ON FULL DISPLAY

Many times, we pay little attention to expressions of hypocrisy. At other times, it consumes a great amount of thought, and is covered by all the news media. We often choose what we will be hypocritical about, paying little or no attention to some things, but then reacting in such a manner that others join us in complaining and sometimes demonstrating about it.

"The Black Lives Matter" is a good example of hypocrisy. When a black person is killed by a white police officer, all hell can break loose; there are demonstrations and sometimes rioting. But, when a black man is killed by another black person, something happening almost every night in Atlanta and other cities all over this country, there is nary a peep from the "Black Lives Matter" people. If "Black Lives Matter" is more than a protest against police officers and the establishment, there should be loud noises made each time one black is killed, regardless of where the killing took place.

Humans have yet to get to the place where we recognize that all lives matter, regardless of the color of their skin or where they come from. In fact, there is nothing more important than one single human being. If we understood this, it would change much of our lives. We would all be involved in making things better for everyone, not just those who happen to think and look like us. The "Black Lives Matter" movement would do well to learn this

Getting to the place where we recognize the value of each person would transform our entire lives.

CHAPTER 93

CHOOSING TO BE IGNORANT

When someone makes the choice to be ignorant, no amount of education can dislodge that ignorance. Ignorance is seen at all levels of society because it is that which leads people to do things that make no sense at all. Indoctrination, a favorite ploy of "educators," politicians and some religions, is far more powerful than education, and often leads to the destruction of life. People often go to their deaths holding onto that which makes no sense at all. And, as we see with ISIS and radical Islam, delivering death to others is a thing of joy and celebration.

Education should teach people to examine things and make sense of them, but that happens all too seldom. What we do is fall in lock-step with those we admire, and begin to posit things that completely defy the intellect. This is seen not only in those with less than a high school education, but, also, with people holding master's degrees and doctorates. The ghettos show this, but, also, the best neighborhoods on the north side of Atlanta. This writer, a former hospital CEO, has seen doctors do many screwy things that defy logic.

Sometimes we make our choice to be ignorant simply by repeating the lives of our parents or guardians. "If it was good enough for them, it is good enough for me." Breaking from the lifestyle of others can be traumatic. Plato drank the hemlock in 399 B. C. and died because his peers condemned him for contaminating the youth by asking them to examine their lives and make their own decisions about what they would do with their lives. Also, he did not worship the gods he was expected to worship. He was supposed to tell the young people to accept the thinking of their elders, but told them to do their own thinking.

Have we not learned since then that life is best lived if we use the 100 billion brain cells each of us has to think about life and what it should be? Sadly, NO. We often turn our thinking over to others, and do not question where this leads us. We walk in the footprints of others and it doesn't bother us at all. We were not made to accept someone else's direction. We were made to carve out our own direction, to express our own uniqueness with the talents and abilities only we have.

CHAPTER 94

BUILDING MY OWN FUTURE

In the counseling office, no-one ever asks what must be done to let other people determine "what my future will be." They come in an effort to learn how to get out from under the control of other people.

They often struggle in their search for a life better than the one they have. Domestic violence clients sometimes say, "He won't let me go see my mother" or "I'm afraid he will hit me if I don't do what he says" or, "If he does not like what I fix for supper, he may throw it against the wall." One famous baseball player said his dad might throw his mom down the steps if he did not like her cooking.

In the alcohol and drug classes, many clients will say, "If I don't drink with them, they don't want me to be with them." After managing to stop drinking, one said, when asked how he had quit drinking, "I had to change friends."

One woman in counseling said, "My husband told me to go get fixed. If I would do that, our marriage would be okay. "He said he had no problems he needed to work on." One client said, "My dad often said when I was growing up, "You are stupid, and can't do anything right." Every job he got, he would mess up and be fired, "Because my dad had prepared me to be a failure."

We have many people who lure us into a trap they set, one where they can take control of our lives, and we have great difficulty breaking away from them. Then, if we try to break loose from their control, they step up their efforts to keep us where they have us.

Taking care of oneself and doing what is personally desired can often bring a fresh new life. Ralph had been valedictorian in high school, but his dad, a graduate of Georgia Tech, said to him, "I will pay for college only if you go to Georgia Tech." So, he went. "What else was I to do? I had no money to pay my own way," he said, and added, "I hated engineering." He flunked out twice. He wanted to study biology. Against the advice of the Dean of the liberal arts college, we accepted him. He transferred, majored in biology, and made the Dean's List every quarter. Upon graduation, he received a graduate fellowship in biology at another university. I said to the Director of Admissions, "If we had not accepted him, I think he would have had a nervous breakdown."

If we are going to find our own way, building the life that is right for us, we must be in control of our lives. Turning them over to others never allows us to pursue our own dreams. It is vitally important that we do what we wish to do. This can never be done when others control us. They want us to walk in their footsteps, and, if they can get us to do that, they can take us anywhere they wish to take us.

This is the promise of socialism, but you never become the masters of your own fate. That always lies in the hands of others who are eager to tell you what to do and when to do it.

The constitutional form of government we have had in the United States offers you the chance to be your own person, doing what you want to do. It gives you freedom from those who want to determine your future, placing that future squarely in your hands. What your life winds up being is what you make it. Sometimes the actions of others limit your choices, but, in whatever your circumstances might be, the final decision is yours to make.

One client, after breaking free from the control of her husband, said of her journey, "It's the hardest thing I have ever done, but it is the best thing I have ever done."

The form of government we have is highly important when it comes to freedom to be what we wish to be. Socialism will take you places other people want you to go. A constitutional government allows you to set your own course and make your own way into the kind of life you build for yourself. You can be what you want to be.

CHAPTER 95

DICTATORS-IN-WAITING

Every country has dictators-in-waiting, politicians who are ready to step in and take control of everything. They are the ones who feel they know what is best for the country and all who live there. The United States is no exception. Current politicians in Washington think they know what is best for the American people and have jammed down the throats of citizens some things that violate our freedoms, totally opposite to the Constitution that has helped preserve the freedoms we have enjoyed.

We have seen dictators throughout history, and we will see them again, but, the question is, "Will we see a dictator eliminate constitutional government in the United States?" This is not a far-fetched question in light of those who currently sit in the seats of power in Washington. They have destabilized this country in a way never before seen. Some of them are poised to pounce if given the opportunity.

The history of dictators has not been good. Although they generally think they are the saviors of a nation, and present themselves as such, what they often do is lead a nation into disaster. In the early stages of their takeover, they usually do some good things for people, and many are duped into believing they have found someone who will take them to the Promised Land.

But, the bright and shining road often disappears, and people realize they are following a false savior.

Whether it be Pol Pot in Cambodia killing millions of his own people, China's Mao Zedong, who said, "All power comes from the barrel of a gun," and then killing 20 to 30 million Chinese; Sheikh Hasina, a serial killer in Bangladesh; Saddam Hussein gassing his own people; Joseph Stalin, making possession of a firearm punishable by death, then killing millions; or Adolph Hitler, who is responsible for 60 million deaths in WW II, the history of dictators is more than ugly.

My mechanic, born in Germany in the 1930's, remembers the bombs falling in WW II. One day, in reference to Hitler and his cronies, he said, "When they took away our guns, we could do nothing." This comment speaks to those of us who love the freedoms guaranteed by our Constitution. Those who developed this greatest of governance documents were aware of the need people have to protect themselves from would-be dictators, those who will always be ready to take control in any generation. We should heed the words of my mechanic.

If we fail to honor the Constitution, it will be replaced by those who do not understand what freedom is all about. If we can be honest with ourselves and take a good look at what the politicians in Washington have done over the past several years, we will clearly see their move to scuttle the Constitution and place governance of this great nation in their hands. Some of the legislation of the past few decades has seen a movement away from their responsibility to serve the people to one where we serve their wishes.

We citizens of the United States could not make a greater mistake than eliminating the Constitution and turning things over to a dictator. Our Constitution places limits on what politicians can do, and these limits have kept us from would-be dictators. Dictators have no limits on the things they do.

There will always be someone knocking on the door, and that is happening right now.

CHAPTER 96

INDOCTRINATION: MORE POWERFUL THAN EDUCATION

Time and time again, indoctrination has been shown to be far more powerful than education. The most educated country in the world in the 1930's believed Hitler could take them to the Promised Land, and, at one time, 96 percent of the German people supported him. "Unbelievable," you might say, but that is what happens when people receive what is called education, but, in reality, is indoctrination.

Indoctrination that goes under the guise of "education" excludes teaching people to think, and can result in masses falling in lock-step behind a skilled leader with a golden tongue. That's where we are in the United States today. We now have the "give me" generation and the "politically correct" generation demanding that they should be cared for by people more successful than they are. When the leader of a nation learns well the art of divide and conquer, and liberal educators flock to support him, those who have not been taught to think for themselves give their lives over to them, and miss what it means for a person to stand on his/her own feet.

If a person earns advanced degrees and, yet, is not be able to think, he/she becomes fodder for the grist mill of the one trying to make them in his image. This writer has known people with master's and doctorate degrees who did not have the ability to deal with things they had not been taught, and could be led to support things that harmed them.

Being led around by the nose is the result of indoctrination, and, with a person skilled in indoctrination, the victim often has no idea someone else is in control of his life.

The United States became the greatest nation in the history of the world because there were enough educated people with the ability to think to move us into unchartered governmental territory. The big tragedy of the Civil War was that enough people had been indoctrinated with the belief that slavery was okay that they were willing to fight and die in a tragic war. Those who are indoctrinated have been a blight on the progress of humans becoming what they were made to be.

In the U. S. today, we have a plethora of politicians and educators, graduates of some fine schools, who are unable to weigh the merits of a Constitutional Republic against all other forms of government, none of which has been able to achieve what we have achieved. In the ivory tower, things can sound beautiful, but, when these things are genuinely examined, i.e. Greece, they are found inferior to the freedom to achieve that is offered in our constitutional form of government.

Socialism is now the great craze of many in the U. S. who have tucked away their thinking apparatus and have joined in the lock-step with those who move to the beat of the indoctrinator. If you have been in school and have been trained to think for yourself, congratulations, but, if you have been taught that you should accept the beliefs of politicians and those who teach, then you have gone through indoctrination, not education. It would be good for you to sit under the teachings of a professor who knows how to teach. Unfortunately, there are too few with this ability, and too many sitting at the feet of those who are highly skilled in indoctrination.

CHAPTER 97

WHEN OTHERS OFFEND YOU

When you claim that others offend you, you may think you are putting them down, but what you are really doing is saying tons about yourself.

Being offended is a personal choice. It comes from a deep-seated fear that what you believe may not be able to stand up against what other people believe, and you feel you must put them down so you can feel superior. The need to feel superior is common for many people.

When you feel you are a free person, using your God-given brain to think about things, you come to a realization that all people should be free to do their own thinking. If you deny this of another person, you have no right to ask them to give you that right.

To deny the other person the right to make up their own mind indicates your desire to force others to believe as you believe, which indicates your belief that you have a hold on truth and they do not. History has shown that no person has a lock on absolute truth, and we all are in need of learning those things we do not yet know. Even in religion, we have a long way to go in learning how to treat others, respecting their right to decide for themselves.

Wanting to feel superior to other people indicates a feeling of inferiority, which is a major problem for many people. It is through this that we turn our lives over to others, and place ourselves in a position where they can do anything with us they desire. Political leaders often count on non-thinking people falling under their sway. When this happens, politicians can lead them around by the nose and get anything they want. This is the source of many leaders in history taking their people into disaster after disaster. It is never good, except perhaps in the military, to place one's life completely at the disposal of another. We must always have the choice of saying, "I will not go there or do that." If we do not have this choice, we cannot claim to be free.

Without the freedom to think for oneself and make up one's mind, our life is far from being what it could be. The pursuit of mental health involves standing on one's own two feet. There has never been a person to come to my counseling office to learn how to turn his/her life over to another. The question they usually verbalize is, "How can I free myself from the control of another?"

The freedom to think for oneself and make up one's own mind has been a hallmark of life under our Constitution. This freedom has led us to become the greatest nation in the history of the world. Of course, many have not chosen this freedom, and their lives have been placed at the disposal of others, and they are not free. But, the chance is still there so long as we remain a constitutional republic.

CHAPTER 98

BEING COMFORTABLE WITH ONE'S BELIEFS

B eing comfortable with one's beliefs and allowing others to be
comfortable with their beliefs is a mark of maturity. Secure
people know what it is be free in what they believe. This is a part
of having one's feet on a firm foundation. When someone works
adequately through all the clutter in life to the point where the
feeling of contentment is enjoyed, they find themselves able to
extend to others the freedom to make up their own minds about
things.

When someone is unable to extend to others the freedom to
believe as they see fit, it is not only a sign of the desire to control
others, but it is a huge sign of immaturity. "When I am comfortable in my own beliefs, I can allow others to believe as they see
fit," is the sign of a good, strong life.

Currently in the United States and around the world, people
on foundations built on sand have risen and sought to either
change or limit what others can believe. This is not only a sign of
the failure of people to respect the freedom of others, but, also,
is a sign that they really do not respect themselves and what they
believe. To be uncomfortable with what others believe is a sure
sign of immaturity.

Many of our politicians, religionists and others are seeking to control what we believe. These are the ones who wish to turn out clones of who they are, and this is nothing other than clear rejection of the freedom we have enjoyed under our Constitutional Republic.

We have seen this desire to control others throughout history. Many have died as a result of leaders pushing their thinking on others. Whether it be the sentence of death handed down to Socrates in 399 BCE because he contaminated the youth by saying, "An unexamined life is not worth living," and because he would not worship the gods he was instructed to worship or the 60 million people who died in WW II because they would not accept Hitler's dream of the Third Reich, the desire to control the thinking of others never ends well.

Political correctness today is one of the strong signs that people have not worked out their own beliefs to where they are comfortable with them. Not being able to extend to others the right to believe as they see fit points to the inability to believe in freedom of the individual. They take the position, "If you do not believe what I believe, you are not acceptable." This is totally unacceptable in this country.

CHAPTER 99

WHAT POLITICIANS HAVE DONE TO ME...
AND OTHERS

The Constitution of the United States says that our government is to be one where citizens are served by government. Somehow or other, politicians, over many years, have twisted things to the point where they expect us to serve them and pay for whatever they wish to do. Rather than trying to help all citizens have better lives, they take from one group of Americans and give to other groups of Americans. They have completely misunderstood that they are supposed to serve all Americans, not just a certain minority.

In looking at their actions over the past few decades, they have really hurt my future and that of millions of other Americans. There are many things they have done that, had they not done, my life would be better than it currently is.

One of the first things to consider is their grab of Social Security monies that had been guaranteed for my retirement. They broke the promise outlined in legislation that the money was to be put into a fund and used only for my retirement. They took it (perhaps "stole" it is a better word to use), and now my monthly check is less than one-half of what it would have been had they not touched "my" money.

Several years ago, Washington politicians made an attempt to dramatically change the housing market by allowing people to borrow 100 to 105 percent of the value of a house with no ability to pay mortgages. This completely changed my neighborhood because people moved in totally unaware that the grass was to be cut, leaves were to be raked, trash was not to be thrown on the streets, homes were to be cared for, and drug dealing had no place in our community (remembering the nine narcotics agents with drawn pistols surrounding the house across the street is a powerful reminder of the failure of this program).

Once the best housing development in this county, it is now one of the worst. A home up the street that was once worth $280,000, recently sold for $40,000 after people moved in and trashed it, and the house below it sold for the same amount. This is the result of politicians in Washington making decisions they should not have made, and the result, for me, is that my house is worth now $150,000 less than it would be had politicians not done what they did. In many ways, politicians during the last few decades have done more harm than good to many American people.

With development of the welfare programs, politicians have paid people not to work. Those who are unable to help themselves should be helped, but politicians wrote such weak legislation that millions of people, fully capable of caring for themselves, chose to accept the government check rather than go to the trouble of developing their talents and abilities through education and training.

It would be interesting to know how many people on the government dole could have been doctors, engineers, teachers, economists, etc., but chose to sit and wait on the free money from Washington.

Liberal politicians (mostly democrats, along with a few republicans and independents) have no use for a constitutional government that asks people to stand on their own two feet, making something of themselves. They want to control what people do rather than supporting them as they make decisions regarding what is best for themselves: thus, the development of the welfare state, where people receive money without having to do anything to get it.

The freedoms guaranteed in our Constitution will never be safe so long as liberal politicians busy themselves trying to take these freedoms from us. They would readily change what made this country great, replacing our chance to dream big dreams with the shallow vision of liberalism.

CHAPTER 100

FAILING TO DEAL WITH THE REAL PROBLEM

The knee jerk reaction of our president and others following the latest tragedy of someone using a gun to kill others is to ban guns. This is nothing other than not knowing what to do, but feeling you must do something.

The problem with using guns to kill people is a mental health issue. People who are mentally healthy do not deliberately use guns except in self-defense or as part of a job like law enforcement or the military.

Taking guns away from people does absolutely nothing about mental health issues. It might cause people to feel good about what they have done, but it has absolutely no impact on helping the mentally ill.

Taking guns away from people can have unknown, but, perhaps predictable consequences. My mechanic of 48 years was born in Germany, and remembers hearing the bombs fall during WWII. He once said, "When Hitler took our guns away, we could do nothing." A defenseless society has no way to stop the onslaught of a misguided or deranged politician. A glance at the history of nations shows that unbalanced political leaders have easily taken their people into one disaster after another. That could be ahead for the U.S. if our guns are taken away.

Several years ago politicians punted on mental health. It was expensive and they wanted to use the money elsewhere. As a result, in Georgia, Central State Hospital, Milledgeville, once the largest mental health facility in the world, was closed. Yes, it had problems that needed to be corrected, but, instead of working on the problems, the entire facility was closed. Running away from problems is often the worst thing that can be done.

Many people needing hospitalization for mental health problems now walk the streets, stay in homeless shelters, pull the triggers, and add to the crime that plagues much of our nation. Counselors, therapists, psychologists and psychiatrists do not have enough inpatient facilities available to meet client needs, and the payment system is woefully inadequate.

It would be nice if we had politicians in Washington and in State Capitols who were able to solve problems rather than run away from them. Running away from problems often makes things worse, and that is exactly what happened in the area of mental health. Taking guns away from U. S. citizens will open up a keg of worms that could lead to some unforeseen problems, and will do nothing to help those needing mental health services.

People are too important to be left with no alternatives available but to act out the deep issues that plague their lives and the lives of those they touch and sometimes kill.

Knee jerk reactions do nothing to solve mental health problems.

CHAPTER 101

TIME TO CHANGE MENTAL HEALTH PROGRAMS

The list is long. There have been approximately 200 mass killings (five or more) in the U. S. during the past nine or ten years. Many people think the government needs to take away guns, but most Americans think not.

When people don't know what to do, they usually go ahead and do something anyway, even if it is wrong. This is true with the people who wish to take guns away from American citizens.

The problem we face with guns is not the guns themselves. The problem is the people who use them. No person in his/her right mind ever deliberately initiates the death of another person. True mental illness or religion based on primitive thought can lead a person to pull a trigger.

Some people say guns are to blame, but guns in the hands of mentally healthy people are not a problem. If we were to remove all guns from Americans, we would still have mentally unhealthy people causing problems. When we work on a problem, our emphasis should be on what is the cause of the problem. Politicians have little understanding of what needs to be done in the area of mental health, and they are likely to do something that has no effect on mental health.

There was a time when our politicians in Washington looked at the mental health programs, found them wanting, and, rather than fixing these problems, decided to close many mental health facilities. This put many mentally ill people on our streets. We refer to many of them as "the homeless."

If we can ever get to the place where we understand there is nothing in the world worth more than a single individual, perhaps it will lead us to provide a mental health program much better than what we now have.

CHAPTER 102

FREEDOM OR LICENSE

The Constitution of the United States and the Bill of Rights place ultimate value on the individual, something not done in any other governing document in the world. This document grants freedom to everyone, but this is not license to do anything one might want to do, as some suppose. It is freedom to be responsible for what we do, and so long as we are responsible, we are free. We had to struggle greatly (Civil War) to take a much-needed step toward this, and we still have steps to take to fully realize this.

Some people think this freedom is indeed license to do anything they desire. But, license tears at the heartbeat of America when people do things without regard to the welfare of others. Too many people do anything they want to do and expect no consequences. We see this daily on the news channels, the internet, and in our newspapers. Our jails and prisons are packed to overflowing with those who have no inkling that life is much more rewarding when lived in freedom. Freedom allows us to stretch our wings and fly as high as we can dream, but being irresponsible clips our wings and relegates us to life that is determined by others. When we break the law, we place our time, and sometimes our money, in the hands of others.

In the past few decades, liberal politicians have been ignoring the Constitution and moving us toward socialism, a system that has never worked as well our Constitutional Republic, and can never work that well. Socialism bows its head to politicians, who claim to know how to take care of people better than people can take care of themselves. All socialistic systems, where individuals serve the system, have come up far shorter than what is available in a constitutional system where the individual is served by the system. Serving the system is nothing other than serving the politicians who are in power. It is far different from the system serving the people.

There will always be a struggle between politicians who wish to subjugate citizens and those who wish to give people freedom to live as they choose.

Extending freedom to people is not a consideration with politicians who feel they know the best road for people to travel. People fly best when they use their own wings.

CHAPTER 103

AMERICANS: A CHOICE HAS TO BE MADE

It is regrettable, but the time has arrived for Americans to make a choice. Since its founding the United States has had governing documents called The Constitution, and the Bill of Rights. When we have followed these documents, we have done well. There have been times, however, when we have struggled to let them be our guides. We find such a struggle taking place now.

A majority of people wish to continue constitutional government, but, for a long time, there has been a growing cadre of people committed to replacing this Constitution and Bill of Rights with something they think is superior, and that something is socialism. They have been successful in capturing the imagination of almost enough voters to abandon the Constitution and Bill of Rights to the history books.

Democrats have done this by working on one of the weaknesses of people, and that is the desire to get something for nothing. The welfare programs have been the vehicles used in accomplishing this: a person, whether needy or not, signs up to receive free stuff, and, when they do this, they are hooked by the democrats. One interesting aspect of this has been seminars offered in churches re how to sign up for free government assistance. The young lady said one day, "I have gotten thirty free phones just by going to where they are given away."

The crowd wanting free stuff has been growing, and, had not Americans who want to continue constitutional government stepped forward and made a change in presidential leadership, we would now be staring at the coming burial of the Constitution.

Yes, loss of our Constitution is the price we will pay if the give-away crowd again wins the presidential office. For this reason, it is imperative that those of us who prefer constitutional government over socialism stand and make a choice to keep it. The give-away crowd, the democrats, have no use for the Constitution. It is imperative that we choose to continue following the Constitution. If we don't, we will continue our slide toward becoming a third-world nation. No good American wants to see this happen. We have the best country in the world, and we want it to stay the best country. But, wishing is not enough. We must put feet to our wishes and do what needs to be done to preserve constitutional government.

CHAPTER 104

AMERICANS: STUPID, INSANE OR BOTH?

For a long time, politicians have been doing things that are plainly harmful to our country. We citizens have been aware of this, and, yet, have gone to the voting booths and continued to reelect them. One of the definitions of insanity is "Doing the same thing over and over, but expecting different results." We may, indeed, have been both stupid and insane to reelect people who have harmed us so much. Sending harmful politicians back to Washington has emboldened them to keep damaging so many of us.

Some of the harmful things are:

1. We have allowed them to steal our Social Security money. We had been promised that this money was to be set aside to fund our retirement. But, they took something guaranteed to be there for us, and used it for something else. Now they tell us the Social Security check we receive is a government benefit. This is theft and betrayal of the highest order.

2. They have changed our country from one where people came to get a chance to work and enjoy the rewards of their labor to one where able-bodied people come to get

a handout of tax money taken by government from hard-working Americans.

3. They created a mess with housing when they made it possible for people to finance 100 to 105 percent of the cost of a house. The end result is that, in some areas, including this writer's subdivision, home values plummeted by 25 to 50 percent. This plunge of net worth is directly traceable to Congress and the presidents.

4. They have spent so much money that our national debt has skyrocketed exponentially to the point where there is no way to imagine how and when we can eliminate this debt.

5. They have made it possible for some people to disregard constitutional law and use what they have brought from other nations. If it is possible for some people to disregard constitutional law, then we are fast becoming an unstable nation like some third world countries where instability keeps life in turmoil for everyone.

6. They have opened our borders to anyone, both good and bad, to illegally enter this country do whatever they wish to do. We know many of these people have been and still are criminals.

7. They have diminished our military.

8. They have attacked our Constitution and Bill of Rights to the point where we are losing our freedoms. Freedom of speech and freedom of religion are already casualties.

9. Our space program has been curtailed, and we are paying the Russians to put our astronauts into space.

10. They have attacked our predominant religion, Christianity, thus revealing they do not believe in our freedom of religion

This is only a partial list of where politicians have been taking us, but it is enough to show that they don't know how to grow a great country.

It is time for the citizens of this country to call a halt to the damage done by politicians in Washington. We need to send home all those who have participated in degrading this nation, and, if we don't, they will continue destroying this greatest of all nations in the history of the world.

If we value our Constitutional Republic, we will go the ballot box and make certain we elect people who understand what freedom is all about.

CHAPTER 105

IF YOU ARE GOING TO UNDERSTAND OBAMA

You will never understand who Obama is or what he has done until you understand that he does not like the United States; he never has and he never will. He went into office with the purpose of dismantling the things that have made us the greatest nation in the history of the world, and elevating the Arab world as much as possible. He has gone a long way toward accomplishing both.

CHAPTER 106

LOOKING ONLY AT THE DARK SIDE

Looking only at the dark side of anything will give a jaundiced view. If you see only bad cops, you can easily conclude that all cops are bad. If you look only at bad tires, you will conclude that good tires are not made. If you look only at bad politicians, you will conclude that all politicians are bad.

To look only at the bad side of anything always gives an incorrect and false view, and it will indicate the failure of the person to be fair and honest in his/her appraisal. We, perhaps today, are seeing more and more people in the United States looking only at the bad side of things and pontificating about what they see. The result of this is as jaundiced and unfair as it can be.

One of the things we must face is that there is no such thing as perfection among men. It does not exist and never will. Any organization you might choose to examine, even the best ones, will have both good and bad people. An exception to this is where an organization exists for the purpose of doing evil, i.e. ISIS.

Christianity has become the target of people around the world. Even the President of the United States has made disparaging remarks about it. Many have joined in the chorus, and reports this week indicate more widespread criticism than previously.

These attacks on Christianity are coming from people who have limited knowledge of what Christianity is all about. A reservoir of "not knowing" moves them forward. Good Christianity is about loving people, never hurting them in any way. There are many people and organizations totally committed to helping make life better for others, but make no noise about doing so, and very few hear about them. They simply don't toot their own horns because that is not important to them

To limit oneself to viewing only the bad people and things in an organization is to reveal a huge reservoir of not-knowing, and gives a false impression of what the organization really is.

Liberals in this country, especially Obama, have been experts at showing we are still short of where we need to be as a nation, but they have failed to see the good things about us, good things that have made us the best of nations.

CHAPTER 107

CHRISTIANITY UNDER ATTACK

Almost every day we hear news stories portraying Christianity as a bad religion. A basic problem with this is that some people, even some who call themselves Christians, do not understand what Christianity is all about. Throughout history, some people have gotten Christianity right and some have gotten it wrong, and today is no exception.

Wrong Christianity makes the news; right Christianity does not, and there are some people, always will be, who relish pointing a finger at those who say one thing and do another. One problem we all face is the fact that not one of us is perfect, and even the best people will make mistakes. When a person makes a mistake, we should not err in concluding that what we see is a true picture of him/her.

Many people throughout history claiming the name "Christian" have been mistaken about what it is, and have done some horrible things. These are the people who delivered such things as The Crusades, the Inquisitions, and slavery, among other things. These things had nothing to do with Christianity, although people proclaimed they did.

At the center of Christian faith is this: "You shall love your neighbor as you love yourself." If this is followed, and millions follow this with no fanfare, a Christian will never knowingly and deliberately initiate harm to another. This writer knows many people who go about quietly doing good things for others. He, also, has known and does know too many people, claiming to be Christian, who have no clue that love of the neighbor is at the center of Christian faith.

Where real Christianity is practiced, we see efforts to do good and beneficial things for people. The Christian Church has been the largest provider of healthcare in the world; it pioneered work in social work and the prevention of cruelty to children; it led in the development of education; it did pioneering work in children's homes; Clara Barton's work of helping others led to the founding of the Red Cross; the Church led in advocacy programs in infanticide and polygamy; the Church led in developing programs for the elderly and disabled; Christian principles helped in the development of the Magna Carta; the Salvation Army is an outgrowth of concern for poor people; the foundation of freedom for all helped in the writing of our Constitution; the Samaritan Purse is an outgrowth of Christian concern for people in war, poverty, famine, disease and disaster; prison reform was led by the Christian Church; civil liberties have their foundation in Christian principles.

Many other good things have been done by the Christian Church to care for people. If it had never existed, the plight of people all over the world would be far worse than it is today. What the Church has done, without desiring to claim headlines, it has done at the same time those who do not understand Christianity have been doing many wrong things. People who do Christian things have little desire in making headlines, and often say nothing about the good things they do.

There is no blood on the hands of people who get religion right. There is often blood on the hands of people who get religion wrong.

For those who think Christianity is a bad religion, make contact with those who get it right. If you do, you will change your mind because you will then see many good things you've never seen before. You may even find that there is nothing better than Christianity done right.

CHAPTER 108

HOW DEMOCRATS TREAT POOR PEOPLE

Democrats decided a long time ago to treat poor people, both white and black, as people without the ability to think for themselves. They knew, also, that, if you give poor people money and things, they will think whatever thoughts you wish them to think. That's the reason for all these entitlement programs, which are, basically, democratic/socialist programs aimed at getting poor people to quit thinking, but voting for democrats so they can remain in political office. Sadly, this has worked, and millions of poor people have stopped thinking for themselves.

This is a slick vote-buying system that depends on the ignorance of poor people. Democrats know that, if you can keep poor people poor, but lead them to believe you are actually helping them, they will vote democratic until the cows come home. So, in their arsenal they have developed many good-sounding programs that actually do harm to poor people, but these programs are worded in such a manner that poor people jump right in and let the government do for them less than could do for themselves.

Treating poor people in such a manner is despicable, but it has worked, and poor people have scrambled to vote at elections in order to keep the free ride that produces less than they could produce if they only depended on themselves. Everyone needs to learn "No-one will take better care of me than me." The world of talent that has been pushed down and hidden within poor people by their acceptance of freebies from Washington is needed if we are to make this a better country.

If poor people continue to believe the words of democrats, they will continue relying on the freebies from Washington rather than on the much better things that can come from their own efforts.

In the political campaigns now taking place, the democrats are already saying things that rely on poor people not thinking for themselves. They are saying many things that are not true, but believe they have the poor democratic vote in their hip pocket

If poor people will start thinking for themselves, they will catch onto what the democrats are doing, and start relying on themselves for their success in life. Each of us needs to get to the place where we can honestly say, "My most important job in life is to take care of myself," and, "If I don't take care of myself, nobody else will." If you give your life over to others, they will abuse it, and that is exactly what has been happening as poor people have given their allegiance to the democrats.

If the truth were known, the only way for liberal democrats to remain in office is to keep poor people poor and ignorant.

Here is a short look at a little bit of history:

1. The 13th Amendment: abolished slavery
   a. 100% Republican Support
   b. 23% Democratic Support
2. 15th Amendment: Right to vote to all men:
   a. 100% Republican Support
   b. 0% Democratic Support

3. 14th Amendment: Gave citizenship to freed slaves:
   a. 94% Republican Support
   b. 0% Democratic Support

Does anything else need to be said about which party is interested in people doing well?

CHAPTER 109

WHAT ABOUT THE VALUE OF POLITICAL EXPERIENCE?

There is a lot of talk about candidates for political office in Washington needing extensive political experience. Is that true?

Well, during the past several decades we've had the greatest concentration of political experience in Washington our nation has ever had, and what has it brought us? Politicians, during this time, have managed to do great harm to the American people. Our nation is no longer the leader of the free world; we have the weakest military since World War II; the quality of our educational programs has declined; race relations are worse than they were 50 years ago; government spending is totally out of control with no ability to repay our debt anywhere in sight; printing presses are filling our nation with money worth less and less; freedoms guaranteed by the Constitution have been taken away; there is no control of our borders; class warfare has been ratcheted up by politicians in Washington; we no longer feel safe in our homes; politicians want to take our guns from us when we need them more than ever before for protection; the value of our property plunged when they made borrowing easy for people who had no ability to repay debt; the stock market fell due to what they had done; they have made untold millions of people dependents of government handouts, which has resulted in vast numbers of fully capable people living off tax money extracted from productive people, etc., etc., etc., ad nauseam.

We do not need to send back to Washington the politicians who have made such a mess out of this nation. If we do, they will but add to the damage of the last several decades.

We need politicians in Washington who have the ability to think and return this nation to the great Constitutional Republic it once was. Replacing it with socialism, as politicians have been doing, has plunged us into being a mediocre nation, and they will continue this plunge if sent back into the government chambers in Washington.

The ability to think has not been an asset evident in Washington for a long time. It's time we sent people capable of thinking about what they are doing, and then take action based on good, sound thinking. This is essential if Washington is to once again serve the citizens of this great country.

Political experience in Washington?? Not worth a dime when it moves toward dismantling this country. The ability to think is far more valuable.

CHAPTER 110

THE STEADY RISE OF A NEW HOLOCAUST

The world reacted in horror when we learned that Hitler had led his people to eliminate over six million Jews from the face of the earth. We fail to understand how humans could do this to each other. Unfortunately, the Holocaust is just the worst of other similar things humans have done to fellow human beings. We might call other horrors by different names, but spreading death among those we do not like often comes easily and springs from the same source. The following is a small sampling of what misguided men have done:

Joseph Stalin, we are told, caused the death of 40 to 60 million
Pol Pot: 1.7 to 2.4 million
Mao Tse Tung: 49 to 78 million
Hitler: 60 million

These were evil men who brought death to millions of people. Most of them had good minds and a lot of education, but educated minds need something that cannot be found in any college curriculum. It is called respect and appreciation for the dignity and worth of each individual. This is found in good homes, and it is found in good religion.

The wrong kind of religion results in such things as The Crusades, the Inquisitions, slavery, the current-day beheadings by ISIS, things resulting from our failure to understand what a human being really is. Any religion that, in any way, suggests, condones or approves of one person hurting another, is a bad religion, and has no place in the affairs of humans. Most of the world has moved away from the kind of barbaric mind that easily eliminates people we do not like, but, sadly, there are still some purveyors of death who believe they are doing the right thing. What's happening with ISIS is an example of this, but so is the criminal in our communities who feel it is okay to kill those who get in their way. The mindset is basically the same.

There is probably nothing more evil than a religion that serves as the basis for delivering death to others. We saw it in the Crusades and the Inquisitions, we see it with ISIS, and it was active in the slave trade.

It seems that the connivings of humans will often leads us to places we do not need to go.

CHAPTER 111

WHEN YOU ARRIVE IN WASHINGTON, CHECK YOUR BRAIN AT THE POTOMAC

There seems to be an absence of the ability to think when our elected officials enter the capitol building in Washington. What causes this? Some people would rather not ask this question, but the deterioration quite apparent in our Constitutional Republic stares us in the face. We are not what we once were.

No longer do the members of Congress represent the people who elected them. For decades, the liberal democrats have been driving us toward socialism, and unknowing Republicans and independents have failed to understand the writing on the wall. It causes one to wonder if they have the ability to understand that our Constitution requires them to serve us citizens, not us citizens serve them. A simple reading of the most important governance document in the world makes this quite clear.

How could this be? Perhaps they believe their socialist ideas will bring us closer to the Promised Land, but the reality is that they have been taking us down a road that leads to the kind of failure Greece is now experiencing. The basic failure of socialism is, indeed, that sooner or later, you do run out of other people's money. It's just a matter of time, we are far down the road, and we are picking up speed.

None of the democrats will challenge our plunge from the greatest nation ever because they have been leading the charge, and many of us wonder if Republicans even know what has been taking place. The brain power that our leaders are supposed to have is absent under the Capitol dome. Many of them sounded intelligent when we elected them, but somehow that intelligence seems not to have made it over the Potomac River because it is not a part of their deliberations in considering legislation. They have ruined this great nation, and it is time they recognized this. And, the president the democrats foisted upon us is leading in the charge downhill.

We don't need brains left south and west of the Potomac. They need to be taken all the way into governance chambers so that we will never again hear such things as, "Let's pass it so we can see what's in it." That is the height of heads without the presence of brains.

The 100 billion brain cells and 100 trillion connections we all have need to be put to use. If we will do that, we will begin to climb back toward the time when the people we send to Washington will actually serve the citizens of the United States.

CHAPTER 112

LIBERALS: EXPERT HORNSWOGGLERS

In looking at why so many good people in the U. S. have been hornswoggled by liberal democrats, we must consider how easily people in the past have been hornswoggled.

History shows us that conniving leaders, those who promise pie in the sky by and by, have learned that some good people are eager to believe that someone other than themselves can give them the kind of life they have been looking for. In the U. S., many good people have been fooled by liberal promises of income without the need to work to earn it. Thus, the rush to sign up for free money flowing through the federal government to them. Many people find the lure of free money to be more than they can resist.

Once the free money starts flowing, people are lulled into not caring what the source of this money might be. They don't concern themselves with the fact that other people have had to labor to produce this money, and that it has been extracted from them by the IRS threat of jail time if they don't pay. The fact that they are just as capable of working to make their own way as are others does not bother them in the least. The thought, "The liberals have given me money and deserve my vote," drives them back to vote for liberals who will keep the gravy flowing.

What happens in this is the destruction of the work ethic and the responsibility of every able person to make our country a better nation. If everyone would assume their responsibility of being a part of strengthening this nation, we would now see a nation light-years ahead of where we are. But, so long as there are those who are content to have others making money so they can live a work-free life, so long will liberals attract their vote.

One of the things liberals depend on is the fact that great numbers of people don't like to think. Thinking is burdensome because it leads us toward weighing our responsibilities against those of other people. When we do this, we are led to the fact that each of us must learn to care for ourselves, not looking to others for money to buy the bread we eat.

Standing on a level playing field is not in the repertoire of the hornswogglers.

CHAPTER 113

WE SHOULD PAY ATTENTION

In the past and still today, when we have tried to make sense of Obama's position regarding the Arabs, we have failed to remind ourselves about something he made quite clear in one of his books prior to being elected. He said that, if the Arabs and the United States ever declared war against each other, he would fight with the Arabs.

What we have chosen to ignore is that many Arabs have been at war with our country for a long time, but we have chosen to not be at war with them. This has been a one-sided affair, and, so far, we are losing.

We need to face the fact that Obama has favored the Arab people far more than he has favored the American people. He has taken every chance he has had to degrade the United States and elevate the Arab nations. In many ways, he, himself, has been at war with the United States, and we have not faced that fact. He did not become president to make us a better nation. He became president for the purpose of diminishing who we have been, and he has been successful with this. No foreign nation could have invaded us and done as much damage as he has done as president.

His political party has supported him and cheered him on as he has become a lawless president, taking freedoms from us that have been guaranteed by our Constitution. In their support of him, they have confirmed that they want our country to be something other than a constitutional republic. He will remove more of our freedoms before his presidency ends if the people in Congress don't change the direction in which they are walking.

CHAPTER 114

IS IT TIME TO CLEAN HOUSE?

I s it time to clean house in Washington and replace politicians who have made such a mess of our country?

I had the good fortune of growing up during the best days of the greatest nation in history. In spite of our faults, we achieved the status of the best that ever was. But, over the last several decades, we have been moving backwards rather than forward as our elected officials have chipped away at the foundation that made us great. I must now say that I live in what was *once* the greatest nation on the face of the earth.

We are moving from a nation where people can build lives according to their own dreams to a society determined by an entitlement mentality delivered to us by liberal democrats. Millions of Americans now do not earn their way, and have signed up for the check from Washington. They have placed their future in the hands of elected representatives in Washington who think they are capable of deciding what is best for everyone.

Our greatness came a result of people taking advantage of their opportunities to dream big dreams and then go on to accomplish amazing things. People clamored to migrate here and have a chance to achieve new and better things. Being able to dream their dreams propelled many to a better life.

Yes, we do have people who genuinely cannot take care of themselves, and we should help them. But, people who are fully capable of getting an education and/or training should be expected to earn their own living.

Liberal democrats, in effect, gave people money so they could avoid working for a living, and forced the productive people in this country to pay taxes for their support. This has destroyed the need to struggle to build good lives which is at the heart of people making something good of themselves.

What we now see are vast numbers of people avoiding the responsibility of being productive citizens, and, thus, contributing nothing whatsoever to making this a better nation. Rather, they are helping to drag this nation down, making it less than what it once was.

The highest dreams liberal democrats have is for people to be dependent on the government. With what they have done over the past several decades, they have succeeded in bringing millions of Americans to grovel at the government trough and waste what could have been productive lives.

The American people need to vote and replace those who have been tearing this great nation apart. If we don't, they will continue to drag us down.

Where do we start? We start by taking a look at the politicians in Washington who have been making subjects of people by giving them money and freeing them from the responsibility of becoming productive citizens. We vote them out of office, replacing them with people who understand that each one of us, under our Constitution, has the responsibility to make something of ourselves, helping to make this a better nation.

If we don't vote to clean house of liberal politicians, correcting the damage they have done to our country, we will be able to say a final "Good-by" to the greatest nation that ever was.

(Liberals are responsible for development of the entitlement mentality that is driving millions of fully capable people to bury their sense of the need to get a job and contribute to the well-being of this country. If we are to restore our nation, we must reject the entitlement mentality or plan to walk where the people of Greece are now walking.)

CHAPTER 115

TREATIES AND AGREEMENTS BETWEEN NATIONS

Many people are ecstatic when treaties and agreements between nations are signed. When Neville Chamberlin, Prime Minister of England, returned with the signed "Anglo-German Agreement" in his hands, he was, in effect, extolled as a great man and savior of Great Britain. King George assured him of the "Empire's lasting gratitude." Chamberlain said this document assured "peace for our time."

In just a few months, German bombs started falling on London.

This is a story of the value of treaties and agreements between nations when men lacking honor make them. Even if they are honorable men, it is only a short time until they are gone, and other men of unknown honor take their place.

We already know that Iran is a member of the Arab block that wants to eliminate Israel from the face of the earth. Anyone who wants to eliminate another person or nation from the earth cannot be considered honorable. We, also, already know something about the integrity of some of the people involved in negotiations for this treaty.

If treaties are only as good as the people who make them, a treaty with Iran regarding nuclear energy may be a huge mistake. One of the governors of Georgia, Lester Maddox, once said of the newspaper, "It is just a fish-wrapper;" in other words, good for nothing but to put dead fish in. Could this be said about treaties?

Perhaps we can be hopeful that this current agreement is a good one and will be honored, but we must remember that the history of treaties between nations is not good. We must remain aware that, sooner or later, whether we like it or not, the Iranians will build nuclear weapons. This will happen with or without a treaty.

CHAPTER 116

PREPARING TO REPEAT HISTORY

She asked my cousin if the Holocaust had really happened. She was in her late teens, and had been taught by her people that it never did.

Humans have a tendency to cover up the bad things we do to each other, to sweep our crimes where they can be neither seen nor remembered. We just don't like to believe that those who have gone before us could actually perpetrate the kind of horrors seen as Hitler tried to exterminate the Jews from the face of the earth. Perhaps Arab people cannot accept the reality of the Holocaust because to do so would mean having to see that their desire to eliminate all Jews from the face of the earth is just as evil as what motivated Hitler.

We don't like to think about things like this because we are afraid that what we inherited from them might mean we have the possibility of doing the same thing. Perhaps what is on the inside of us is no better than what was on the inside of them, and we don't want to face it. Our humanity may be no better than was theirs. So now we have part of the world's population being told the concentration camps and furnaces never did exist.

Yes, there are some things that should be swept under the rug, but we dare not pretend we are better than the peoples who have preceded us. Sweeping all their evil where it can no longer be remembered will result in our unawareness that humans, even today, are capable of extreme cruelty to each other.

We need reminders that we are humans, and to cover up the sins of the past is but a prelude to repeating them. The Rebel flag should never be hidden where it cannot be seen. Perhaps we do not need it on a flag pole in a state capitol, but hiding it to erase all memory may be the worst thing we can do.

We must face the fact that we are who we are, and the reminders in history of the potential within us will help us manage not to repeat the awful things of the past. Yes, failing to remember history is a certain way to repeat it.

CHAPTER 117

WE DON'T WANT TO DEAL WITH THAT

So long as the race-baiters, like some opportunistic politicians and Al Sharpton, keep people riled up about things like the Confederate flag and political correctness, so long will they be able to avoid doing what needs to be done. Lacking the skills to help people learn to live together, they keep the flames of hate burning, and our entire nation suffers. They don't want to do what needs to be done because they lack the skills required, and are getting elected and enriched by stirring the pot.

Many of us, perhaps most, are eager to avoid dealing with some of the most critical things in life. We do this because we'd rather not face the hard reality of what is. We want it to be what we want it to be rather than what it really is.

Our Civil War was the product of failure to grapple with the right of all people to be treated with equality and dignity. To see people as they are and not as we want them to be is often too difficult for us, and we go to great lengths to protect our distorted beliefs.

The Second World War was the product of a mind that wanted to get even and to impose a system of life that could be controlled by one man. The result was the death of 60 million people.

Some of the most critical issues in life are avoided by emphasizing other things. It is not unusual to hear someone say about another person, "He is doing that because he does not know what he is supposed to be doing." We often think that just being busy is the only thing that matters, and we busy ourselves doing what we want to do rather than what we ought to be doing.

Thus, we find ourselves embroiled in getting rid of the rebel flag, in political correctness, and many other things. So long as we can stir the pot and keep people upset with these issues, we don't have to deal with the real issues that come when we look inside our own lives and find them lacking. We don't like to look at the ugliness that lurks there. When we allow the rabble-rousers to ratchet up our disdain for the bad things others do, we can avoid real issues, such as 93 percent of black deaths being at the hands of other black people (per Andrew Young). This is where a lot of work needs to be done, but we prefer not to go there.

The value of black people is just as great as the value of white people, but this reality has not yet become a part of the psyche of even black people, and, so, they kill each other at an alarming rate. The stamp of inferiority once placed on black people by a minority of white people has been taken up and paraded on blacks by blacks themselves. This is where some gut-wrenching work needs to be done by black people, and is something that cannot be done for them no matter how loud people can be in dealing with things that matter so little.

Our interest in developing respect for each other has lagged far behind scientific achievements in providing things that make life comfortable, and, also, in developing weapons that kill each other. We haven't been too concerned about getting along with others because we have successfully avoided dealing with the subject of value in each human being.

Until the time comes when we understand that all people have value, we will continue saying about the important things in life, "We don't want to do that."

CHAPTER 118

ABANDONING THE CONSTITUTION

The Constitution of the United States was written to protect citizens from the kind of politicians we now have in Washington. Those who wrote the Constitution were good students of history, and were aware that political leaders without constraints would take away freedoms and do things that are harmful to people.

From the current president to many of our legislators, and now the Supreme Court, we have people who are disregarding constitutional guidelines, and the result is the removal of some of our freedoms. History shows that, once people's freedoms begin to be taken away, it is only a matter of time until more and more are gone.

Some of our politicians in the past have flirted with ignoring the Constitution, but there have been those who have called their hand, and constitutional government remained in place.

Over the past few years we have experienced what can happen when politicians have decided that they are better able to govern on the basis of their limited wisdom rather than on the Constitution. The result is a nation that no longer gives freedom to citizens to make their own decisions, but, rather, who are forced to accept what politicians in Washington decide is best for them.

The United States is no longer the bastion of freedom it once was. We no longer lead the world in exercise of freedom, and it is getting worse from day to day.

With the administration, members of Congress, and the Supreme Court moving away from constitutional guidelines, we find our nation rapidly falling apart economically (debt that is totally absurd), militarily, in international relationships, respect for each other, citizenship, religious freedom, and other things that have made us the envy of the world.

If we citizens do not make the corrections needed in our next national election, we will be subjects of those in Washington who think they know what is best for each and every one of us. Thomas Sowell, political philosopher and Senior Fellow of the Hoover Institute, Stanford University, recently wrote, "When any branch of government can exercise powers not authorized by either statutes or the Constitution, "we the people" are no longer free citizens but subjects, and our "public servants" are really our public masters."

It is no accident that, under the Constitution, we became the greatest nation in the history of the world. William Gladstone, four-time Prime Minister of England, said of our Constitution, "...it is the most wonderful work ever struck off at a given time by the brain and purpose of man." Although we have often struggled with making freedom available to all our citizens, we, none-the-less, have been a nation superior to all others.

Current politicians in Washington are abandoning the guidelines of the Constitution, and the loss of freedoms we are now experiencing is only a taste of what is ahead for us if we citizens don't elect politicians who understand that the Constitution, although it is not perfect, is far better than any other governance document that has sprung from the mind of men.

CHAPTER 119

THE PRICE OF LIBERALISM

Many people are now riding on the welfare train, and left-ist liberals are trying their best to add more cars to the train. Many people have clamored to jump onto that train, and the seats are full. More passenger cars and seats are needed as more and more people clamor to climb aboard.

What the people riding that train do not know is that their destination is not a good one. The train is headed in the wrong direction, but the liberals are keeping quiet regarding the destination.

The seats on the train are occupied by people who have been convinced by liberals that their contribution to making this a better nation and world is not needed. "It is okay to personal-ly take wealth rather than help produce it; your talents are not needed in today's world. There are people who will work hard and pay taxes, and it is okay to have the government transfer some of these taxes to your bank account so you can live and do well," is a message that rings a bell in the ears of those who fail to understand that their effort is drastically needed if they are to become what humans should become.

People with good minds and bodies have thrown themselves into the category of uselessness when it comes to helping make life better for others. They have chosen to be takers rather than givers, and the contributions their developed minds and talents could make to the lives of others have been left behind.

The destination the people on the train are not concerned about is one that takes them and their offspring to a land where life is controlled by liberals, not by themselves. So long as they ride that train, so long will they have no voice in what is best for them. That will be determined by the liberals who are busy figuring out ways to keep the passengers on the train from doing the job their maker prepared them to do. Accomplishing personal goals by development of talents and abilities is never a product of passengers on this train. Most of them will make no contribution to improving life for others, but the liberals don't want them to know this. Also, liberals don't want people to understand something Margaret Thatcher understood very well when she said, "The problem with socialism is that you eventually run out of other people's money." That's when things coming crashing down, most recently seen in Greece.

CHAPTER 120

RETREAT INTO BARBARISM

Retreat into barbarism seems to ever be with us. At any time, we are able to point to some area of the world and see people who have chosen to act as if humans have not yet been civilized, which means "characterized by taste, refinement and restraint" (Merriam-Webster).

ISIS is a profound example of this right now. They are functioning at a primitive, barbaric level with modern weapons in their hands. When we think about evil, this is evil in its purest form.

It is easy to retreat into the barbaric level in the absence of personal values, because, when you see yourself as worthless, you project that onto others. To value yourself is to value others, and, when you value others, there can be no desire to hurt them.

To constrain others so that their lives are diminished or eliminated is to violate their basic sense of freedom, which is at the heart of human development. To take away the basic freedom of an individual is to violate the very creation of that person having been made a distinct, separate, and unique individual who will never again be repeated in the history of the world. To undo what the Creator has done is one of the greatest sins humans can commit.

CHAPTER 121

THE NEW WORLD ORDER

Must we travel down this road again? Mankind has traveled down it often, too often. It is a road that takes us to places we do not need to go, often ending in disaster.

Napoleon had a dream of ruling the Middle East, Europe and Russia. Last century, the name given it was "The Third Reich." Now the U. N. and some of our political leaders are calling it "The New World Order," and are pushing for it to become a reality.

There is little difference between The New World Order and what has gone before. The biggest difference is the means by which it is to be achieved. The end result, however, is basically the same. It is a system of world domination by a small group of people with a supreme leader.

Achieving this New World Order would require the elimination of freedom for all people in all nations. What is acceptable would be that which is determined by the supreme leader in council with his/her advisers.

The thirst for freedom lurking within the hearts of people will never allow it to happen. Resistance to a world order will bring resistance in many places, and, pushing to implement it, whether calling it "Theory 21" or something else, will end in great disaster.

The feeling of omnipotence, aroused by the desire to control others, is hard to resist by those who do not understand what life is all about. Mastery of others, central in all who wish to control the world, will always end in disaster because no-one is wise enough to know what is best for everyone.

The U. N. and our leaders who are now working for The New World Order lack understanding of the disaster toward which they are nudging us, and, because of this, do not need to be where they are.

SECTION FOUR

Finding Our Way

CHAPTER 122

MY EGO: IN THE HANDS OF OTHERS?

Why do I get upset, why is my skin so thin when others do and say things that offend me? Is the control of my feelings in their hands or is that something I am supposed to control?

Could my Maker have intended that my life be made miserable by the crowd or does my well-being reside entirely within my own ego, something that is entirely within my control?

I have found my life to be miserable when others lead me where they are going or do things I don't like. I find myself tied up and consumed in their journey, and lose sight of my own destination.

I really don't have time to walk down their road. It is only my road that I must travel if I am to reach the goal for which I was intended.

Yes, I must be aware and respectful of the pain of others, but I must not make it my own. My ego is in my own hands, and my joy comes from my successes, not the consequences of others. Others will drag me down. I am the only one who can and will propel me forward.

I am aware the crowd wants me to be a part of them, but when I join them, I lose my identity; their identity becomes my identity. My identity, however, is too important to place in their hands. They will take me places I do not wish to go, and I will lose sight of who I am. I am not responsible to them for who I am. That is between my Maker and me. I will respect others, but their pattern for life will not be mine. That is for me alone to decide.

I look for abundance in my life, and that comes only from pursuing my own dreams. Others would have me walk in their footsteps, but, if I did, their rewards would be my rewards, and that is not good enough for me.

It is only those things I desire that can be good enough for me. The way of life for others and their rewards will never meet my needs.

⊷ ⊶

No-one is in charge of my happiness but me.

⊷ ⊶

CHAPTER 123

THE NEED FOR RENOUNCERS

Renouncers are people who choose to put aside what is believed, and move on to something that is better. In the Axial Period, 900 BC to 200 BC (named by Karl Jaspers), great advance was made in Greece, Israel, India and China, as people like Plato, Isaiah, Buddha, and Confucius raised questions regarding the way life was lived. They thought something better was available to humans; the old ways and beliefs were not adequate in their world. Without knowing about each other, these men developed a new way of thinking, and, not knowing about each other speaks volumes regarding the development of human beings.

These thinkers became renouncers as they challenged the way life was to be lived and the way things were to be done, and led in the development of things that were better. They challenged the belief that the arrangement of God, king, and people was the way life was to be structured. They took the position that life should be lived on the basis of individual thought, that individuals were directly responsible for thinking and building their lives as they thought best. There was no need to go through the group or the king (group think) to decide what is best in life. Each individual is responsible.

We need renouncers in our world today, people who will do their own thinking regarding what is best for them. We need to quit following the drum-beater who wants to take us down his/her road, and find the way that is best for us. We are free individuals who are responsible for our own lives and we need to follow our own drum beat. This is the only way in which we can pursue the life that only we can live.

CHAPTER 124

ESCAPING THE NEED TO THINK

In the movie, "Gone With The Wind," Scarlet, at one point, said she did not want to think about something, then added, "Tomorrow is another day."

Many people today don't want to think about things. We'd rather put off our thinking until another day. However, a problem we face is that failure to think about things today may open the door for other people, who have been busy thinking, to pull the wool over our eyes. When Obama campaigned for office in 2007, he said some things Americans should have thought about, but did not. For those who were paying attention, he told us he wanted to change our country into what he wanted it to be, which, by the way, is different from what our Constitution says it should be. He also said that, if the United States ever went to war with the Arabs, he would fight with the Arabs. He was quite plain in this and other things, but, because he was a good-looking black man who could read a good speech, we fell under his charm, and did not think about what he meant. So, we did not think about the meaning of his words.

Democrats, ever on the road to control what America becomes, saw Obama as the one who could finish the race into socialism, supported him in the things he desired. This has resulted, during the last eight years, in undoing some of the things that distinguish us from all nations, things like freedom of speech, freedom of religion, freedom to own guns for sporting purposes and for our protection, many things that remove us from being a Constitutional Republic.

If Americans had thought seriously about the words that came out of his mouth, we would not have had so many of our freedoms attacked, and we would not have deteriorated so much in becoming like some of the third-world nations.

Sometimes people prefer not to think about things, but there are occasions when, absent thought, we can be led to places we do not wish to go, and that is what has happened to this nation during the past eight years.

Whenever we hear a politician talk about things he wishes to do, we must pay attention to what he means.

CHAPTER 125

WANTING THINGS THAT CANNOT BE

I f we are honest, each of us would have to say we desire things that cannot be. We dream of the person who can love us and make our lives complete. We long for the perfect job where the challenge and money exceed our expectations. We covet a relationship with the Maker of the world and everything in it. We want our God to accept us and complete our lives. In our wildest dreams, we walk through the world where everything comes up rosy.

Humans have been seeking Nirvana ever since they were created, but Nirvana has never appeared. We are stuck with reality, but our dreaming does not diminish. Some people do marvelous things serving the needs of others in an attempt to enter into a world of their dreams where all is peace. Some do horrendous acts of evil after being falsely told by their religion that, in doing so, they will be given 70 virgins in the hereafter (we know where their minds have been).

Our expectations are that the excellent life will come from someone giving it to us, and, in our concentration, we fail to see where the real source of what we are longing for is to be found. In looking outside for our Nirvana, we do not see the only place it can come from, and that is deep inside each of us as we develop the vast potential placed there by our Creator.

Even though the pages of history reveal the futility of following the charismatic leader who promises to fill our hunger, we, none-the-less, fall victim to the one who arises and promises to give us our hearts desire. We are quick to believe someone else can do a better job of satisfying our hunger than we can do for ourselves. World War Two would never have happened if people had not believed the lies of Hitler.

The truth of the matter is that true happiness comes from the inside of each of us. No-one else can give us what we can give can ourselves. The successful basketball player, or any athlete, is never successful on the basis of what someone else can give him. It is only in the development of what is on the inside that gives outstanding performance. And, so it is, outstanding performance in any area of life comes only as the result of each person doing his/her own thing, taking what is on the inside and developing it as best each can. This is the only way to the Nirvana we all desire.

To you who are hungering for someone to give the life you dream about, turn your eyes inside, see the beauty and grandeur that is there, and develop it as best you can. You will not be disappointed by the end result, for you will then have the best life can offer you.

CHAPTER 126

THERE ARE REASONS WE ARE THE GREATEST NATION

Yes, we've got problems, but so does every other nation. In spite of our problems, we became the greatest nation in the history of the world.

The United States is the most admired nation in history. More people desire to migrate here than to any other country. People of other countries send their children here for education more-so than to any other nation. We have built the best economy the world has ever seen. Our military is superior to that of all other countries (without the U.S., the two world wars would have turned out differently). We lead the world in scientific development. We send more foreign aid than any other country. We have offered more freedom to people than any other nation. Each person born in this country has an opportunity to be successful by earning an education and/or training. We have more foundations offering charity than any other nation. More wealthy foreigners and others come to our country for healthcare than to any other nation. We are world leaders in innovation. We lead the world in development of the internet. We produce more movies and music than any other country. We have the best healthcare in the world; any person with or without money needing healthcare can go to an emergency room and be seen by medical professionals (the law requires that all persons presenting themselves in the E.R. must be seen).

It is no accident that the United States became the greatest nation in the history of the world. Human beings are humans with all their frailties wherever they are, and, if unrestrained, personal goals can take over life. Those who developed the foundations of this great nation were aware of this, and were smart enough to develop documents that would keep us from falling into the traps of every other nation in history where a small group of people or one person could usurp control over everything and everybody.

Our Founders developed the Constitution of the United States and the Bill of Rights because they understood who humans are. These documents have served us well because we have, to a great extent, honored them as our guides. Honoring and abiding by them became a way of life for most Americans. When people tried to do things contrary to these documents, others reined them in. Even with the many frailties we have exhibited, honoring our founding documents has made us what we have been.

These documents were written to protect us from people like Barack Obama and his democratic followers, who have chosen to disregard their guidelines. They have chosen to project their ideas about government as superior to these founding documents, and we now suffer under the results, which is great deterioration of life in this country, plus a failed foreign policy. Many of the freedoms we enjoyed eight years ago no longer exist, and the tables have been turned regarding what is considered good and bad.

We have learned the hard way that there are always people who stand ready to control our lives if allowed to do so. We have learned that the kind of freedom we have demands our constant attention. We let our guard down, and Obama and his people pounced. The result has been deterioration in almost all aspects of American life, and restoration to the great nation we once were will be difficult.

There will always be people who will rise up and proclaim, "Follow me and I will take you to the Promised Land." We need to remember, however, that, of all those throughout history who have proclaimed this, not a one of them has ever found and delivered the Promised Land, and there will never be anyone to do so.

William Gladstone, four-time Prime Minister of England, said of our Constitution. "…it is the most wonderful work ever struck off at a given time by the brain and purpose of man." Knowledge of the past history of governments will reveal this to us, and knowledge of what politicians in Washington have done to our great nation in recent years will make it even clearer.

CHAPTER 127

LIBERALISM: KEEPING PEOPLE INFERIOR AND POOR

Liberals do not want black people and poor whites to be successful because, if they are successful, liberals will lose their ability to feel good about themselves by giving things to the poor. The Great Society Program, with all its give-a-ways, was structured to keep people poor. It rewarded people for doing nothing when it should have rewarded them for accomplishment.

Did the liberals know the give-away programs would result in people not trying to be successful? Yes, they knew that very well, and they knew, also, that, once you start giving people money and things, you can control what they do in the voting booth and in other areas of their lives.

In language everyone can understand, "The liberals used and abused millions of black people and poor whites with free money from Washington."

Liberals have treated blacks and poor whites as inferior people incapable of caring for themselves, and have presented themselves as the heroes who have come to their rescue.

Perhaps we need to remember the words Frederick Douglas spoke in 1865 when asked what should be done for freed blacks, "I have but one answer from the beginning. Do nothing with us...

If the apples will not remain on the tree of their own strength…
let them fall…And if the Negro cannot stand on his own legs, let
him fall also. All I ask is that you give him a chance to stand on
his own legs." He said this because he knew that, if blacks were
given a chance to succeed and were required to do for themselves, they would be successful. This is something liberals today
do not believe.

Liberals have developed the give-away programs in
Washington so that blacks and poor whites do not have to stand
on their own legs, and these recipients of the free money and
the rest of us are all the worse off because of it. But, the liberals can step forward and say, "Look what good boys and girls we
are because we have put money and things into the hands of the
needy."

CHAPTER 128

FREE MONEY OR SHALL I EARN IT?

A few years ago, my son had surgery that resulted in the loss of a body part. As a CEO of my fourth hospital, and familiar with medical malpractice lawsuits, I recommended he sue the physician. A case like this could have been settled out of court for a million dollars or more.

My son chose not to sue. He had been an honest auto technician, and his honesty meant he did not make the kind of money many techs make. I thought perhaps he had done the wrong thing by not suing.

Just a few years after this, he returned to college and earned a mechanical engineering degree. Upon graduation, he was hired by a company that makes rockets used in the space program. He has responsibility for production of one stage of rockets that lift satellites into space.

A few months after he began work building rockets, I asked him the question, "If you had sued and won a million dollars after that surgery, would you have gone back to college and earned your engineering degree?" He quickly said, "No, I would not." Almost at the same time, both of us said, "This is much better."

Money that comes into our hands without us working for it is one of the worst things that can happen to a person. It basically kills our initiative to learn/train and make something of ourselves. We receive free money and we quit trying to accomplish anything with our lives. Free money leads us to bury our uniqueness and talents, and the world misses out on what we could do to make life better for ourselves and others.

This is the sad story of what the welfare programs have done to millions of people fully capable of making something of themselves. If people with their great potential had said, "No," to the free money from Washington, they would have gotten busy developing their talents, and would now be enjoying a better life than is provided by that free money. They, having good jobs, would now be able to say with my son, "This is much better."

CHAPTER 129

THE VALUE OF TREATIES AND
AGREEMENTS

After meeting with Hitler in 1938 and signing the "Anglo-German Agreement," Neville Chamberlain returned to England in triumph, and King George assured him of "the Empire's lasting gratitude." Chamberlain said this document assured "peace for our time."

Chamberlain was not aware that, after signing the document, Hitler said to his Foreign Minister, Joachin von Ribbentrop, who protested the signing, "Oh, don't take it so seriously. That piece of paper is of no further significance whatever." Several months after this, Germany started bombing London.

This is a story of the value of treaties and agreements between nations when men lacking honor make them. This is where we question the value of any treaty that may come out of the efforts of our President and his Secretary of State. We already know for certain that our President has difficulty with the truth, and his Secretary of State has had problems with integrity. We, also, know that Iran is a member of the Arab block that wants to eliminate Israel from the face of the earth.

No one who desires to eliminate anyone from the earth is an honorable person.

If treaties are only as good as the people who make them, a United States treaty with Iran regarding nuclear energy may be a huge mistake.

CHAPTER 130

NO GROUND TO STAND ON

What has happened to the American people? Even with our past failures, we were the most stable nation in the world. But, now we are floundering, being led by people who bring histories of extreme personal instability. When a person does not have his feet on firm ground, he is easily swept away with weak philosophies.

The fundamental rights of man become tenuous when threats to freedom arise. When people do not have their feet on solid ground, an opportunist can befuddle them with glitzy presentations that turn out to be nothing but a false hope.

The American people have allowed themselves to be beguiled by one man and a group of people who fail to understand the meaning of freedom, who think limitation of freedom is better than freedom itself. They should be reminded that the greatness of our nation comes from the freedom to be whatever we desire, which is guaranteed by the Constitution. The greatness we have achieved as a nation has come from men and women who followed the Constitution. When tempted to violate our laws, which has often happened, politicians have drawn back, and we have enjoyed the best life ever lived by humans.

As we now have someone leading us who disregards the Constitution, we are losing our freedoms, and, if corrections are not made, our great freedoms will be but memories.

CHAPTER 131

LEARNING TO LIVE WITH EACH OTHER

Must we continue to look at each other as adversaries, and build our systems to further take advantage of and kill each other? Are we destined to never get along with each other, continuing to build structures to protect us from each other? Will we learn what history has to teach us or will we, like members of ISIS, decline into a primitive, barbaric state where brutality is without limits?

Each of us has within that force which, if not controlled, can wreak havoc with our lives and the lives of others. We saw in Hitler's concentration camps the depths to which humans can sink if life is not respected. Inhumanity to each other is the result of supposing ourselves to be superior, and those who do not meet our standards as worthy of elimination. We think that savagely eliminating each other allows us to stand tall, beat our chests and shout out, "What great people we are; we are in control!!!"

We must ask, when we have finally reached a time in history where it is possible for all people to be fed and provided with things necessary for a comfortable life, will a process of human decay set in whereby we will retreat to a life where only a few can enjoy the good things? To eliminate anyone from our concern is to take a step back in the progress of mankind.

Perhaps we can ask a question such as this: Does the growth of ISIS signal a decline in humanity that is just the beginning of a plunge back into a world where life belongs only to those who are the fiercest destroyers of other humans? Those who would do such things rob people of freedom and liberty. Movements like ISIS major on killing others to eliminate them. Movements like the Third Reich, communism and socialism herd people into both mental and physical camps where survival depends on gifts from those who seek to control all of life. If we forget that it is in freedom and liberty that mankind finds his best life, it is easy for us to be beguiled by those in either camp and lose the best things available in life.

We can never have the best life if control of it is placed in someone else's hands. Unfortunately, people are trained to turn their thinking over to others, and, when this happens, life is always inferior to what one can develop for himself/herself.

We have seen in Hitler's furnaces what man can to do man, and, yet, we have not learned to avoid the distorted thinking that leads to one or more men thinking they know what is best for everyone. We still see this as the center-most philosophy of socialism where men think they know what is best for everyone. We still go like kids to the slaughter because we have turned our thinking over to those who shout, "I know what is best for you. Follow me and I will take you to Nirvana." But, in spite of all those throughout history who have promised Nirvana, the world has yet to see Nirvana.

To be dragged into a belief that someone can take us to Nirvana is the result of not knowing the possibilities our Creator has placed within each of us. We are born with the capacity to build a good life for ourselves, but, when we turn our lives over to others, they use us to accomplish their goals, not ours. What happens is that we allow someone to destroy our lives mentally and emotionally while we are still physically alive, and we lose what is best for us individually. It is a short step to madness, as we saw in Germany and we now see in ISIS, from life controlled by others.

ISIS and like movements are involved in dehumanization, and to so devalue the lives of others speaks loud and clear that they do not value themselves. To understand the value, dignity and holiness of oneself is to see others in the same light.

Those who believe that man is made in the image of his Creator can never accept the message of ISIS and other like-minded people that certain lives do not matter. The road may be rough, but belief that man is the creation of a divine being will prevail. Nihilism may be at the center of life for some, but they are far outnumbered by those who believe every life has meaning and is worthy of continuance.

The evil dreams of misguided people may claim the day for a while, but, in the end, the image of God will prevail. We cannot and will not allow the purveyors of death to have the last say. Those of us who value human life will, in the end, have the last say.

The concentration camps and the beheadings, etc. of ISIS will never prevail because the march of human freedom will never end.

The rise of ISIS and their barbaric killings should serve as a reminder that this evil is always a possibility for humans. If we are not careful to constantly keep in mind just how valuable each of us is, in spite of our frail humanity, we will make it easy for evil men to have their way. Constant attention to the worth of humans must always be a part of our agenda.

Countering the march of madmen is essential if we are to find a way to get along with each other. We dare not allow ourselves to hide from the evil before us.

CHAPTER 132

RESIGNATION TO THE WILL OF OTHERS

Looking at the way liberal democrats have supported Obama in his relentless work of destroying the Constitution of the United States and severely damaging "The Greatest Nation," it is not surprising that they would so easily jump onto the efforts of Republicans to speak for the people who elected them.

Obama has blatantly violated his oath of office while his supporters have cheered him on. We are a more divided nation than we were six years ago. Our foreign policy is in shambles. Our unprotected borders have allowed into our country those who wish to destroy us. Freedom of speech is being taken away. Our second amendment rights are seriously threatened. The majority of voters in this country have been ignored. Gross lies have been used in the development and passing of legislation. The malcontents have been given a strong voice. Those on the lower end of our socioeconomic system have been given government money so they will remain where they are and produce votes for those who are keeping them where they are.

The current resignation to the will of someone who wishes to destroy our nation should not surprise us. History has shown that people easily and quickly follow a golden tongue without paying attention to the content of his words. "Divide and conquer," a favorite ploy active right now in Washington, has always worked. The world experienced this in the 1940's as well as multiple other times in history, and the results are usually catastrophic.

If we resign ourselves to the onslaught of those who wish to destroy this country, it will be destroyed, and a time of chaos will prevail. There is already more division among our people than experienced during the last 50 years, and, under Obama and his liberal democrats, this deterioration will continue. It would have been good had they tried to make our good things better, and work on correcting things that needed to be corrected. Throwing out the constitutional system that has worked better than any other system in history is a colossal mistake. Our nation will suffer a long time for the things now being done by people who do not understand constitutional government.

CHAPTER 133

THE ROAD FROM FREEDOM TO CHAOS
IS SHORT

At any moment in the history of the world, humans have the choice of continuing the development of freedom and culture, refashioning it to make life better for everyone or of sinking back into the chaos of a primitive world.

A good picture of sinking back into primitive chaos can be seen in the activity of ISIS as they go about destroying life in the most primitive of ways. They have chosen not to make life better for people, but, rather, to make it worse, or even by ending it. That is what people do in the absence of freedom.

All of us, at any time, have the possibility of retreating into the chaos of a primitive, barbaric life. We see in our evening news reports the unbelievable savagery in the communities in which we live. We see it internationally in what ISIS and other organizations are doing. We have the choice of moving forward, striving for a better tomorrow for mankind or we can retreat into primitive chaos where life means little to nothing.

What we see in ISIS is a rejection of the idea of freedom. First of all, to be a part of ISIS, you have to give up the idea of thinking for yourself, accepting the misguided belief that delivering death to others is okay. You have to become a part of the destruction of human life, an idea that is totally alien to all that is right and good. This is a retreat into primitive, barbaric thinking of the worst kind. It has developed in a part of the world that has fallen behind the western world with its emphasis on the dignity and worth of every human being. The fact that a small percentage in the western world has been attracted to join ISIS is a testimony to the fact that humans still have a lot of work to do in helping in the understanding that freedom never takes away a person's right to determine what life shall be.

One of the contributions of the western world has been its emphasis on making progress an indispensable part of life.

Humans have been in the world a long time, some claim for millions of years. However, it was not until approximately 5,000 to 3,000 B.C. that enough progress was made for writing to be developed. With writing, we have the beginning of history, and all that goes before can be referred to as pre-history. Archeologists can help us guess what life was like in pre-history, but writing made it possible for us to read about actual history. We know for certain that from 3,000 to 1,000 B.C., chaos was a part of life. Our guess is that prior to 3,000 B.C., which we may refer to as "primitive," chaos was perhaps even more prevalent. Even after the beginning of writing, the development of humans has been awfully slow.

The fastest growth in human development has taken place in the Western world during the last four centuries. When we look for the reason for this, this progress seems be tied to the growth of freedom. It is on the basis of freedom, in particular the beginnings of political liberty that made it possible for people to stretch their minds and imagine things never before dreamed of. This has been the genesis of our scientific development.

Today we are seeing in what ISIS is doing a retreat into what primitive life must have been like, and it is sad to witness their barbarity being attractive to many. ISIS takes over control of people, and brings a full retreat from the idea and reality of freedom. Retreating from freedom and movement toward chaos will always be a part of those who think they know what is best for others. A brotherhood of free men will always be superior to a country where one man, supported by a cadre of followers, says, "I know what is best for you. Follow me." Removal of freedom is one of the worst things that can happen to a people.

Chipping away the freedoms we have enjoyed in the United States is the basis for the growing chaos we are experiencing. Removing more of our freedoms will result in more and more chaos coming into our lives. The threats being made against our people and nation would not now be occurring if the administration in Washington had not been removing our freedoms over the past few years. Most of these threats are coming from nations where freedom has never been a part of their lives. They have found there that chaos can quell freedom, and they wish to spread their experience. Unfortunately, some people in our country are encouraging them to do this. The end result will not be pretty.

To do something to or with a person without that person's insight and consent is inhumane. This was one of the travesties of Hitler burning Jews in the ovens. What ISIS is now doing with the beheadings, etc. of people is equally as evil.

The introduction of freedom into the lives of people is what made possible the growth of the western nations. Removing that freedom will be one of the greatest tragedies in the history of the world, and the work of ISIS and other wan-a-bees, will eventuate in a return to the barbarity of primitive life.

ISIS and others who would remove freedom from mankind would have us retreat into a world of chaos where success is measured, not by human progress, but by how cruel you can be. If the people of America ever abandon the Constitution, it will only be a short time until all our freedoms are gone.

CHAPTER 134

SCIENCE AND TECHNOLOGY HAVE NOT DELIVERED WHAT MAN NEEDS

Science and technology have come a long way. We can sit under the tree outside and, using our cell phone, talk with someone on the other side of the world. We can step on a plane and get to the other side of the world in just a few hours. We can watch our TV and see a rover navigate the Mars landscape. Moon rocks were picked up and returned to earth by our astronauts. A doctor in Germany can direct surgery as it is being performed in New York. I can sit at my computer and find information on any subject known to man. We can do marvelous things because we have made unbelievable progress in science and technology. Having been born in the 1930's, I am amazed at what our minds have produced.

But, we can also send a bomb anywhere in the world and kill hundreds of thousands of people in the blink of an eye. We have military on stand-by to be deployed anywhere in the world on a moment's notice. We are prepared to kill whomever we think poses a danger to us. We keep millions of guns in our homes for protection from people who have no respect for our lives.

Yes, we have come a long way from what life was like three thousand years ago, but, somehow, we have failed to develop life so that we are not a threat to each other. We need something to quell those things inside that continue to separate us from each other, but we look here and there and throw up our hands because we cannot find it.

Science and technology cannot deliver it. Religion has been with us for thousands of years, but that, also, has not kept us from each other's throats.

Are we destined, as human beings, to live with no hope of finding how to do only good things for each other? Surely this is not the destiny of the human race, to always be looking over our shoulder lest someone is there to do us injury.

We've tried many different religions, and we still hate and kill each other, so we must raise the question if the answer is in religion. But, then we search and still cannot find the answer. Perhaps we need to reevaluate what we expect of religion. Do we expect it to give us a check-list of how to treat each other?

Perhaps we need to realize that a checklist of do's and don'ts is not enough to bring what we are looking for. Maybe we need to consider that things which come out of our minds will never be sufficient, and we need that which changes the way we look at each other. This would require a fundamental restructuring of the way we see each other. Perhaps we need to begin seeing that we all walk on the same level of value, and we need to work to make life better for each other. There can be no room for the desire to injure another person.

The only thing on the horizon is some kind of religion where we can treat each other as brothers. Fact is, this religion already exists, but we don't give it a chance because we choose to see each other as threats, those who would take from us what we have.

If we can ever get science and technology and the right religion together, we will be on the threshold of brotherhood. Can I tell you how to get there? No, I cannot. This is a personal journey each of us must make. But, I can say, if you ae seriously willing to look, you will eventually find.

CHAPTER 135

EVIL IN ITS PUREST FORM

What we are now seeing in the murders by ISIS is evil in its purist form. The life of a single human being is the most important thing in the world, and to initiate the end of that life is as bad as it gets. That is the message we hear when we get religion right. The problem with us is that we often get religion wrong.

Blaming the evil we do on God or Allah or any other divine being has been a favorite thing to do throughout history. It has been done in every religion as humans have sought excuses for the evil they do. People who do their evil have often been given a pass when they have claimed, "God told me to do it." If we, at one time, could see laid out all the dead who have been killed throughout history by people who justify their killings by pointing to God, we would be utterly shocked and amazed at what we would see.

We need to learn that God does not participate with us when we initiate harm to others, no matter how vociferous we might be or by what authority we might claim. Because human beings are slow learners, it has taken a long time for this message to sink in, and multitudes still don't understand. If we could ever get to the place where "we love others as we love ourselves," there would be an end to our senseless killing of each other.

We need to see that our cruelty to each other is nothing more than personal agenda that has gone wrong. It seems that we are almost always able to find a way for personal agenda to trump the good things religion requires of us. The question, "What is the best thing for me to do at this moment?" just about always gives way to, "What do I need to do to take advantage of this situation and elevate myself?"

Our belief systems, religious or otherwise, are what leads to our cruelty to each other. Unless we get these belief-systems straightened out, we will continue to add to the purest form of evil, which is in initiating the killing of each other.

If your belief system, call it religious or not, gives you permission to initiate harming others in any way, you need to get in touch with how valuable human life really is. The right religion will make that known to you because it places ultimate value on the life of a single human being.

CHAPTER 136

TRUE COLORS ALWAYS SHOW

It should come as no surprise that Obama has done everything he could to build up the Muslim world and tear down the United States. He told us in one of his books that, if there was ever war between the Muslim world and the U.S., he would fight with the Muslim world. He told us where his heart was, that is where his heart still is, and that is where it always will be. Too many Americans failed to pay attention to what he said, and opened the door for him to harm our great country, and this harm will continue so long as he is president.

His veto of the pipe line is a simple example of where his heart is. Vetoing the pipeline guarantees the continued flow of American money into the hands of the Muslim world, but the pipeline would create approximately 42,000 new jobs. Building it would help every American reduce their fuel expenses, thus keeping more of our money in our hands.

Rudolph Giuliani said it well when he said Obama does not love America. Obama will always feel this way, and his actions will continue to be in favor of the Muslim world. It is not within his power to love America. His schooling in the bad things Americans have done has blinded him to the many more good things we have done.

Many of Obama's actions have indeed hurt this country, and, so long as liberal democrats support him, so long will the quality of life in this country deteriorate for the majority of American citizens.

Only a small minority of Americans understood Obama's remarks about fighting with the Arabs. A large majority paid no attention to what he said, being mesmerized by his ability to read a good speech, never paying attention to the fact that he did not have the ability to make a speech without tele-prompters.

Regardless of the way a person presents himself/herself, we should always consider carefully the words that are spoken and written, because, regardless of the presentation, the true colors will always show.

CHAPTER 137

SAVAGES AMONG US

The cry of savages has been heard throughout history. Whether it be, "Allahu Akhbar," shouted by Muslims, "It is the will of God," shouted by Crusaders as they killed the enemy, "Urrah," shouted by Russian Soldiers as they charged German guns, "Banzai," shouted by Japanese in a last, desperate military charge, the goal has been the same: to kill as many of the enemy as possible.

Savages are now making themselves known in the Middle East as they destroy human life. The claim that they are doing this because of religion is a claim made by savages down through history. "It's not my fault. This is what God wants us to do," has been heard again and again.

Perhaps we need to be reminded that each of us has within the possibility of doing savage things if we fall under the sway of political or religious leaders who are bankrupt when it comes to knowledge of God. Each of us needs to be careful who it is we follow, for there are many who would control us and lead us to do savage things. Each of us should do our own thinking, but too often we follow those who wish to think for us. This is how, in the modern world with all its advancements, we can be drawn into savagery.

No religion or political position worth its salt encourages or engages in the destruction of human life except in one situation, and that is in defense. Good religion and good politics both do what it can to make the lives of others better. We were not made to kill each other, but that's what we do when we practice bad religion or bad politics.

We often couch our war-cries in religious trappings, thinking that so doing makes what we do okay. However, using religion in an attempt to justify our killings is nothing but evil on our part. Religion should bring out the best in us, and prompt us to do good things for other people, but that, too often, is not the case

It is all too easy becoming a part of the evil of killing others. The thrill of war beckons to us, and we join in this evil and kill as many as possible.

Initiating the death of anyone can always be considered evil in spite of what some politicians or religionists claim. No God worthy of worship would ask anyone to kill for him/her. To justify killings places one in extreme evil. No good political program will lead to the deaths of people.

The bottom line is: initiating the killing of other people cannot be a part of good religion or good politics. Good religion is always interested in doing good things for people. Good politics does the same.

CHAPTER 138

CHOOSING OTHER THAN THE CERTAIN MINIMUM

Being satisfied with less than the best is characteristic of too many people. There was the highly gifted ninth grade basketball player who had the gifts to be a huge star. But, he never became a star, never a starter, even in the twelfth grade, because he would not work hard developing his skills. He was satisfied with less than the best.

On the other hand, we have others like Michael Jordan, who was cut from his high school team. He did not accept the judgment of the coach, and chose to work hard in developing his skills, becoming, in the minds of many, the best basketball player of all time. Developing his skills brought both great wealth and fame.

Countless people with every skin color do not develop the vast potential latent within them. Sometimes this is because their circumstances negate the dreams of being successful. Sometimes people erect roadblocks and encourage them to follow the star of another person, forsaking their own dreams. The message, "You can't do that," often becomes a sound continually reverberating in their minds, and kills any enthusiasm for self-development they might have.

Perhaps the saddest of all are those who knowingly abandon any efforts to develop what is on the inside of them, and accept the minimum life has to offer. It has been said that 25 percent of gifted young people drop out of high school. This is not only personal failure on their part, but failure of adults to help them understand and appreciate the opportunities before them.

Our federal government is one of the worst problems we have in this regard. The strong message, "If you don't do anything to get an education or training, the government will send you a monthly check so you can get along." For the person who has difficulty dreaming his/her own dreams, this is one of the most devastating messages they can receive because it gives them an "out" when it comes to doing something positive with their lives.

We need to teach all our citizens that, unless you are mentally or physically handicapped in some way, you can make something worthwhile of yourselves, accomplishing things that only you can accomplish. It is true that there are no two people in the world exactly alike, and this uniqueness offers each person the opportunity to do something no-once else can do.

Each of us needs to find our niche in life, and do what only we can do. That is the only way for us to free ourselves from being satisfied with the minimum, and move on to the success awaiting each of us.

CHAPTER 139

WHENCE ALL THIS CRIME?

S he came into the Laundromat with a pistol on her hip. This
was during the week of 01/ 05/15 in a small town in North
Georgia. In over 20 years, the owner had never seen anyone
come into his place of business with any kind of weapon. He
asked her why she was wearing a pistol, and she said, "I've never
done this before, but the crime has gotten so bad, I feel I need
to carry protection." This scene is being repeated in many places
in our country as lawlessness is on the increase. It is far different
from what it was in years past when walking the streets, even in
Atlanta, presented no problem.

It is long past the time for us to ask what has happened to
bring such deterioration to a nation where most people once
chose to obey the law? If we do not address this question, we
stand a good chance of sinking into a nation of citizens afraid to
be anywhere without guns to protect ourselves.

Dr. Clay Christensen, professor at Harvard Business School,
asked a Marxist Chinese student completing his degree, "Have
you learned anything that was surprising about democracy?"

The young man said, "I had no idea how critical religion is to
democracy. One hundred to one hundred fifty years ago, people

attended church and synagogue where rules were taught by people they respected. They learned that they were accountable not only to society, but to God, and they voluntarily chose to follow the law."

Responding to the young man's comments, Dr. Christensen said, "If you take away religion, you can't hire enough police."

Many people today scoff at religion, as did the American official following the Iranian revolution, "Whoever took religion seriously?" The increase in lawlessness in this country fairly well tracks the decline in religious practice. At times religion is far less than it should and could be, but religion has made us a much better nation than we would be without its challenges to be good people.

Where can we find an institution that will teach people to respect each other and voluntarily obey the law? There seems be nothing other than religion that will do this.

CHAPTER 140

THE INQUISITION: WITH US AGAIN?

Today we don't burn them at the stake for believing the wrong things, as the Italian, Giordano Bruno, was burned for believing the wrong things. He was a Dominican friar, philosopher, mathematician, poet, and astrologer.

Bruno was tried for heresy in 1600 C.E., found guilty and burned at the stake for not believing what he was supposed to believe.

In our modern world, we do not burn people at the stake. We just attack and fire them for believing the wrong things. This current effort goes under the name of "political correctness," but it shares the same source, which is none other than mind control. It says, "You believe what I want you to believe or you are history."

This is the current mantra emanating from Washington, and it has captured the minds of people all over the country. Unfortunately, the mayor of a city in Georgia has fallen in lockstep with those who cannot give other people freedom to think and believe as they choose. He fired an employee who wrote a book that contained thoughts the mayor disapproved.

The trial and burning of Giordano Bruno is considered a landmark case in the history of free thought. We would do well to understand that denying others freedom to think and believe what they choose to think and believe will always limit human progress.

It is only as we accept each other in our differences, respecting the freedom each has to do his/her own thinking that we can build the brotherhood we so much need in our fragmented world. The current popularity of terrorist organizations and their destruction and killings is a strong commentary on the results of wanting to control what other people think and believe.

We do not need a return to the kind of group-think that led to so much separation, misery and death as seen in the Inquisitions. Human progress does not come by denying anyone the right to think and believe.

Censorship was supposed to have ended a long time ago, but it has been edging its way back into our lives with the new name "political correctness." They used to burn books. Will we now see the mayor attempt to burn this former employee's book? If he is consistent, he will do just that, and, further, he will advise all employees of the city where he is mayor, if they plan to write a book, they will need his approval.

SECTION FIVE

Maintaining Awareness

CHAPTER 141

BRAINS ARE FOR THINKING

The reason our Maker gave us brains was for thinking, but many people would rather not begin the process. We would, rather, turn our thinking over to others.

Letting others do our job of thinking and deciding what life will be like is one of the most devastating things that has happened throughout history. One of the best illustrations of this was the Second World War and all its atrocities.

It is inconceivable to a thinking person that millions of people could fall prey to the words and leadership of Hitler, but they did. He led the Germans in attempting to purify the Arian race by sending Jews into the gas chambers and furnaces, and millions of lives were destroyed. Hitler did this through the words he spoke, and people learned to shout, "Heil Hitler." It was not appropriate to think for oneself. Doing so brought the assassination of Dietrich Bonhoeffer, and many others. Sixty million deaths happened during WWII, and it was all because of the desire of one man to build his Third Reich and control the world.

People who allow others to think for them are easily led down paths of destruction. Millions of unthinking people throughout history have been taken down paths that look rosy, but which turn out to be filled with all kinds of pitfalls and death. Many people have met their demise in horrendous acts of savagery and death because they have allowed someone to think for them.

The framers of our Constitution were good students of history, being fully aware that giving unlimited power to an individual with a golden tongue eventually leads to abuse of power and sometimes destruction, i.e. Hitler and many other leaders. For this reason, they included in our founding document three separate branches of government, clearly stating that all three branches would serve the citizens of our country, "We The People." This was for the purpose of protecting citizens from those who would abuse power and turn our country into whatever they might desire.

Until the last several years, politicians in Washington, sometimes against their wishes, have honored the guidelines of the Constitution, and this is what has propelled our nation to being the greatest nation in the history of the world. We have had significant struggles, but we have made progress in moving toward freedom for all. Now, however, we have experienced what happens when one or more branches of our government disregards constitutional guidelines, and the result is that many Americans now experience life that is not free at all. The executive branch has walked away from our governing document, part of Congress has supported this, and control of much of our lives is being taken away from citizens as one man seeks to impose his thinking on all of us.

We should all be reminded that history powerfully teaches that allowing someone to do our thinking always ends when this person's dreams come tumbling down (they always come tumbling down), and the rest of us are left picking up the pieces.

Those who wrote our Constitution understood that a person wanting unlimited power will always abuse that power. Honoring and following The Constitution of the United States is necessary if we are to remain free and reclaim our place as the greatest nation ever to exist on the face of the earth. If we will once again use our brains and do our own thinking, we will reclaim our freedoms and our greatness. We will not allow one person or small group of people to take our freedoms from us.

CHAPTER 142

SOME THINGS NEED TO BE SAID

In light of many of the things that have been happening in our country over the last several years, it is time for some things to be said.

1. White people cannot do for black people what black people need done. Rising to the level of equality is not something that can be handed to people. It is something that comes from personal effort, perhaps best seen in sports. No-one qualifies to play in the NFL or the NBA without dedication and effort. So it is in everyday life: no-one qualifies to walk with successful people who are not successful themselves; equality must be earned.

2. Elevating common criminals to a place of honor is never a sign of progress. Honoring, celebrating and extolling criminals, which blacks do, makes the black community appear to be inferior.

3. Living off the labor of others when you are physically and mentally able to take care of yourself is wrong. It was wrong during slavery, and it is wrong today.

4. Giving money to poor white and black people has not raised them and does not raise them. After billions of

dollars being given through the Great Society programs, many blacks and whites still have not learned to be self-sufficient.

5. Most white people would like to walk side by side as equals with black people. This might come as a surprise to some, but life would be easier and better for everyone if this was true. Whites already enjoy rubbing elbows with many blacks who have earned their status through education and/or training.

6. Liberal politicians and race-baiters have probably harmed blacks and poor white people more than they have helped them. By encouraging dependence on government handouts rather than on what they can do for themselves through study and/or training, the result has been burial of vast intellectual possibilities by many of our citizens.

7. Police are not the enemies of people, black or white. They show up where most of the crime is taking place. If blacks will quit committing crimes, which includes killing each other, the police will not be in your neighborhoods.

8. Celebrating ignorance never achieves anything worthwhile. Multiple numbers of black students have said that, when they make good grades, other blacks deride and make fun of them. This is a sign that ignorance is preferred over education. Such things as this will keep blacks in the lower classes. Making fun of people who achieve has got to stop.

Blacks have excelled in sports because they have done what was necessary to be good athletes: they have practiced. In most cases, they could, also, excel in academics, but have not yet decided to study and prepare. Once they do, they will walk side-by-side with whites and other groups who are now ahead of them. Being unprepared never gets anyone a job.

One thing everyone needs to realize: every life is important, and degrading or destroying any life diminishes life for the rest of us. No-one in his right mind enjoys seeing life become tenuous for anyone. None of us should ever place ourselves in situations where life may end, and that is what many do.

When people do the wrong things, they lose protection that is afforded those who do not break the law. Don't do illegal things because that is going to bring the cops, and that's as things ought to be.

Most cops are good people trying to do a good job. They do not wish to participate in the death of anyone.

The check from Washington does not bring equality. In fact, it does just the opposite. A person receiving tax money taken from those who earn it can never expect to be equal to the ones who earn it. You will never be considered an equal until you earn your own way.

Achieving success has been available to everyone in this country over the past 60 years. Some people claim the fallout from slavery is holding them back, saying, "I can't be successful because I am a victim of slavery." This is not so because millions of blacks have learned to turn from the past and face the future. They have learned that doing things because of one's past is a formula for defeat. Facing and dealing with today and tomorrow for what they are will always be the prerequisite for success.

Education and/or training are at the heart of success. This is the same for both blacks and whites, and brown and red and yellow, and all others. If you have not gotten education and training, you have no right to expect to make big dollars. Big dollars are reserved for those who have paid the price of preparation and hard work.

As a white man, I live in a community that has now become over 50 percent black. Our crime rate has soared, and we whites have had nothing to do with this. Two houses across the street are examples of the problems blacks face. In one house, black people are a credit to the community. Both adults have a college education, and one is now in graduate school. Both own their own businesses and do well. One child is completing an engineering degree, and the other is planning college and graduate school. They keep their property well. They are fully equal with the best in the community.

The other house has seen people come and go. Individuals in one family who lived there were drug dealers. Once there was a total of nine drug agents with drawn pistols surrounding the house. In the last eight years, the people living there have cut the grass about three times. The occupants of that house have never been equal to the good people living next door or to anyone else in the neighborhood. Education and/or training have been available to them, but they chose not to get it. Their situation has nothing to do with the aftermath of slavery. It has to do with the choices they have made.

One of the great needs in our country is good families. Recently this writer was in a continuing education course where he met a black lady who had grown up in The Bluff, a now boarded-up, crime-filled community in northwest Atlanta. People have been surprised when she has told them she has a PhD and drives a Mercedes. She came from a good family and made good decisions. The road to success she has traveled was available to all who grew up in The Bluff, but poor quality families and wrong decisions were made by most. Neither the fact that her ancestors were slaves nor her growing up in a poverty area kept her from succeeding. She left the past behind and moved forward with success, something everyone born with a good mind could have done.

Yes, it is time for black people to leave their horrible past behind. Continuing to gaze on the evils of slavery days will never prepare one for the future, and will never bring the equality so many are seeking. Earning your way to equality is something you must do; whites cannot give you equality. This author is white, and it was my education and training that prepared me for the jobs I had, and, without this, the jobs I had would never have been available to me. My best friend first through third grade quit high school, and none of what I have accomplished and enjoyed has been available to him.

For those who are still being encouraged by politicians and race-baiters, better known as agents of hatred, to keep your attention on the evils and shortcomings of the past, it is time to turn and face the future, developing and using the minds with which you were born. Base your life on who you are and what your developed talents can bring. You will be surprised at the good life awaiting you. You are too important, and what you can give the world is too important, for you to keep gazing into the past.

It would really be nice if we could all be equals, but everyone will have to do their part for that to happen.

CHAPTER 143

IT IS TIME

It is time for the American people to "catch on" to what the democrats have been doing for decades.

In the 1960's they developed a program that has resulted in millions of fully capable people removing themselves from the labor market. "Why work when I can get a check from Washington?" is a statement often made by welfare recipients. In my own state at the present time, we cannot find enough skilled laborers to fill the jobs available. All the while, countless numbers sit at home awaiting the gift from Washington, being convinced their talents and abilities are not needed.

Welfare programs have led to a big waste of talent. Although a small percentage of people lack the mental ability to help themselves, and we should help them, there are millions who, because of the availability of welfare money, have done nothing to educate and/or train themselves for worthwhile jobs. The biggest thing these programs have done is produce votes for democrats. Poor people don't realize it, but the welfare system boils down to a vote-buying program for democrats.

At the center of the stage as this is written, is the CIA program of protecting America. Democrats have produced a stilted record of CIA efforts to protect this country, and it has done more harm than good. They think this will embarrass the republicans, but the biggest thing it does is put the lives of Americans in danger in many places around the world, and will probably lead to the murders of some good people. Reports are coming in that ISIS is already using this democratic review to recruit people who will commit themselves to fighting the United States.

Six years ago, the work of democrats resulted in the election of Obama, a man who swore to defend and uphold the Constitution, but then immediately began to attack and seek to destroy it. This president has been fully supported by the democrats: he could not have done what he has done to tear down this country without their support.

The racial divide in this country has been made worse by Obama, and the democrats have remained silent while he has done this. Exacerbating the problems between blacks and whites should have brought howls from the democrats, but they remained silent, and things have grown progressively worse.

Putting all these things, and many more, together will bring one to the conclusion that democrats are not interested in building a better Constitutional Republic. Rather, they wish to tear down what we have had and replace it with something far inferior, socialism/communism.

Having a Constitutional Republic with its freedoms is what has made us the greatest nation in the history of the world. It has given people an opportunity to get education and/or training, roll their sleeves up and go to work.

No nation will ever be perfect because all are made up of imperfect people. Our nation, with all its opportunities, best gives people a chance to do good things with their lives, succeeding if they are willing to pay the price of success.

It is time for the American people to "catch on" to what the democrats have been doing to degrade and destroy our Constitutional Republic. Shame on the democrats!!!

CHAPTER 144

KEEPING AMERICA SAFE

Keeping America or any nation safe is not work for Sunday School teachers. All nations seeking protection from those who wish to destroy them do things that would make the average citizen cringe. That's the way life is, and always will be so long as people are people. Some people are good and would not hurt a fly, but others would hurt or kill simply because they don't like you.

To those who are releasing information re our system of protecting the people of this country, you have joined in the effort to discredit and tear down our country, something that is a hallmark of our present administration in Washington. If we cannot use whatever measure is necessary to extract information from those who planned the 9/11 attack, then we would be open to this happening again and again.

To those who feel it is their duty to reveal how we protect ourselves, you are doing more harm than good. Chances are you have not uttered a peep about the beheadings done by ISIS and other people who are mistaken about their purpose in life. This reveals you as a hypocrite.

When people communicate that they plan to kill you and take over your country because you do not worship their version of God, you should pay attention if you want to survive. These people are serious, never playing by the rules, and getting approval for protection programs to be used against them is totally out of the question. Being courteous and kind to those who work hard to annihilate you is a certain way to bring on annihilation.

It would be good if everyone was nice and respectful of each other. This always is a better way to live, but this has never existed and will never exist in a world made up of human beings. We must deal, not with pie in the sky bye and bye, but with reality, which is far from what we desire.

By releasing the report on how we extract information from those who would destroy us, the democrats are placing the lives of Americans around the world in jeopardy, and are identifying themselves with those who wish to tear down our country. This is not acceptable for the American people. Reports are already coming in that ISIS is using this report by democrats to recruit more people to fight the United States.

It has been said that a strong country can only be defeated from within. This effort to make America look bad is but another step in destroying our nation. Releasing this report is one more step in bringing down the destruction of the greatest nation in the history of the world. The American people deserve better than this from the elected officials in Washington.

CHAPTER 145

THE LAW AND ME

Most of the work I do is with people who have broken the law or appear to have broken the law. With a few people, it seems law enforcement personnel (the police) have overreacted, but this seems always to be in a situation where clarity is well-nigh impossible. There are bad cops, but the vast majority are good at what they do. But, one thing is certain: I will never be arrested so long as I observe the laws of our land.

CHAPTER 146

A LESSON TO LEARN

Quite often we are given a lesson to learn, but we do not pay attention.

We see the results of failed parenting, but our minds go elsewhere. We don't like to look at what we see, so we look elsewhere, and our lives get entangled in protecting us from the obvious.

The Michael Brown case is a sad reminder that we fail in our most important of jobs, rearing the children our Maker gives us.

Reports are that Michael's mom was not married to his dad. She was living with a boyfriend, but they did not allow Michael to live with them. He was living with his grandmother.

It has been reported that, after Michael was dead, his grandmother sold T-shirts to memorialize him. Michael's mother thought she deserved the money, and she and her boyfriend had friends attack and beat up the grandmother.

This is a story of Michael, who apparently never had a chance to learn about love, a story repeated almost everywhere in our society as people give birth to children they do not want and do not love. These are the children with the absence of any chance to develop stability in their lives, and we see them struggling to make sense of life, often failing wherever they go, ending up in jail or prison or dead.

If we continue to turn our eyes from the obvious lessons of life, we will continue to see and listen to TV reports of failure and tragedy. Our children are worth more than this. We, too, are worth more than this, and we have the power to do something about it. Our children cannot make us give them good parenting. We adults are the only ones with the power to become responsible enough to love and care for our children, but we must keep our eyes on the problem, facing it head-on and doing something about it.

We can learn the lessons of good parenting. But, will we???

CHAPTER 147

LOOKING SUCCESS STRAIGHT IN THE EYE

White people cannot do for black people what black people need done. Politicians and race-baiters have trapped black people into believing their lives can be made right by extracting money from whites and given to them. But, it has not worked, and never will. The work black people must do does not involve the exchange of money from whites to black. In fact, money has nothing to do with it.

The work black people must do is something only they can do. Yes, slavery was a terrible sin committed against their ancestors, but white people alive today have never owned slaves, so railing against them brings no benefits. Demonstrating against them or destroying their property does nothing to get even with slave owners. Such things only compound the problems blacks face.

Perhaps it would be good if we all could be reminded of what brings a good, satisfying life. Ecclesiastes 3:13 (NIV) says it well: "...that everyone may eat and drink, and find satisfaction in all his toil – this is the gift of God." Toils for himself/herself is what brings a good life. This is where black people need to do their own work; white people cannot do this for them.

The existence of slavery or the Jim Crowe laws has nothing to do with the latent potential deep within the brain of each black child at birth, a potential, if developed, could match the brains in other races. Countless are the numbers of black people who have chosen to not let the past limit their futures. They shucked the limitations of their past, did not listen to the politicians and race-baiters, and moved into the future as equals with whites and others.

Living off another man's dollar never brings a good life. Those who have helped black people wallow in the tragedy of slavery and its results have committed a crime against them because it has helped them avoid the real work they need to do.

Where have the black preachers been? Aren't they supposed to help their people through the wilderness? They have, however, been silent regarding what blacks must do to lift themselves, many times helping them stay in a state of misery.

MLK Jr. had a dream in which he said, "I have a dream that one day this nation will rise up and live out the true meaning of its creed: 'We hold these truths to be self-evident, that all men are created equal." The race-baiters and liberal politicians have robbed millions of blacks by couching their language in such a way that millions of blacks have believed them and stepped right into the trap that was laid for them.

Black people can be successful when they turn a deaf ear to the race-baiters and listen to the voice within that says, "I am just as capable of preparing myself as any other person on the face of the earth. Success awaits the one who is willing to shut out the voice of the race-baiters and develops the talents within.

CHAPTER 148

LEAVING THE PAST BEHIND

The struggle to leave the past behind is often seen in the therapist's office. It can be one of the most difficult things a person can do in finding a new way to live.

Too often our lives are weighed down as we drag the deficits of the past with us. The young man said, "Can't you see that I am stupid and can't do anything right?" He was dealing with being fired job after job. He was asked, "Where did you hear that you are stupid?" His reply was, "My dad used to tell me that all the time when I was growing up." Whenever this young man would get a job, his father's words were like a tape playing in his mind, and he would screw up because he believed he was stupid. He had to choose to let go of the past before he could concentrate on his strengths and become a success.

Involved in letting go of the burden his dad had placed on him was the act of forgiveness. He could not go back and face his deceased dad. The past was the past, and his past could not be fixed. His job was to fix himself, and only he could do it by choosing to turn from the past and move into the future on the strengths he had. He had covered-up those strengths because of allowing his dad's deficits to control him.

Today in the United States we live in an environment where the deficits (sins) of the past claim the attention of our entire nation as we witness the events in Ferguson, Mo., Baltimore, Md., and other places. A good future for millions of people is being lost because the tapes of past injustices are playing loud and clear, leaving little to no time for consideration of the strengths of today and moving successfully into the future.

It's like getting into a car and trying to back down the street looking only at where you have come from. Doing such is a certain way to have a wreck. The only way to drive down the street is to look where you are going and use the power of the automobile and your driving abilities to get to where you wish to go. So it is with life today. We must look to the present and the future. That is the only way for us to travel and get to where our strengths will take us. We must learn the lessons of the past, which many times are bad, but we must be aware that we cannot change the past. It is what it is and will always be what it is. The only thing we can change is the future, and that is possible for all of us.

Just as the therapist could not free the young man's past because that was something only the young man could do, so no-one other than those who now hang on to past evils can free themselves from that evil, whether it be slavery or something else. The liberals and race-baiters who continue to direct attention to what the past has done to people must cease helping them wallow in their misery proclaiming, "Woe is me." Telling them over and over again that they are damaged material and cannot do well because of the past, is a certain way to help them remain in the past

Leaving the past behind would free millions of people to face the future on the basis of the many talents and abilities that lie deep inside, strengths now hidden by attention to the past. Many people like Thomas Sowell, Dr. Ben Carson, Kenneth Frazier, Ursula Burns, Robert L. Johnson, Kenneth Chenault, Herman

Russell, Et. Al, chose to leave the past behind and do something with their inner talents. They left the limitations of the past and have been extremely successful.

Those who still wallow in the past, letting it determine their future, can choose to let it go by turning and facing the future on the basis of who they are and what undeveloped talents now lie hidden under attention to the past. No-one can make that choice for them. It is something they have to do for themselves, and, if they will do it, their lives will immediately get better. No-one can make the past what we might wish it to have been, and the only way it can be left behind is to exercise the act of forgiveness, which frees an individual to move into the future unencumbered by sins of the past.

Yes, in order to have a good future we must face it for what it is, learning the lessons of the past, but, moving into the future on the basis of who we are. Concentration on the past will never give us a successful present or future.

CHAPTER 149

ON THE SAME ROAD...AGAIN

Must we travel down this road again? Mankind has traveled down it often, too often. It is a road that takes us to places we do not need to go, often ending in disaster.

Napoleon had a dream of ruling Europe and Russia. Alexander the Great fought his way into control of vast lands. Last century, the name given it was "The Third Reich." Now the United Nations and some of our political leaders are calling it "The New World Order," and are dreaming of it becoming a reality.

There is little difference in this "New World Order" compared to what has gone before. The biggest difference is the means by which it is to be achieved. The end result, however, is basically the same. It is a system of world domination by a small group of people with a supreme ruler.

Achieving this New World Order would require the elimination of freedom for all people in all nations. What is acceptable would be that which is determined by this supreme leader in council with his/her advisers.

The thirst for freedom lurking within the hearts of people will never allow this to happen. Resistance to a world order will happen in many places, and, pushing to implement it, whether calling it "Theory 21" or some other fancy name, will end in disaster.

The feeling of omnipotence aroused by the desire to control others is hard to resist by those who do not understand what life is all about. The desire to be masters of others, central in all who wish to control the world, will always end in disaster because no-one is wise enough to know what is best for everyone. We have already had too many misguided men who mistakenly believe they are wise enough to determine what life should be for others, and we do not need anyone else thinking they qualify for the job.

The U.N. and our political leaders now working for this New World Order lack understanding of the disaster toward which they are nudging us, and, because of this, do not need to be where they are.

CHAPTER 150

POLITICAL CORRECTNESS OR POLITICAL CONTROL

Many people are not aware of the reality that "political correctness" is one of the major steps toward political control. It is nothing less than getting people to think the thoughts political leaders want them to think.

When someone tells you what you can and cannot think, and you accept this, you have become a pawn in their hands. They can get you to do anything they want you to do.

Although there have always been efforts on the part of politicians to get people to think what they deem is acceptable, this effort has been ratcheted up in the past several years. This has happened because people have abandoned their responsibility to think for themselves. In so doing, they have become pawns in the hands of those who think they know what is best for everyone.

The end result of political correctness is always subjugation of life to the whims of those who wish to pull our chains whenever they wish. History has shown this to be true in many places. The hara-kiri of soldiers and the kamikaze pilots of World War II resulted from a long history of mind control which had been engrained in Japanese life so long that there was no question about the practices. Those who died in these ways had no ability to question if killing themselves was right or wrong.

To lose the ability to think for oneself is simply placing one's life in the hands of people who do not respect the fundamental dignity that belongs to all people. God gave us our minds to use personally, not to place in the hands of those who believe they have been appointed to determine what is best for others.

CHAPTER 151

LEARNING ABOUT THE WORK OF A CHIEF EXECUTIVE OFFICER

Perhaps it is time, during this political season, to take a look at the work of a Chief Executive Officer (CEO). This is currently a problem in Washington, and, if we don't correct what we voters have done, it will get worse.

A CEO has the responsibility of carrying out the wishes of the governing body (board). If he/she does things the board does not desire, he/she should be fired. This needs to be applied in politics as well as in business. A CEO does not have the freedom to add expensive programs without the approval of the board. A CEO does not have the freedom to close a business. Only the board can do that. A CEO does not have the authority to move a company to another state or to a foreign country. Only the board can make that decision. A CEO cannot do things based on a personal agenda that ignores the wishes of the board.

When a CEO is hired, he/she inherits the financial structure of the company, which includes what everyone is paid. Changing that pay structure or other obligations may be difficult because of the effect it will have on the bottom line (profit or loss). If he/she changes things without board approval, he/she should be fired.

According to the Constitution of the United States, the citizens (voters) in this country are supposed to be the governing body of our government. We currently have quite a few politicians in Washington, both in the Oval Office and in Congress, who have thumbed their noses at their governing body, and have done things a majority of board members do not want.

It is time for the governing body to remove those individuals who have done things contrary to the governance outlined in the Constitution, and replace them with people who understand what constitutional government is all about. The coming election in November presents us voters with an opportunity to begin our needed work.

CEO of four hospitals

CHAPTER 152

ENJOYING "WOE IS ME"

Crying "Woe, is me," seems to be one of the favorite pastimes of some people. There is an appropriate time to cry, "Woe is me," but it is often cried when we have failed to build good lives, and wish to gain the sympathies and/or support of other people.

A lot of people who have not built the life they desire sure do enjoy being able to say, "Woe is me." They are not hard to see because they are just about everywhere, and take pleasure in gathering with others of like mind every time there is a chance to cry, "Woe is me."

We are seeing a lot of this in the crowds that are gathering to protest Trump's election. We are seeing it in the "crying rooms" being provided on college for those who are distraught over Trump's election. Gathering to cry "Woe is me" is nothing short of gross immaturity, and has no place in the way the United States is structured.

What people do is an expression of what they are on the inside. If we are good people on the inside, we will show we are by the good things we do. If we are bad on the inside, we will do bad things. What we do is an exterior expression of what we are is on the inside.

Too many of us are attracted to the bad things which go on around us without giving thought as to whether these things are either good or bad. That, in and of itself, denotes a lack of stability on the inside.

CHAPTER 153

MY THIN SKIN

Why is my skin so thin? I wish it were not so, but it is. When others say and do things I do not like, I get all upset. They offend me, and my life becomes miserable. Of course, that's also true with most of my neighbors.

Must I permit this? Am I to go through life wearing my feelings of hurt on my sleeve when I can protest and gain support from other people in shutting them up? We'll make them feel bad for making me feel bad, and we'll control what comes out of their mouths. It seems there is a lot of support for me wanting to shut them up.

Now wait a minute. I wonder about this. Is the control of my feelings in the hands of other people or are my feelings something I can control and am supposed to control?

Is it possible my maker intended that my life be made miserable by how the crowd reacts or did he give me the chance to determine my own feelings of well-being? Are my feelings supposed to reside entirely within my own ego, entirely within my own control?

I have found my life to be miserable when others lead me where they are going. I find myself tied up and consumed in their journey, and lose sight of my own destination. I really don't have time to walk down their road. It is only my road that I must learn to travel if I am to reach the goal for which I was intended.

Yes, I must be mindful of and respectful of the pain of others, but I must not make their pain my own pain. No, my ego is in my hands, and my joy comes from my successes, not the consequences of what others do or feel. Others will drag me down. I am the only one who can and will propel me forward.

It has finally dawned on me that my happiness is not dependent on what other people think, say or do. My happiness and well-being come only from what is on the inside of me, and I can control that. If other people choose to be offended by the words or actions of others, that's their problem, not mine, and that's okay. I will own my thoughts and feelings, not theirs.

CHAPTER 154

SUCCESS: AVAILABLE TO EVERYONE

B eing successful is no accident. Being unsuccessful is no accident. It takes planning to be either successful or unsuccessful. This has been true for people born in the U. S. for the past 60 years. What is required for being successful or unsuccessful is within the reach of everyone regardless of their birth circumstances.

Being successful involves a plan that includes preparation through education and/or training. Being unsuccessful also involves a plan, but one that usually does not include education and/or training.

It is easy to spot those who are planning to be successful. They are the ones who take advantage of every opportunity presented them to gain knowledge and/or to acquire skills through training. It is also easy to spot those who are planning to fail. As an example, in the transitional community in which I now live, they are the ones who walk the streets after school, who frequent as many clubs as they can, and party at the drop of a hat. They spend their spare time interacting with their friends rather than interacting with books and skills-building activities. And then you can see them in line demanding that the minimum wage be raised. Had they only taken advantage of and developed the potential they had within, there would be no reason to protest their low wages because they would have jobs paying more than low wages.

Some people might protest and say their community and family placed no emphasis on education and training. That may be true, but we are all ultimately responsible for the decisions we make, and, we must remember that untold numbers of people have risen from the worst of circumstances to become highly successful, building amazing reputations and amassing great wealth.

We generally do what we plan to do. If our plan includes accomplishments, we will do those things which bring accomplishments. If our plan has nothing in it but having a good time, that is about all we will accomplish, and we will reside in the kind of neighborhood where others of like mind reside.

We need to understand that all of us who were born with good minds, which is the overwhelming majority of us, and have the potential to be successful – but only if we develop what is on the inside of us. Each of us is a wonderful work of art, and, if we will but recognize this and begin developing what we have, we will be able to paint a life of exquisite beauty.

CHAPTER 155

AMERICAN CITIZENS: "REDUCE THE SIZE OF GOVERNMENT"

The politicians in Washington are supposed to work for the American people, just like the Chief Executive Officer (CEO) of a company is supposed to work for his/her governing board. We, the citizens, are the governing board of those we elect and send to Washington to serve us, but the politicians have gotten it all wrong. They should not do anything we, the "board," do not want them to do.

A CEO does not decide what new programs to begin or the programs to discontinue. That decision is made by the governing body, which instructs him/her to do what they desire. If a program is added or deleted, the governing body is the one behind that decision. On this basis, far too many programs have been added by politicians without American citizens wanting them added. This has resulted in the addition of programs with debt that is impossible to pay.

It is past time to cut programs not wanted by the American people, and we should elect politicians only if they will commit to reducing or eliminating programs and expenses. They have refused to do this in the past, and we should remember this when we step into the voting booth.

Now, the question becomes, "Who will do this, and are there people with some experience in reducing or ending programs?" That is something we voters must consider or the out-of-control spending in Washington will continue. We must not only write and talk about this, but we must act on it. Failure to do so will be even more catastrophic than what we face at the present time.

The questions we must ask are: "Who will commit to do this?," and, "Are there people with experience in doing this?" If there are some running for office, we must make sure they go to Washington with a mandate to cut, and, because of what the liberal group in Washington has already done, they must cut severely.

It seems the democrats have been making as many Americans dependent on government as they possibly can. Once a person becomes dependent, freedom to choose is eliminated, replaced by a system that leads to people being told what to do. Freedom becomes a thing of the past, which is one of the goals of socialism.

The only way for citizens to reduce the size of government is to elect people who will do this.

CHAPTER 156

WHY WE DO THE THINGS WE DO

People always have a way of showing what they are on the inside by the things they do. The person who is a good person will be a good person every day, occasionally making mistakes simply from being a human being. The person who is a bad person may look like a good person for a while, but the time will come when his true colors show.

Many people, ministers, politicians, news reporters, policemen, socialists, liberals, conservatives, husband, wives, kids, etc., try to explain why people do certain things. Most of the reasons given fit into the category of "It's not my fault." We are good at fleeing responsibility. This has been going on since the beginning of recorded history, and probably before.

It's tough looking ourselves in the mirror and seeing the culprit for the wrongs we do, but the truth is that we do whatever we do simply because of what is on the inside of us, not what is on the outside. The golfer who puts down the wrong number on his scorecard does so, not because he has seen other people do it, but because he is a cheat. Such an action comes from the inside.

The man who enters a store with a gun and robs it is a thief, not because he is hungry. If he then kills anyone, he is a killer, not because he has lived in the ghetto, but because he makes a choice.

The man who blames his drinking on his drinking buddies, "They don't want me with them unless I am drinking," is trying to escape the reality that he puts the bottle to his mouth and drinks; they did not pour it down him. He chose to drink the alcohol and got the DUI. He may wish to blame it on his friends, but he made the choice to swallow it.

The rioters in Ferguson rioted because they are rioters. Those who looted did so, not because of anything anybody else did, but because they are thieves. There were thousands who could have jumped in and smashed the windows and taken what was on the inside, but they did not because they are not thieves.

Yes, we do the things we do, not because of others, but because of who we are.

CHAPTER 157

WHEN MY NEIGHBOR THROWS ROCKS

When my neighbor throws rocks at me and my family, what am I supposed to do? Nothing? And, when he does it again, should I still do nothing? What then if he injures one of my family, and later he throws a big rock and kills one of my family members?

When I turn to my other neighbors for help, rather than helping, they turn their backs. No-one to help there. Then the local police won't help me either, and I find the entire community is not bothered by my neighbor's rock throwing. In fact, some of them have publicly stated they wish for me and my family to be dead. Thus, I realize there is no-one to help me but me.

So, with silence from many directions communicating approval of the rock-throwing, I decide the protection of my family is in my hands, and I take the needed action. But, guess what. Everybody around me, even the police, say I am doing the wrong thing because the action I take hurts some of my neighbor's family, and even kills. They castigate me for having the courage to do what has to be done. They label me a bad guy, but say nothing about my neighbor doing bad things to me. He was totally free to keep throwing rocks until I tried to protect my family, and then everybody jumped in and said I should never have done what I did.

Am I supposed to allow my family to be hurt and destroyed by people who have sworn to kill us?

This is the position Israel's neighbors, along with the encouragement of many in the Arab world, and the silence of the rest of the world, have put them.

The Holocaust of last century came from the same evil mindset, resulting in the deaths of six million Jews, and this has now been labeled one of the greatest crimes in history. What Hamas and others in the Middle East wish to do to Israel is just as wrong and as evil as was the Holocaust under Hitler.

The international community, through the U.N., has been a failure when it comes to fairness to Israel. It has done little to nothing to stop Hamas from hurling death at Israel, but then has jumped on Israel when they go it alone in trying to protect themselves.

If we do not straighten out our sense of the value of each and every human being, Jew, Arab, and everyone else, we will continue hurling the instruments of death at those who do not please us.

CHAPTER 158

HATE: ON THE RISE, AGAIN

Once the poisoning starts, where does it end? When it does start, it travels along like a tsunami, engulfing the bad people in its path, but, also, many good people.

Must we go through what the people of last century went through with disaster upon disaster before it subsided? The world suffered and cried deeply as the evil of the 1930's and 1940's consumed it. The hate of one man swept up a good nation, and led to the death of six million Jews and 55 million others around the world.

Today the poison of hate is at the heart of the conflict in the Gaza strip, with Hamas and others in the Arab world having made it quite clear they wish to eliminate all Jewish people. And now, many groups have identified Christians as deserving of death, and some are already being eliminated. Racial and religious hatred is the motivating force behind the shedding of much blood and the snuffing out of lives.

Man's inhumanity to man is being loosed again. It is being taken up by those who do not understand the purpose of life. The cry, "Death to those we don't like," seems to be winning out over, "You shall love your neighbor as you love yourself."

Those with their feet in sand easily respond to the purveyors of death because the foundation of their lives is not strong enough to withstand the onslaught of hate. They have no appreciation for the dignity and worth of each living soul. "You must conform to what I want or you will die," is easier for them to respond to than "giving a piece of bread to the hungry" or "a cup of cold water to the thirsty." They know how to respond to the human emotion of hate, but responding in love is an unknown to them. We all know instinctively how to hate, but love often eludes us. Hate can turn good people into beasts with ravenous appetites for blood.

Will the good people now in the world stand up and oppose this evil? When good people remain silent, it is only a matter of time until calamity visits us. And, when leaders do not condemn the purveyors of hate, but, on the contrary, help bring division, those with feet on shaky ground are easily led by the ones who make the most noise. It happened in Germany during the last century as good people were mesmerized by the one they thought was their savior. Those who now shout, "Kill the Jews and the Christians," are attracting people who have no concept of what the word 'love' means. Is there anyone who will rise up and get people's attention, helping them see that disaster is always the fruit of those who devalue human life?

The easy thing to do is to make bullets and bombs and eliminate those we don't like, but, afterwards, it is only a matter of time until we do it again. Killing each other seems to be easy for us. On the other hand, helping each other have a better life each day is difficult, but, once we begin this, it, too, becomes easier to do each succeeding day.

Instead of "Death to the infidel," it would be much better to hear, "How can I help make life better for the people around me?"

If we could somehow lose our attraction for those who hate, and learn to love our neighbors as we love ourselves, there would be no use for the bullets and bombs rolling off our assembly lines, and we could end our inhumanity to each other.

Those of us who know something about love must speak out. We must raise the voice that says, "Love is the only thing that really works, so let us be done with hate." Silence encourages those who do not understand the value of life. We must help everyone understand that human suffering at the hand of each other must end because it is evil.

Violence and death came to six million Jews because of Hitler's hate, and this eventually resulted in 60 million deaths. The doors to this kind of calamity for the world have again begun to swing open as we hear "Death to Jews and to Christians," and the chorus is getting larger and louder. If we are good people, we must rise up and not allow a tragedy similar to what happened in Germany last century.

CHAPTER 159

CONTROL, MASTERY AND MATURITY

It is a mark of gross immaturity to seek control of another person or group of people. We have been haunted throughout history by those who think they should be masters of what other people think and do. Wars have been the result of one man or several circumscribing what is and is not permissible. At the present time in the United States, we are experiencing an escalation of immaturity by people who think they should control the lives of others

One of Webster's definitions of mature is, "of or relating to a condition of full development." This being true, much of the political leadership, along with many others in this country who feel others should be what "I want them to be," have a long way to go. As history so powerfully teaches, this is a certain way to calamity. We are already seeing this as pronouncements from leaders are diminishing our freedoms.

The governor of California has taken the position that the words "husband" and "wife" must be omitted from all marriage ceremonies. This is going to call for speech police who will have to be present at all weddings to assure the absence of those words, and then arrest those who use them.

This is the course of people whose development was arrested when they were kids. It speaks powerfully to the inability to understand the need we have to get along with each in spite of our differences. One of the strengths of our nation has been its ability to solve problems that arise from a desire to control what other people say and do. One of the reasons for establishment of our country was to get out from under the control of the King of England. Now we have politicians who desire to increase the control of those they consider to be their subjects. "You do as I want you to do, and, if you don't, I will punish you."

There will always be among us those who do not understand the desire and the need to be free from the control of other people, and the fact that freedom from this dominance is a good, healthy thing. Freedom offers the only way for people to become who and what they were made to be, and this is a personal decision, having little, if anything, to do with what others want for them.

Once control of other people is successful the first time, it is only a matter of time until control of something else is desired, which is usually followed by calamity of some kind. Napoleon took over 600 thousand soldiers into Russia in order that they might help him do what he wanted to do. He failed miserably, and returned with less than 50 thousand. In the last century, Hitler wanted to make the world what he wanted it to be, and the result was 60 million people killed.

Wherever you see leaders take the position that it's "My way or the highway," you see the deterioration of life for all. Unfortunately, the political realm is not the only place this is seen. The terrible Inquisitions in Europe were begun and led by church people who took the position that their beliefs must be the beliefs of other people. If you said you do not believe what you are told to believe, you could be severely punished or even killed. This is an excellent example of where the road to control others leads. There are many religionists today who require that others believe what they believe. This was true of Jim Jones, and the result was mass suicide.

One of the marks of maturity is being free from the control of others. People in the therapist's office struggle to be free to make their own decisions. One client said, "Learning to be myself is the hardest thing I have ever tried to do, but it is, also, the best thing I have ever done."

Control and mastery of others cannot be a part of free societies. It is and always has been the product of those who do not understand the deep yearnings people have to be free from the dominance of others. The current climate in the United States is one that eliminates the possibility that freedom will grow. Instead, it is a guarantee, if continued, that our freedoms will be diminished and eventually eliminated. Somewhere in the removal of freedom, thought police will be needed to keep us under control.

CHAPTER 160

TREATING FAILURE AS SUCCESS

I f you want to see an example of failure that many see as success, consider this: the unemployment rate in the African American community climbed from 12.6% to 13.00% in August, 2013 (Department of Labor, Bureau of Labor Statistics). In 1964, when the Civil Rights legislation was passed, the unemployment rate for African Americans was 9.6% (Department of Labor, Bureau of Labor Statistics). This is a tragedy, and it is calling out loud and clear that many things legislators have been doing for the past 50 years have done more harm than good.

The liberal politicians in Washington thought they could do for blacks what they needed done, and they have been thumping their chests over the years, saying, "What good boys and girls we are in giving blacks what we have given them." The tragedy in this is that they do not see the dreadful things they have done to African Americans. The programs they have developed have failed, but they cannot understand this.

We witnessed real progress in the African American community under the leadership of Martin Luther King, Jr. Black people did the heavy lifting then, and they were successful. But, the politicians in Washington stepped in with the Civil Rights

Legislation of 1964, followed by the "entitlement programs," and took the initiative from far too many of them. Doing this halted the real progress of blacks, and the result is seen in increased unemployment rates.

African American people need to quit looking at themselves through the eyes of misguided politicians who picture and treat them as people unable to care for themselves. The lives of the Tuskegee Airmen, Dr. Ben Carson, Thomas Lowell, and countless other African Americans speak loud and clear to the fact that they can earn an education and/or training and perform as well as white people when given equal opportunity to study and prepare.

What brings success to people is not what is given them, but what comes from inside them as they get more and better education and earn their way through developed skills and experience in business. People can achieve much more for themselves when they develop what is within rather than when they accept what others give them. This is a lesson the politicians need to learn, and, if they can learn it, they will end their give-away programs and replace them with an environment in which people are provided incentives to do for themselves what only they individually can do. It will be at that time when our elected officials will cease celebrating their failures, and will be in position to celebrate the personal achievements of millions of people they are now harming with all their free stuff.

CHAPTER 161

SOMETHING TO REMEMBER NOW & WHEN WE VOTE

It is extremely important that we remember the following, both now and when we step into the voting booth:

Obama could have done nothing he has done without the strong support of liberal democrats. They recruited him, they got him elected, and they supported him as he went about destroying many of the good things in the greatest nation the world has ever known. Liberal democrats bear ultimate responsibility for what has gone wrong, and they need to be removed so they can no longer continue their destructive work.

CHAPTER 162

WHAT HAPPENED TO ALL THE GUMPTION?

When I was young, it wasn't unusual to hear someone say, "He sure does have a lot of gumption." It's been a long time since I last heard it, and I wonder why. It seems like today there is not enough gumption around for people to take note of it. A lot of people seem to have never heard of it

Well, what does gumption mean? According to Webster, it means "common sense, horse sense; enterprise, initiative." Wiktionary adds: "boldness of enterprise, initiative or aggressiveness, guts, spunk."

According to this definition, there isn't much gumption in the American people anymore.

CHAPTER 163

THE HIGH COSTS OF BRAINWASHING

B rainwashing comes with unbelievably high costs, and people get taken in without being aware it is happening to them. Brainwashing happens often, and has been effective throughout history. It has been done in many places by many different people to accomplish personal agendas, agendas usually hidden from those who are being brainwashed.

Brainwashing, simply, is getting people to abandon their ways of thinking and accept ways of thinking you desire. When brainwashing is complete, the one doing the brainwashing can get people to do just about anything he wishes.

Examples jump out at us from the pages of history:
There was Pol Pot and the Khmer Rouge:

20,000 mass graves
1.886 million victims of execution
Up to 2.5 million deaths out of a population of eight million

Pol Pot wanted to create an agrarian communist revolution.

There was Mao Zedong with his Chinese Communist Agenda:

> 49 to 78 million deaths in his Great Leap Forward Program
> There was Joseph Stalin's Communist agenda that led to approximately 60 million deaths (estimate by Alexander Solzhenitsyn).

There was Hitler, who exterminated 12 million, six million being Jews, and who led us into WW II with its 60 million deaths.

None of these men could have accomplished their destruction of human beings by themselves. They had to convince other people to do their dirty work for them, and this they did through brainwashing. They were all skilled at getting other people to do what they wanted them to do.

These are only four men among many in history who have been able to get others to abandon their ways of thinking and do what seems unimaginable. Where brainwashing is successful, seemingly good people will participate in unbelievable horrors that are without limit.

Can people in the United States be brainwashed? You can bet your last dollar they can be. Both poor whites and black people have been hit with a double whammy during the last 80 years. The first thing was the government in Washington, with the Social Security program, removing from them the responsibility of taking care of themselves ("Let us do it for you."). This was followed by multiple welfare and entitlement programs that led millions of healthy Americans to abandon useful and productive work in favor of the free check from Washington.

The second thing was the brainwashing by liberals as they convinced people to change their ways of thinking about the most successful form of government and nation the world has ever known. It was no accident the U.S. became the greatest nation, but liberals began to attack almost everything that made it great: our religion, our freedoms, our morals, our wealth, the Constitution itself, and any other thing that would capture their minds.

This double whammy has, indeed, captured the minds and support of millions of people who do not realize that their allegiance has been bought by politicians who have been intent on reducing us to the level of a socialist country that has no resemblance to the great nation we once were.

Our Constitutional Republic, in spite of our many frailties, offered freedom and opportunity to those who wanted to make something of themselves. As a result, people from all over the world came here, jumped into the task of pulling themselves up by their bootstraps and accomplished things no people had ever accomplished.

The agenda in a Constitutional Republic is for the government to serve the people. Thus, the people are more important than government. In socialism, the agenda of government is to be served by the people, which means people are expendable if they don't serve the purposes of government. This is why the millions of people mentioned above could so easily be exterminated.

An excellent example of the work of liberal, socialist politicians can be seen in the housing debacle many Americans are still reeling from. They bombarded us with the message that everybody deserves a house to live in, people quickly believed this, and we experienced the greatest housing disaster in the history of our nation. This, regrettably, was followed by the world-wide economic collapse. The brainwashing was effective, and it resulted in financial disaster for millions of Americans and people around the world. Liberal, socialist-minded politicians were the cause of this.

This was followed by liberals convincing more than half our population to vote for someone without credentials, someone who could bring changes that would elevate people to where they wanted to be. The brainwashing was effective, and now we have attacks on the Constitution, on Christianity, on morals, on citizenship, on families, on privacy, on education, on freedom to say and do as we have been accustomed, on many other things that have made us a great nation, all for the purpose of changing us into a socialist, communistic nation run by politicians.

We are no longer the envy of the world as the erosion of our freedoms and the rewards of our labor have been replaced by growing control of our lives from Washington. Politicians have decided they can run our lives better than we can, and they are taking away our opportunities to build the lives we desire for ourselves. Sadly, brainwashed Americans are supporting them in about everything they want to do.

In many countries at the present time, we are seeing cartoons making fun of the stupidity of Americans for choosing leaders who have little to no understanding of what people can do for themselves if government will just stay out of our lives.

Yes, the brainwashing from Washington has been effective over the past 80 years, and we now have huge numbers of our citizens willing to abandon their previous ways of thinking about freedom and opportunity, and adopt the kind of socialist/communist thinking that has proven so disastrous in other countries that were led by people who thought they had a better way for people to live.

We in the United States have gotten a good start toward the kind of disasters that come when citizens have abandoned their desires about life, turning them over to misguided politicians. If we do not correct what politicians have been doing to us for the past 80 years, all of our freedoms will disappear, and we will be total subjects of the liberal politicians in Washington. Brainwashing is, indeed, costly.

CHAPTER 164

A FLOURISHING LIFE

There Is something within that propels each of us to reach for the stars. We want to do well and have those things which bring a good life. A newborn baby does what is necessary to satisfy hunger; it cries and the mother responds. That is the beginning.

Each of us is equipped to strive for a good life. Aristotle believed that all things, including humans, have something within that drives them to become what they were made to be. The rose will become the beautiful flower it was made to be if it receives proper nourishment and is allowed to thrive. So, too, human life will be fulfilling and good if it does what it was made to do.

The Greeks had a word to describe possibilities: eudaimonia, which "…is a Greek word commonly translated as happiness or welfare; however, 'human flourishing' has been proposed as a more accurate translation" (Wikipedia).

Perhaps this human flourishing is what Jesus had in mind when he said, "I have come that men may have life, and may have it in all its fullness" (John 10:10b, New English translation).

Everyone has the potential for eudaimonia. If "human flourishing" is, indeed, available to all people, what has happened?

Why aren't more people flourishing? A simple answer is: they fail to do those things which cause them to flourish. A sociologist might go into all the social problems people encounter, and claim many people live in environments that rob them of any chance to flourish. But, we must often escape our environments if we are to enjoy human flourishing. We have to do that which qualifies us for this eudaimonia.

A person cannot sit back, do nothing, and expect to have a flourishing life. Those who wait for others to provide their flourishing will never receive it. We must actively participate in those things that develop our minds and are moral and good. We cannot expect this human flourishing to be ours if we fail to do those things that earn it.

Yes, the environment can be problems the socialist addresses, but the reality is that many people have risen above the limitations of where they came from and have flourished magnificently. They have learned that what is on the inside of a person is what determines how life will be lived. They have become aware that no-one has to be a victim of his/her environment.

CHAPTER 165

FREEDOM TO FLY HIGH

Henri J. N. Nouwen once said, "...it is easier to own life than to love life." When you own a thing, you can do anything you want to do with it. This is the tremendous attraction of those who wish to control the lives of other people. "You be what I want you to be and everything will be okay," is the subtle message behind those who feel it is their responsibility to foist on people things they do not want. A big problem with this is, once control begins, there is no end to it; it must continue until everything is controlled. This is why those who seek to control can never rest easy until control is totally in their hands. Step in government, and we see the unending meddling in all aspects of our lives. There will be no end to it until everything is controlled out of the headquarters of government.

When a person loves life, there is no room for control by or of others, thus the extension of freedom to everyone. For people to be free, they must be able to determine what life will be for them. They might be offered things by others, but they ultimately have the opportunity to either accept or reject them, and there will be no attempt to punish them because of their choices.

In our Constitution and Bill of Rights, citizens are given freedom to conduct their lives as they wish. They can make good choices or they can make bad choices, and sometimes they hurt others because of their bad choices, and they and the ones they hurt suffer. The history of the United States, however, is that we have made more good choices than any other nation in the history of the world, and that is why we have stood head and shoulders above the rest.

When freedom to choose is taken away, what one person has to offer out of the abundance of his/her aspirations and talents is put to sleep, and the days ahead become that of trying to please those who are in control. This eventuates in the future being determined by the limitations of leaders as they clip the wings of those who dream big dreams, thus resulting in lives being less than they could be.

For centuries, people clamored to come to the United States because it offered them the opportunity to spread their wings and fly high. With liberal Democrats having decided they would rather have a system to control the lives of citizens, they have been in the process of taking away our freedoms through the introduction of socialism, a system which eventually determines what life will be for all citizens. This is attractive to those who have limited dreams and little initiative, but it is anathema to the people who wish to make something of themselves, dreaming big dreams that eventuate in far more good things than can come out of the minds of political leaders. Freedom to fly high is the great gift we have had in this Constitutional Republic of ours.

CHAPTER 166

A WORD TO POLITICIANS

First of all, I am not at all interested in you telling me about the weaknesses and bad things about your political opponents. When you talk at me about them, you lose me completely, and I can forcefully tell you I do not vote for politicians on the basis of what they say about others. You will never get my vote by badmouthing anyone.

There are some things which do interest me, and on these I will make my decision to vote for you or one of them. Things I will consider are the following:

1. Have you read and do you believe in the Constitution of the United States?
2. Do you believe in the freedoms guaranteed by the Constitution and Bill of Rights?
3. Do you believe in representing the citizens of the United States or do you think it is okay for politicians to disregard what we want?
4. Do you feel every able-bodied and able-minded individual in this country should be held responsible for learning to care for themselves, thus making a contribution to the betterment of our nation?

5. Will you help us again become the greatest nation in the world?
6. Will you serve the people rather than yourself and other politicians?
7. Will you work to set term limits for all politicians in Washington?
8. Will you pass laws that apply to all members of Congress as well as to citizens?
9. Are you interested in and will you work for a balanced budget?

If you want my vote, you must address these and other concerns I have. My thoughts and feelings are that professional politicians over the past 60 years have done much to cripple our great nation. We lost our way in providing an environment where "all God's children" could sit down at the same table and call each other brothers. Much legislation has divided us rather than united us. Progress in equality and brotherhood were yanked away from millions of people when politicians in Washington started doing for people what people should be doing for themselves.

We have been the greatest of nations in the past because our strength was based on "we the people." Politicians in Washington have altered this by trying to place our nation's strength on themselves, and we have become much less than we once were.

The job of politicians is to serve citizens, and I will be looking and listening to learn if you can help in this. If you talk about your opponent, I can learn nothing about your interests and strengths, and you will not get my vote. If you can convince me you will serve us citizens, I will gladly vote for you.

CHAPTER 167

LOOKING FOR THE PROMISED LAND

Many people go through life looking for The Promised Land, but never find it. They believe that someone will come along, lead them there, and all their hopes and dreams will be fulfilled. This is why people stay ready to follow the person who claims, "Follow me, and I will help you realize the kind of life you have always dreamed about."

And, so, we quickly and easily follow the person who can convince us he/she will give us what we are looking for. This has been true throughout history, and it is true today.

In the United States, we have seen excellent examples of this, the last of which came onto the scene several years ago, when an unprepared and virtually unknown man stepped forward and claimed he could correct the wrongs of the United States. He was a nice-looking man, and was a master at reading a prepared speech from the teleprompter. Many people fell under his charm, and he was elected President of the United States.

At first, as usually happens, he gave people things they were looking for, his popularity soared, and people believed they had indeed found the one who would deliver things they had longed for all their lives. The money flowed where it had never flowed before, and people said, "Yes, we have found our savior."

But, the dreams came crashing down as people began to question where he was taking us. He, with the help and full support of other elected officials sitting in Congress, began to do things that were not in keeping with a free society and nation. We began to lose some of our freedoms as things we did not want were forced on us. Political correctness eliminated freedom of speech, freedom of religion came under attack, a movement arose to take our guns away, we were forced to allow males to enter women's dressing rooms, our borders were opened to allow anyone to cross over, and many other things that headed us away from freedom toward subservience to the person who projected himself as knowing what is best for all.

Fortunately, enough Americans caught on to what was going on to call a halt to it. They turned down for president a person who said she would continue the agenda of this man, choosing, rather, a man who said he wanted to "Make America Great Again."

Perhaps we need to look seriously at what it takes to arrive in The Promised Land. The Promised Land is not something that anyone else can give you, as many believe. It comes only through a personal journey. You take a look at your individual dreams, and make decisions regarding how you can personally get there. When you decide where you want to go, you evaluate things you must do to get there, and then prepare, prepare, prepare. You do this with training, education and a lot of hard work. It isn't the work of other people who will get you there. It is strictly the work you do. Many people want to get there without doing the necessary work, but that just not happen.

The great promise of the United States is that your future is in your hands. It is there where entrance into The Promised Land is found: in personal preparation and effort. Bob came to the counseling office, distraught over three failed marriages, still in the third one. He talked about each wife, and the difficulties they had. The first one had affairs, the second one worked long hours, never having enough time for him, the third one spent them into bankruptcy. He had two boys, and relationships with them were rotten. To top it off, he hated his job, never finding one he could enjoy.

For three sessions, Bob poured out his misery. On the fourth visit, the counselor said to him, "I want to ask you a question I refer to as the miracle question. This is it: If a miracle could happen tonight, if all your troubles were completely gone, and you could do anything tomorrow that you really want to do, what would that be?

Without a pause, Bob shot back immediately, "I would be a concert pianist."

This was the first time he had said anything about music. The counselor said, "Maybe we need to talk about that."

Bob began his story. He began taking piano at the age of four, and just fell in love with it. When in high school, he made plans to study music in college, and become a concert pianist. In the eleventh grade, as he began to make application to college, his dad, a physician, said to him, "You can't make a good living as a pianist. I don't want you to study music in college, and I will not pay for you to go there and major in music."

Bob said, "What was I to do? Dad made plenty of money and could have sent me anywhere. He told me I should major in medical technology, that I could get a job in any hospital in America with this degree. What was I to do? I had no money to pay for college, so I went and did what he wanted me to do. After graduation, jobs were easy to get. Over the years, I worked in several hospitals, but never found one where I could enjoy the work.

"Then I decided to set up my own business, and I did. I made decent money for several years, but did not find happiness there. I decided to become an attorney, and I became one, passing the bar the first time I took it. Since then, I have been working in my wife's office. She is an attorney. But, I don't enjoy the job. She and I just don't get along well together, and I want to get out of this marriage."

The therapist asked if he would still like to study music, and he quickly said emphatically, "Yes, I would?" The therapist then said, "Are there some colleges you know about where you could go and take piano?" He said, "Yes."

The therapist then said, "If you really want to do that, see what you can find."

The next week, Bob returned with information on several colleges where he could take piano, and already he had chosen his favorite.

Although it was too late for him to become a concert pianist, he returned to college and breezed through his course. After graduation, he was hired by that college as a piano instructor. His entire life changed as he now was involved in something close to what he originally wanted to do. His days were no longer miserable as he lost himself in music.

Many people have dreams of what they wish to do, but, for various reasons, are unable to pursue their dreams.

One of the things, though, that makes the United States the greatest of all nations is the fact that, if you decide what you want to do, there is usually a way for you to do it. You can do what you wish to do, and get paid for it.

Your Promised Land is in your hands. It cannot be given to you by anyone else.

CHAPTER 168

CAPTURING PEOPLE: AS EASY AS CAPTURING WILD PIGS

R ecently I read a story about herding wild pigs. The first problem is how to capture them, and following is how you do it:

1. First, identify an area they frequent.
2. Second, when they are not present, spread some corn on the ground.
3. Third, day after day spread more corn on the ground.
4. Forth, when they are not there, build one side of a fence when they are not present, but spread more corn on the ground.
5. Fifth, build a second side of the fence, and spread more corn on the ground.
6. Sixth, build a third side of the fence and put more corn on the ground.
7. Seventh, build the forth side of the fence with a gate, leave the gate open, but spread more corn on the ground.
8. Eighth, spread more corn on the ground, leave the gate open.

9. Ninth when the pigs are eating, close the gate, and you will have captured them.
10. When you have them captured, you can do anything you desire with them.

Um, I wonder if this is how liberal politicians have been able to capture and control so many people with their entitlement programs. The entitlement programs are the equivalent of spreading corn on the ground. They have trapped millions of people who have no ability to free themselves.

This is one of the best explanations I have heard about unsuspecting, good people being captured by the politicians in Washington. They've given here, and a little there, and more over here. When they have done enough, the deal is closed and vote for the democrats are assured.

CHAPTER 169

LET'S QUIT BEING OFFENDED

Being offended is a personal choice, but we in the United States and around the world have raised it to a fine art. Someone says or does something I don't like and I say, "I am offended," and crowds join me and commiserate with me. "Oh, woe is me and woe is us," we proclaim.

Being offended is similar to being angry. It arises within the person. Two people can hear something or be treated a certain way, and one becomes angry while the other one does not. What's going on when one person, hearing the same thing, does not get angry, but the other one does? Something on the inside of one reacts with anger, and the other is not bothered at all. This simply means that something on the inside of one person is what produced anger, but that something was not in the other person. It was not the thing that was done or said that produced the anger. It was something on the inside that was the problem.

Someone may call me stupid, an idiot, a redneck, a honky or anything that may come to mind. When that happens, I have the choice to not let it affect me or I can have a fit and cause a scene by labeling that person whatever I wish. The choice is mine, no one else's. To place my feelings in the hands of other people who are ignorant and lacking decency is a certain way to guarantee my unhappiness.

If I have my feet on the ground and my head screwed on right, I can allow another person to act the fool or say stupid things, and it does not bother me. I am in control of my life, and my feelings are what I produce, not what others produce. In other words, other people do not determine how I act or what I shall be. If it bothers me, then I must look at what is wrong with me.

If someone can pull my chain and get me to react, that person then and there is in control of my life, not me. Emotionally mature people do not allow others to control thoughts and feelings, understanding that their lives are what they make of them, not what others make.

Being offended indeed is a choice.

CHAPTER 170

OBAMA GOT PART OF WHAT HE WANTED

Obama became president having in mind degrading the United States to a level below what it has been. He wanted to make it more like the other nations of the world. In other words, he wanted us to become like third-world nations.

What we are now seeing in the demonstrations, riots, and destruction of property by those who do not like the outcome of the presidential election, actions that might be done in third-world countries. Reports are that they plan to disrupt the inauguration any way they can.

This does not look like what good Americans do. It looks like what people in third-world nations do.

When Obama was elected, many people reacted negatively, but they did not riot and destroy property. Being greatly disappointed, they sucked it in and moved on, keeping in mind what needed to be done, and, when the appropriate time came, they took action at the ballot box.

What we learned in America many years ago was that reasoned discussion is far better than conflict. We had to fight a Civil War because we did not know this. It is quite clear to people who know history that thinking together is far superior to conflict.

Allowing disagreements to propel you to the streets to riot is an indication of failure to use the brain your Maker gave you. It was given for thinking purposes, but many people have not learned this.

Are we going to convert our country into a third-world nation? Perhaps those who are demonstrating, rioting and destroying property want that, but that does not fit under the guidelines of our Constitution, where we have a means of dealing with life without demonstrating and damaging property.

If people want to act like they live in a third-world country, perhaps they can find one outside our borders.

Obama is bound to feel good in that his legacy has, indeed, moved some Americans to adopt the habits of people wo live in third-world nations.

CHAPTER 171

FINANCES SHOULD BE BETTER

The people Trump has brought on board constitute the richest people who have ever been in charge of our government. This is some of the best news regarding what is happening on Capitol Hill we have heard in many years.

These men and women understand finances better than the ones who have been there. They have gotten rich because they know how to read financial statements. They understand what debits and credits mean, and that, if the debits are greater than the credits, you go bankrupt. None of them got rich by going bankrupt.

The people who have been in Congress seem not to have had any inkling regarding what profit and loss mean, and have added many more debits than credits, having run up a debt of approximately 20 trillion dollars, something that is beyond the ability of people to understand.

Given the financial mess these people have inherited, it will be amazing to see them get the federal budget under control, but that is what they must do. If they cannot, this nation will go belly-up, which would lead to things none of us would like to see.

Hopefully the reckless spending of our government is going to change. If it does, that will be some of the best news we could receive.

CHAPTER 172

THE NEWS MEDIA AND MIND CONTROL

Have we not learned anything from history regarding the subject of mind control? We saw it in Germany as Hitler took over the minds of the German people. We saw it in Japan where control was so pervasive that becoming a kamikaze pilot was eagerly accepted by men who then went to their deaths thinking they were doing well.

Mind control has been used by individuals and groups of individuals throughout history to achieve control of people's lives and get them to do anything they wish. The success of mind control is usually short-lived, and is often quite destructive.

This writer thought we would never see effective mind control in the United States, but he was wrong. It has reared its head and taken control of many people, some of them supposedly well-educated.

People in the media are perhaps the best example of those whose minds have been victimized. The media is supposed to report unbiased news as it happens, but, for the past several decades, it has twisted the news to achieve a consensus of thinking by people to support a change in our form of government. It is clear that, with few exceptions, the media would relish a move to replace our constitutional government with socialism. They were fully behind democrats who wish to have nothing to do with the founding documents of this great nation, our Constitution and Bill of Rights.

The pervasiveness of this mind control is easily seen in the percentage of news people who were fully committed to the election of Mrs. Clinton, who promised to continue the agenda of Obama, which would have changed government in Washington to one completely controlled by whoever was in the Oval Office.

Media people are supposedly some of the best educated people in this country, but their group-think is so pervasive that one must conclude that their education was not education at all. Rather, it was writing about news through the eyes of persons who did not like the United States, and who wished to see the Greatest Nation replaced by something much inferior. In other words, news people were drug around by their noses to report something the way they were told to report it.

This mind control has led the news media to give no resistance to the removal of our freedoms. This, in effect, means most of the news media does not believe in the freedoms offered in the Constitution and Bill of Rights, and desires that they be replaced.

Should we call the media victims of mind control or willing participants in the destruction of this nation? It appears that they willingly accepted the mind control of those who want to eliminate our form of government, which, therefore, identifies them with those who do not understand what this nation is all about. In other words, they do not believe in freedom for people to think their own thoughts and make their own decisions.

CHAPTER 173

NOW, WHAT DO WE AMERICANS DO?

One of the really troublesome things about the democrats in Washington these past eight to ten years has been their eager support of Obama and the things he has done. We haven't heard a single one of them protest about what he was doing or where he had this country headed (at least this writer never heard it).

If they did not agree with what he was doing, we should have heard some kind of protest, but we heard nary a thing, which leads this writer to believe they were a central part of the charge into socialism/liberalism. There was nothing they did that would indicate their objection.

What are we to conclude about this? Are they a bunch of "yes" men and women who have no courage to challenge the destruction of the Constitution and Bill of Rights or have we reached a time when they actively support its destruction. Whatever, they were on the train headed for socialism, and they seemed eager about where they were going, so eager that they fully supported a person with a questionable background as their next leader.

The American people will have to decide what to do with the democrats: continue to encourage them in their attempts to bury the Constitution, which many citizens would like to do, or put them out to pasture in the back forty where they will be out of sight and out of mind, where they will be of no danger to the American people. To think that they would get in line to support our founding documents is quite a stretch.

We need an atmosphere in Washington where questioning of ideas and plans is okay regardless of where they originate. Full speed ahead without adequate questioning, which often seems to be the way things are done there, can carry us into troubled waters, where we have too often been. Intelligent people are not afraid of questions, because questioning can often lead us to something better.

If we get the right people in Washington asking the right questions, we will move in a direction that is good for all Americans, not just a minority. That would be a refreshing change to what often comes out of Congress and the Oval Office.

CONCLUSION:

Over the last several decades, and particularly during the past eight years, we have been powerfully reminded that the politicians we send to Washington may not believe in the Constitution of the United States, and may have no interest in preserving the freedoms offered by this document and the Bill of Rights.

The United States has been great a nation, but we have been diminished by politicians who are supposed to make us a better nation. This has happened because politicians have risen who think they have a better way than following the Constitution. When we look at history and the rise and fall of nations, we are confronted with the fact that the demise of a nation usually happens because of what takes place within that nation, not because of what other nations do. This is precisely why we have retreated from the nation we once were.

Liberal democrats made the decision decades ago that the citizens of our nation should serve government, and they began to entice people with offers that appeared quite attractive: "The purpose pf government is to take care of you, to give you whatever you need," was and is their basic message to poor black and white people.

It is vitally important that people who understand the Constitution and Bill of Rights be continually aware of the presence at all times of people who wish to make our country in their own image. There is always someone who thinks he/she knows what is best for everyone, and is willing to force that way upon people. Unless we remain continually aware of this, we can become victims of the person with a golden tongue who can paint a beautiful picture with words that mesmerize us.

We Americans let down our guard, and the liberal democrats came close to burying our constitutional form of government. They came within a hare's breath of burying the documents that led us to being the greatest nation in the history of the world. Those of us who believe in the Constitution and Bill of Rights must remember that there will always be people who think they have a better way than what we have.

If we desire a life that is different from the one we have, it is up to us to build it. The ones we build on the hopes of others will never deliver what we long for, and that is realization of our own dreams. Our happiness and fulfillment always come from us doing our own thing.

In the recent presidential election, citizens rejected the liberal juggernaut that would have put our Constitution and Bill of Rights in the history books. Now we must maintain vigilance to make certain these documents remain the foundation of our great nation.